The Gift of a Bride

A Tale of Anthropology, Matrimony, and Murder

SERENA NANDA AND JOAN GREGG

ALTAMIRA
PRESS

A Division of
ROWMAN & LITTLEFIELD PUBLISHERS, INC.
Lanham • New York • Toronto • Plymouth, UK

AltaMira Press
A division of Rowman & Littlefield Publishers, Inc.
A wholly owned subsidiary of The Rowman & Littlefield Publishing Group, Inc.
4501 Forbes Boulevard, Suite 200
Lanham, MD 20706
www.altamirapress.com

Estover Road
Plymouth PL6 7PY
United Kingdom

British Library Cataloguing in Publication Information Available

Library of Congress Cataloging-in-Publication Data

Nanda, Serena.
  The gift of a bride : a tale of anthropology, matrimony, and murder / Serena
Nanda and Joan Gregg.
    p. cm.

ISBN 978-0-7591-1150-9

  1. East Indians—United States—Fiction. 2. Anthropology—Fiction. 3. New York
(State)—New York—Fiction. I. Gregg, Joan Young. II. Title.

PS3613.A579G54 2009
813'.6—dc22   2008048562

Printed in the United States of America

∞™ The paper used in this publication meets the minimum requirements of
American National Standard for Information Sciences—Permanence of Paper for
Printed Library Materials, ANSI/NISO Z39.48-1992.

Daughters and sons are one's own, but the daughter-in-law is other.

—*Indian proverb*

The Gift
of a Bride

✿ Chapter One

Senior civil officer invites correspondence from North Indian professionals only, for a beautiful, talented, intelligent daughter, 5'3", slim, fair, MA in psychology. Prefer immigrant doctors, between 26–29 years, living in the tri-state area. Reply with full details and returnable photo.

Julie Norman thoughtfully reread the matrimonial ad that her friend Shakuntala had placed in a New York City Indian-American newspaper on behalf of her daughter, Amrita. After Shakuntala and Amrita had vetted the responses, Shakuntala had asked Julie to meet the men who seemed like the best possibilities as a first step in arranging the marriage.

"I must do my duty as a mother," Shakuntala had told Julie on her recent fieldwork trip to India. "It is the right time for us to marry Amrita off to a good boy. She prefers someone already settled in America, and I would prefer New York or New Jersey so we will not seem so far away. Amrita is, after all, our only daughter, so I must at least try to fulfill her wishes." Julie, of course, had agreed to help.

Shakuntala had placed several ads, offering a few details about her requirements and requesting phone numbers and "biodata" along with a photograph. Amrita had already turned down several of the responding candidates on the basis of their photographs. One candidate was

3

"too ugly," another "too fat," another combed his hair in a fashion so out of date that even Shakuntala could see he was hopeless. Still another lived in some small town in Arkansas. This detail irritated Shakuntala to no end. "Does he think we are so backward here in India that we think Arkansas is part of the tri-state area?" she e-mailed Julie, expressing her contempt. Julie had a good laugh over that, but she also knew that for some families, marrying their children abroad trumped all other considerations, and they were willing to give up a few bargaining points. But Shakuntala was not in that category. Amrita was beautiful and well educated, their family was from a highly ranked *Kshatriya* subcaste, and their older son was married and well settled in India.

Julie had called several of the numbers Shakuntala passed on to her as possibilities. The first candidate seemed only interested in whether Amrita was a good cook and whether she would be capable of looking after his mother, who was quite elderly and lived with him. "Lose this guy, Shakuntala; what he wants is a maid, not a wife," Julie had written. Shakuntala was grateful for the advice and e-mailed Julie some more telephone numbers that had made Amrita's short list. "Not like the old days, Julie," Shakuntala added in a postscript, "when our parents just looked to see if the boy was a good provider while the girl had nothing to say in the matter. Well, we must change with the times. Now we cannot force our choice on our children, so they must have the right of veto." *Right,* thought Julie, *from arranged marriage to assisted marriage!*

The second candidate Julie called lived in Chicago. Naturally, Shakuntala would only consider a professional man, so this guy, apparently a statistical researcher for some big corporation, might qualify even though he didn't live on the East Coast. When Julie reached his home phone, however, the man who answered said that his brother had left recently for India to get married. "So that's that," Julie sighed with some relief.

After e-mailing Shakuntala with that report, Julie received a letter in reply with the matrimonial ad in front of her, along with the man's name and telephone number. He had described himself as a PhD in some scientific field, working on the faculty at the state university of New Jersey. Julie had to call several times before reaching him, and he always seemed to have an excuse for not coming to New York to meet her. *Not auspicious!* He lived in what Julie, who didn't have a car, thought of as the wilds of New Jersey, which meant anything beyond the PATH train to Newark. So, as much as she wanted to help her friend, Julie made it clear to the "professor," as she now thought of him, that she could only meet him if he came to New York.

"I have an uncle in Queens," he told her, "but I really don't visit much, so it's not very convenient for me to come to the city." They had hung up without making any definite plans, and things seemed to have stalled.

Julie was about to e-mail Shakuntala to scratch this candidate also, but then two days later, the "professor" had called. "I'm stopping over at the Port Authority Bus Terminal on my way to a conference in Washington," he told her. "If you are free, I could meet you there around eleven in the morning."

Julie's first class didn't begin until 2 P.M., so she figured the meeting time would work. *"Surely an hour should be more than enough to give him the once—or maybe twice—over,"*

Arriving punctually, Julie approached a lone Indian man sitting with a coffee at one of the tables in the simulated outdoor café he had indicated was convenient. He was casually but neatly dressed and good-looking—though even sitting down, Julie could see he was kind of short. *A minus right there,* Julie thought at first, but immediately revised this notion. Amrita was not tall, so the "professor's" height did not make him a complete washout. Also, he was fair, a definite plus point, as they said in India. Fair skin had always been essential for girls and often included in matrimonial advertisements, but now it was an increasingly important trait for boys as well.

"Are you Professor Sood?" Julie asked as she tentatively approached his table. When he nodded, she introduced herself and took the chair opposite his. "Thanks so much for taking the time to meet me," she began, restraining her annoyance at the need to be so polite and deferential. She kept reminding herself that these qualities were important factors in the boy's evaluation of the girl and her family. As their go-between, Julie would be measured by the same standards.

Julie started the conversation by briefly talking about her fieldwork in India, explaining how she had met Shakuntala and her family. "I study Indian marriage and family," she said, diplomatically omitting her research on the *hijras,* a marginalized community of transsexual performers who dance and sing at weddings and whenever male—and now female children—are born. Some Indian people she met were very interested to hear about her research, but others looked aghast, so she had learned to be discreet in discussing it.

In any case, Professor Sood didn't seem very interested in her work and merely nodded, so Julie decided to get right to her questions. The most important ones involved his present employment, immigration status, and living situation in the States. She was sure Shakuntala had checked out the basic facts about his family through her network of relatives and friends in India, but Julie wanted to hear his story herself. It was not so much that people actually lied as that they exaggerated, and the whole point of the meeting was to get a feel for a candidate's character and personality.

"I hope I don't seem too nosy," Julie said, aware that it was something she had to say regardless of whether he minded or not, "but Shakuntala is like a sister to me, and her daughter is very precious to us both. So," she continued, with a small smile to soften the bluntness of the question, "do you have a girlfriend already, or maybe even a wife, here in America?"

"No, not at all," he replied quite seriously, without surprise and apparently without having taken offense. He was probably just as aware that there were plenty of Indian men who had these relationships and never informed their families back in India, even as they were being considered for an arranged marriage there.

"Could you tell me a little about what you do?" asked Julie.

"I'm on a postdoctoral fellowship in the engineering department," he answered. "I worked in Holland for five years but decided to take up this offer in America, where they are doing more sophisticated research." He gave a few details of his work, some esoteric thing about strength of materials that lost Julie after a few minutes, so she turned to the all-important question of his immigration status.

"Are you a U.S. citizen?" Julie asked. After 9/11, one couldn't be too careful about an immigrant's status. "Not yet," he replied, "but the chairman of my department is hoping to sponsor me for a green card, and my plan is to remain permanently in the United States." *Hmm. This could be a problem.* Even with the emphasis on family reunification since the 1965 U.S. Immigration Act, Amrita might have to wait a long time after the marriage to get a U.S. visa. There was a huge backlog in processing immigration visas, and the costs had also gone up tremendously. And with all the anti-immigration rhetoric, the laws could change at any time. Of course, if the new immigration-reform bill passed, with its premium on skills and education rather than family ties, the "professor" would surely make the cut. But still, it could take time. Not an impossible obstacle to the match, but a serious difficulty.

"I'm curious," Julie continued, "how come you're not married already? You seem like a good catch."

"Oh, I'm not so much in demand," he contradicted. "There have been many inquiries, but these good families in India all want a real doctor; I'm only a PhD." Julie was a little taken aback by his candor, though she found the matter-of-fact way he evaluated his own worth as a marketable match quite touching and a point in his favor.

"Do you live with some family here?" she inquired, another important question that could have a big impact on a new bride's happiness.

"I live with my elder brother and his wife," he said, "and I plan to live with them after my marriage, at least for a while. That will help me save money and also help me adjust to America." That sounded unpromising. Part of the point of a girl marrying someone in America was to get away from living in her husband's joint family. The hope that Amrita could live independently with her husband, following the American custom, partly explained why Shakuntala was not completely averse to her daughter marrying abroad. Seniority was important in the Indian family, and living with an elder brother and his wife could be as confining and demanding for a young bride as living with her in-laws.

With all her admiration for Indian family values, Julie knew that she would never be able to adjust to living in such an extended household. But she concluded that if everything else was okay, Shakuntala was probably resigned to that sort of arrangement for her daughter, at least temporarily.

In response to Julie's question about his family in India, Dr. Sood answered, "My father owns a pharmaceutical business in a small town in Punjab." That was a plus point, as the place he mentioned was near Shakuntala's own "native place," though Shakuntala and her husband had lived in Mumbai for years.

"My younger brother is an engineer with Tata—you know, the big Indian textile firm; they are in Ahmedabad, and my sister is a social worker in Bombay, or Mumbai, as you know they call it now. She is married to a computer systems analyst."

All this was on the plus side, Julie thought. A boy with unmarried sisters would put more pressure on the girl's family to give a big *dowry* in order to help arrange the sisters' marriages. "Of course, under the Indian constitution dowry is illegal, but still, the demands are there. Not that one minds giving," Shakuntala had told her, "but these days some families make outrageous demands—it is almost like a form of blackmail. People have become so greedy." As the mother of a daughter, this was a big consideration. "We will check thoroughly into the family background," Shakuntala told Julie. "One needs to be very careful, even among good families."

Julie kept this is mind as she chatted with Dr. Sood about inconsequential subjects for a few minutes longer and then thanked him for meeting her. "The people who placed this ad for their daughter are very, very good friends of mine, and their daughter is a lovely person. I don't have to tell you that these days so many boys who have settled in America aren't completely honest about their situation. We all want Amrita to have a very happy married life."

Making no response, Dr. Sood looked at his watch, prompting Julie to do the same. By mutual consent it seemed time to go. Julie rose and waved a casual good-bye, thanking him again for his time and headed for one of the terminal bakeries to pick up some pastries. Despite her mom's gripes that the bus station's renovation and the Times Square clean-up had Disneyfied and corporatized the area beyond recognition with fake "ye olde shoppes," Julie reflected happily that it was now possible to wait for a bus with a decent cup of coffee and a croissant minus ankle-deep litter. George Segal's sculptured "Commuters" and George Rhoad's audio-kinetic "42nd Street Ballroom" always brought a smile to her face, and certainly Forty-Second Street's little theaters and cafes were a definite improvement over the porn movie houses and other tawdry venues that had characterized the area in the bad old days.

Walking to the subway, Julie mused on the meeting with Dr. Sood, feeling ambivalent about actually involving herself in an arranged marriage "up close and personal." It was an awesome responsibility that she hoped she would not have to shoulder again soon. But she also reminded herself that anthropology is *participant*-observation, not just sitting like a fly on the wall; you couldn't get to the heart of a culture that way. As she settled herself in her seat for the twenty-minute subway ride,

Julie thought about the many factors Shakuntala would have to consider: Sood's immigration status, his intention of living with his brother and sister-in-law, and his personality as Julie reported it. She had found him boring, not a good match for Amrita's outgoing personality. But she would only e-mail Shakuntala with her impressions; it would then be Shakuntala's decision.

Julie owed Shakuntala a lot for her help in her Indian fieldwork. Shakuntala had helped Julie understand the intricacies of Indian culture and had also introduced her into the women's group that had become key to her research on marriage, family, and gender. Acting as her intermediary for her daughter's marriage was the least she could do in return. In his classic book, *The Gift*, Marcel Mauss really was spot-on about the importance of reciprocity, and not just in tribal cultures. Take and giveback applied to anthropological fieldwork as well as to a lot of other relationships in the contemporary world, no matter how much Americans prided themselves on being so independent.

As Julie exited the subway station and walked over to the NUNY campus, her mind turned to the book she was writing that she hoped would pave the way for her promotion to associate professor. Its subject, the changes in patterns of marriage and family life in the Indian diaspora in the United States, was an important one. The global connections involved in the study made it more difficult to pursue than the more locally focused studies of the old-time anthropologists, whose fieldwork was usually limited to people in remote places with few if any connections to the outside world. But with the world now a global village, contemporary anthropologists increasingly studied more complex, interconnected societies and participated in multicultural social groups dispersed across continents.

For Indian girls such as Amrita, a life in America seemed to offer a promise of some independence, while for many Indian men living in the States, marriage with a girl from India seemed an ideal way to combine traditional Indian values with some modern trimmings. Even in the best of situations, marriage required great adjustments, Julie considered, and immigrant women, of all classes, faced a great deal of stress in an alien situation that most knew only from film fantasies. The burden of uncertainty was even heavier in an arranged Indian marriage that took the bride a continent away from her parents. For the girl, especially, it was a risky undertaking, since even with the best efforts of her parents to inform themselves about a future husband and his family, it was a chancy business. Even in today's India, where the boy and girl might have several opportunities to meet without a chaperone, in many arranged marriages the husband and wife would hardly know each other well.

But then again, Julie reflected with some anthropological objectivity, even in the American tradition of romantic love, a wife really wouldn't know her husband until she married him, and sometimes not even until she'd been married for years. Julie hoped to explore some of these themes in her courses and walked to her office with anticipation, looking forward to her first class in the new semester.

✿ Chapter Two

"Hey, Glenda," Julie sang out as she stepped into the anthropology office. "What news on the Rialto?"

Julie was dressed for the fiery furnace outside in a cotton sleeveless shift with only a little knit shrug over her shoulders, but the office was cool, and Glenda, the very professional departmental secretary, had made no concessions to the season. Her dark blue suit jacket was half-buttoned to show a white blouse adorned with what Julie thought her mother would call a jabot, and Julie would bet she was wearing stockings with her pumps. With the phone scrunched up between her shoulder and her neck, Glenda was answering a student's inquiries about the department's majors while she sorted the mail. She signaled Julie to wait just one minute and when she hung up, answered Julie's inquiry about the latest news.

"Oh, you were away the last couple of weeks, weren't you? So you don't know about the three-day blackout in Brooklyn, something with the sewers, manhole covers flying all over the streets, everyone's refrigerated food spoiled at home and in the stores too. Since Con Ed promised to reimburse stores for their lost business and spoiled produce . . ."

"Well it's about time Con Ed took responsibility," Julie interrupted.

"Yes, Julie, mostly you're right, but look, here's one storekeeper who claimed $900 for spoiled produce . . . only it was a clothing store," Glenda finished with a sly wink. Julie laughed out loud. Under that churchy look and neat gray cap of curly hair, Glenda had a sharp, even caustic, sense of humor directed at all factions and classes. Her focus was the well-being of her family, a handsome, unmarried son, an Iraq War veteran who was an electrician for the city, and a smart, hip daughter, Andrea, majoring in human services at Hunter College. Which reminded Julie, "Glenda, could you please call that Badi Bahen group? It's a woman's organization that works against domestic violence among South Asian immigrants. I'd like them to send over a speaker for my gender class, maybe late October or early November."

"You got it," Glenda replied, writing a note to herself.

Julie entered her class with her notes and books well organized and quickly introduced herself. "I'm Julie Norman, and this is Anthropology 223, Sex and Culture." The few titters reminded Julie of the department's discussion over the course's title. Since it focused on both culture and gender, it fulfilled both a humanities and a social-science requirement. Its segments on domestic violence were especially useful to the many NUNY students contemplating careers in law enforcement and public service, so it always attracted its share of students. But everyone agreed that "Sex and Culture" sounded, well, sexier and would have wider appeal, a major consideration in designating course titles. Julie smiled briefly at a few students whom she recognized from her previous classes. She had a small faithful following: Loretta Milano, one of her best students, sitting in the front row, was already applying her coursework with Julie as a volunteer on a domestic-violence hotline. Glenda's daughter Andrea often sat in on her classes, and there were a few others whose interest in anthropology had deepened over the years.

Julie thought she might take a small group of them for a coffee after the planned Badi Bahen lecture so they could extend their discussion of domestic violence against immigrant women. Maybe the group could even offer some internship positions. Of course Julie also lost a number of students before the school's drop date due to her reputation as a grinch who insisted on rigorously cited term papers and as a strident grader who took attendance at every session.

She began with a paraphrase of Woody Allen's injunction that "showing up is 80 percent of success." "If you aren't here you can't participate, and if you can't participate it will affect your grade. And that's participation in spirit as well as body, so no cell phones or text messaging in class. Unless you're a neurosurgeon or a drug dealer . . . any of you in either category please raise your hand." From a tank-topped, tummy-baring duo in the furthest reaches of the room, a stage whisper erupted, "No cell phones—that's so five years ago! She's giving me toxic stress here." Julie ignored the sally—she knew her classes weren't for everyone; nothing personal on either side, right?

"Yes, right," her mom had agreed once when they had discussed it, "but the student who threatened to kill you over his grade was a wee bit over the top."

"A disturbed person," Julie countered. "Most of the disgruntled ones are satisfied just to drop my class without losing their tuition money."

Julie briefly ran through the syllabus and the course requirements: "I begin class punctually; you folks are paying a lot of money for your education, and I owe you every minute of the time you're paying for. These are double-period classes, so make sure you've put enough money in the parking meter, eaten your lunch, and done the necessaries before we start; if you overstay our short break, you don't get back in." Julie knew she couldn't really enforce this but gave it a shot every semester anyway.

"Give us a break," a student groaned from the back row. Julie let it go and rolled on. "We start with the classics, in this case, Margaret Mead's

Sex and Temperament in Three Primitive Societies. Although Mead's work has been widely criticized, it was the first important breakthrough in illuminating how culture shapes gender roles, including sexuality.

"I've done my fieldwork in India, so the impact of Indian culture on gender roles forms an important part of the class material. But we'll also consider culture and gender roles in the United States. When most of you hear the term *anthropology,* you probably think of other, exotic cultures, but anthropology also contributes to our understanding of our own society, especially the different cultures of America's many immigrant groups. So, what you learn here may even be of some personal benefit to you."

Julie then outlined the topics to be covered for the semester, calling attention to her own interest in domestic violence. "Domestic violence," she explained, "grows out of specific cultural patterns, but it is also rooted in widespread, if not universal, patterns of male dominance. We'll be applying this dual theme to a number of societies, and it's a topic some of you may want to choose for your term paper. Feel free to ask a lot of questions, and I look forward to some exciting discussions."

When Julie had first started teaching, she'd thought of each class as "showtime" and had tried to give fascinating lectures, but she soon realized that both she and her students learned a lot more by talking to each other. However, she kept a firm hand on the rudder and encouraged her students to back up their opinions with evidence from their reading, or at the very least, logical reasons. References to "human nature" did not cut it. "A lot of what we talk about here may challenge your most basic beliefs and habits, and even seem offensive to you," Julie continued. "We're all ethnocentric; we think our own culture is best, especially when it comes to our values and our morality relating to sex, gender, marriage, and family. These core patterns of culture provoke our most intimate and intense emotions; they're so deeply rooted that we tend to view them as inherently natural. But one of the things I hope you'll learn in this class is that what we call human nature is in very large part due to cultural learning. This is really the heart of cultural anthropology: to see what makes other cultures tick, to understand them as insiders, and then to use that understanding to view our own culture as outsiders. Without that contrast, it's difficult to be objective about our own values and behavior.

"Now, I like to make the course requirements clear the very first day," she added with a small smile, "so that you know what you're getting into."

"Or out of," said a student in the back row, picking up his books and walking out the door, waving a small good-bye. Some of the students looked a little shocked at his rudeness, but Julie really meant what she said. "Please don't feel shy to leave; I don't take it personally, and there's no point staying in the class if you're not prepared to do the required work. Your grades are based on quizzes, term papers, and exams that demonstrate that you've digested the reading and incorporated our class discussions into your responses. The term paper must be your own work; I'll talk a little later in the semester about correct citations. Very often I think—*"did she really think this?* Julie was honest enough to wonder "—students don't mean to plagiarize, but they just don't know how to correctly refer to the work of others. I know politicians do it all the time, but we're not running for office here.

"Any questions? Okay, see you next time."

🪷 Chapter Three

Our great sages speak to men and women in their own language, elevating their minds through the telling of the story of the Ramayana.

—*C. Rajagopalachari*, translator, Ramayana

A few weeks later, without saying a word, Julie turned off the lights as she entered the classroom and switched on the overhead projector. An image of the goddess Kali flashed on the screen, her black face grimacing savagely, her sharp tongue dripping with the blood of demons. With her wild tangle of locks and a garland of skulls hanging between her pointed, shriveled breasts, the Indian divinity grabbed the students' attention every time, Julie thought with satisfaction, a menacing image indeed.

"Oh, gross," she heard a female student whisper, while another male student got a few laughs by saying, "she looks just like my sister."

Julie let the image linger on the screen in the darkened room for a few seconds longer, then turned on the lights and wrote the name Kali on the blackboard.

"As you know, "Julie began her lecture, "one of the important ways we learn about the gender ideology in any society is to look at how men and women are portrayed in mythology, religion, and folktales.

"Hindu goddesses have many names and forms," she continued, "but are also understood as a single power and presence. Sometimes the goddess is simply called *Devi*, which means goddess, or she may be frequently addressed as *Mata*, or mother. Like real women, the goddess has no one form that captures her complexity. In fact, also like real women, the characteristics of the goddess are contradictory and even logically opposed. Two major forms of the Indian goddess representing these contradictions are Kali, the fierce and even frightening image in front of you, and her opposite, Gauri, also called Parvati, 'the Golden One,' who is benign and docile."

Julie added to the overhead projector the image of Parvati, the docile form of womanhood, with her voluptuous, feminine figure, radiant golden skin, gentle smile, brilliant jewelry, and tightly braided hair.

"These contrasting images of the goddess express two major dimensions of Indian women," Julie continued, "and each of them is associated with norms and expectations, but also underlying fears about women's nature." Julie spoke slowly as most of the students assiduously took notes. "As in many cultures, including our own, in Indian culture women are viewed with ambivalence, and the many aspects of women may even be contradictory. Ideally, in India, women are docile," Julie continued, "but they can also be angry, violent, and destructive. In fact, female rage and destructive capacity are often thought of as worse than male rage. In Hinduism it is the goddess Kali, in her warrior form, who destroys the demons, the forces of anarchy, with her *sakti*, or power.

"Only when Kali sees her husband, Shiva," Julie wrote the name on the blackboard, "does she become controlled and beneficent. Women in India thus have a dual nature: they are held responsible both for defeating the forces of disorder and also for promoting creativity and fertility.

Even Kali is referred to as 'Mata,' emphasizing her role as protector of her devotees. Thus, an important aspect of gender roles in Hindu culture is that women's power can establish order and well-being only when it is channeled by male control, particularly through marriage."

"Hey, when's the next flight?" Jimmy Warren, a bright student but clearly the class wiseacre, called out from the back. "Oh, grow up," yelled Martha Gleber from her front row seat. Martha was an outspoken feminist who never let any misogynist remark pass unanswered.

"Okay," Julie said, encompassing Jimmy and Martha with a friendly but determined look, "Let's get back on track. As I was saying, the view that women must be under the hypervigilant control of men is basic to gender roles in India. This is partly based on the belief that women are by nature open to sexual temptation. Thus, they must be controlled to protect their own purity, which in turn protects the purity of their husband's bloodline. This emphasis on maintaining the purity of the husband's bloodline also underlies the hierarchy of caste and is an especially important consideration at the time of marriage.

"The concern about women's purity forms one of the major themes of the great Indian epic, the *Ramayana*, whose message is the triumph of good over evil. Written by Valmiki over a thousand years ago, this great drama of Indian culture has been rewritten and reinterpreted many times and is read, performed, enacted in ritual and art, and known to every Indian today. Like all great epics, the *Ramayana* teaches righteous action, called *dharma* in Hinduism, through depicting characters that are models of both good and bad behavior. Central to the *Ramayana* is the story of Rama, the king of Ayodhya, and his wife Sita. Sita faces many trials that test her purity, and she passes all the tests. The story of Sita's trials and her devotion to Rama makes her the ideal representation of the pure, devoted wife, filled with compassion and grace, with whom all Hindu brides identify."

Julie paused again, and then Annie, a particularly attentive student, raised her hand. "It's confusing," Annie said. "If women in India, like

Sita, are so revered and, like Kali, so powerful, why do Indian women seem so oppressed?"

"A great question," Julie responded, "which goes to the heart of some anthropological theories about the relationship of women to power. One theory, called the private/public dichotomy, claims that women's power resides in—and is mainly limited to—the private, or domestic sphere, growing out of their roles as wives, mothers, and homemakers. But while these powers can be substantial, they are perceived in many cultures as inferior to the *public* power of men—who dominate in politics, economic production and exchange, and the defense of the society. But the theory raises the question of different kinds of power: while women's power may not be dominant in the visible, everyday world of practice, is it possible that women have subtle or hidden powers, behind-the-scene powers, so to speak, that are revealed in the domain of mythology, religious belief, and folk culture?"

As Annie prepared to respond, there was a spontaneous outburst from Martha Gleber. "It's outrageous—women deserve as much power in public as men do; all this symbolic stuff is just a sugar coating on oppression."

"Many others share your view," Julie nodded to Martha, but then turned to call on Karim, a Muslim-American student from Palestine whose thoughtful and formally articulated opinions earned him the serious attention of both Julie and his classmates.

"I agree that from the Western viewpoint women in most societies, including Islamic cultures, do occupy a seemingly lower, even oppressed position, compared to men—" Karim turned to address his explanation to Martha, "—but many anthropologists and historians are revising this idea. Just because the sphere of women is different, even separate from men, does not mean it is inferior or subordinate. A woman in the household and family does wield real power. Women may greatly influence men's decisions even in their public activities. History gives us examples of this, like some emperors of China and sultans in Islamic culture. And even, I think, sometimes like the presidents in America."

"Good examples," Julie affirmed, "but are these perhaps rare exceptions in most societies, rather than the rule?" Martha vigorously waved her hand again and assertively preempted Karim's reply. "Well, what about that head-scarf business; you call that power, not having the right to wear your hair any way you want to? And the veils, too, are a clear sign of oppression to me."

"I know a lot of Westerners think the *hijab*, and especially the *burka*, are just signs of oppression," continued Karim in his measured way, "but I personally know many women who choose to wear this clothing to express themselves specifically as *Muslim* women. Especially in the West, they may wear the *hijab* as a sign of pride in their Muslim identity and even an expression of their power to defy the majority culture."

Before Martha could respond again, Julie recognized Barbara Mason, an older black student whose participation in class, like Karim's, was always thoughtful, measured, and undogmatic. "As an African-American woman I see this a little differently. From my reading about Africa and my experience in American culture, I see our women as having an important collective experience that our men, who are always competing with each other in jobs, for example, don't have. And in America, anyway, with slavery and discrimination, black men have been even more oppressed than black women. So, African-American women have gained a sort of power in the public sphere by default, yet they have power in the private sphere too, taking care of their children and old folks. But this double power at the expense of black males isn't a good thing for African-American society."

"These excellent observations help us understand the intersection of power, culture, and history," Julie affirmed. "It's key, as Barbara illustrated, to understand that the treatment of women doesn't occur in a vacuum; it's shaped by culture, economics, politics, and history. In

India, for example, as in many other societies, there have been great historical shifts in the position and power of women. The ancient Indian Vedic era did not restrict women to the extent they were subordinated in the later Indian agricultural state, which became more politically centralized. These growing restrictions were codified as the Laws of Manu in 200 BCE. Child marriage became the ideal; virginity and chastity were strictly required of females, but not males; females were placed under the perpetual guardianship of first their fathers and elder brothers, then their husbands. Women lost their rights to property and inheritance, the right of divorce, custody over their children, and the right to participate in public life."

Here, Prithi, a student from India, shyly raised her hand. Julie was eager to hear her comments because in spite of her obvious interest in the class material, she did not often participate in discussions.

"That's so interesting, yet in India we have had a female prime minister, but in America there was such a fuss made about a woman trying to run for president."

"A true and curious comment about America, Prithi, and not just in relation to India," Julie added. "England, Pakistan, and Egypt have also had women prime ministers. We ought to think more about this cultural contrast. In India, women's rights expanded under British colonial rule, and some of the more extreme disabilities they suffered were abolished. But it was really under the leadership of Mahatma Ghandi and other men and women in the Indian Independence movement that women gained even more legal rights. Independent India encouraged its women to participate in the new democracy, which they did with great enthusiasm. And with heroic women leaders like the Rani of Jhansi, who fought military battles against the British, some might say that warrior queens as well as submissive wives have played important roles in India. Maybe the question we should ask is why America, which so publicly praises individual achievement and equality, has been so slow to bring women into the political sphere. Raising these issues really brings out the complexity of the relationship between gender and power in a variety of cultures."

Julie paused for a moment. "I'd like to take up this contradiction between private and public power and explore further the notion of the oppression of women in the Indian context. From my fieldwork, it seems to me that this oppression is not as monolithic as it may seem. Indian women have a number of different domestic roles, and the power inherent in each is also different. For example, as wives and daughters-in-law, Indian women are under great pressure to obey and please their husbands and their husbands' families, particularly the mother-in-law, the *sas*, who is often the real power in the home. As a new wife and daughter-in-law, a woman seems to have very little, if any, power. Yet at the same time, a wife is held responsible for her husband's welfare. So in one sense, women have what might be called the ultimate power: that of protecting their husbands. But if this is a great power, it is also a great burden. Therefore, a woman who becomes a widow is regarded as having failed her husband in this crucial task, and she becomes an inauspicious and even dangerous figure with no real place in society. In the old days, she might throw herself on her husband's funeral pyre, or remove herself to a home for widows. Things have changed now, of course, but not completely, and such beliefs still hold some sway.

"On the other hand, when a wife bears a child, particularly a son, she gains power in the household. And when she herself becomes a mother-in-law, she gains even more power. So if all goes according to the ideal, the Indian woman will be able to wield some power in a family. And since the family is the center of Indian society and culture, this power cannot be lightly dismissed. Popular culture in India partly recognizes this in the festivities associated with marriage, where the women entertain themselves, without any men present, singing songs that mock men and their pretensions to power."

Julie regarded the students intently as she went on. "As I've said before, our study of the relationship between women and power will focus both on gender roles in the context of a specific culture and aspects of gender roles that are similar across cultures. One very widespread, nearly universal aspect of gender roles is male dominance and the ways in which patriarchy, as it is called, leaves women vulnerable to violence. This is an increasing problem in all societies: more women are becoming victims of violence, whether as sex workers, as victims of war, or within their households. But some women seem more vulnerable than others: women who have fewer options—because of poverty, or migration, or ethnic marginality—and we need to see how specific cultural and social situations impact women's ability to resist violence. Understanding this is an important contribution we can make as anthropologists.

"However, as anthropologists today address violence against women, we face a dilemma. If culture is the key to behavior, how can we impose our own views about a woman's right to *not* be harmed, or to control her own reproductive rights, or to participate equally with men in society on traditional cultures that don't permit such rights? Does each culture have the right to make those decisions for itself without interference from well-intentioned—Julie made air-quotes here—outsiders? A few years ago, for example, a Chinese man in New York killed his wife because he believed that she was having an affair. An anthropologist testified in his defense that in a traditional Chinese setting an adulterous wife's murder would not be considered a criminal act. The judge was impressed enough by the cultural evidence to hand down a sentence of one year's probation. Many Asian women's groups were outraged by this leniency."

A prelaw student, Rafael Suarez, raised his hand, explaining that he had read about that case and was disturbed by the outcome. "It's not the only case like that we've learned about in our law class. There seem to be a lot of cases where a guy beats up, or even kills, a woman, and if the guy's from some ethnic culture, his lawyer says, 'his culture made him do it.' Like among Latinos, there's this macho thing, right? So should some Hispanic guy go free after mauling his wife because his macho culture tells him it's okay to beat up on women? To me, it's just an excuse. And if some judges go for it, what kind of message does that send about respect for our law?"

"Thanks, Rafael; exactly the dilemma I was thinking of, and we'll consider this 'cultural defense' later in the course," Julie responded. "Because of my own research interests, we'll explore violence against women, including domestic violence, within the Indian immigrant community, but of course this is a problem that arises in almost all ethnic groups and mainstream America, as well. And in my view, the root cause of this problem is the power imbalance between men and women. Powerful individuals—whether a man acting on his own, or even a woman acting on behalf of a patriarchal family structure, such as the Indian mother-in-law or the older women who manage the genital-operation rituals for girls in Africa—take actions because they can, because their cultures give them the authority to do it, and because even people who think it is wrong look the other way."

Glancing at her watch, Julie paused. "Okay, it's almost time, and I want to take the final few minutes to talk about an assignment in connection with our next class. Since domestic violence is a significant context of contemporary violence against women, I'd like you all to reflect on this issue by doing some journal writing about a case of domestic violence you might know of from personal experience or through the media. You might want to consider how your story relates to some of the issues we've discussed today. If you like, you can hand in your journal entry anonymously, and I'll be happy to comment on it."

Here Julie noticed Loretta Milano exchanging a significant glance with Alicia Romero, the woman sitting next to her. When Loretta whispered something in Alicia's ear, her friend frowned but then nodded.

"Our next class," Julie went on, "will present a film about an Indian victim of domestic violence whose story profoundly impacted legal issues of domestic abuse both in England and the United States. Following the film, there'll be a speaker from Badi Bahen, an organization dedicated to fighting domestic violence in South Asian immigrant communities."

As Julie gathered her notes from her desk, she saw Loretta and Alicia approaching her, with Loretta pushing her friend forward slightly. "Excuse me, Professor Norman," Alicia said hesitantly, "I know sometimes you do permit visitors to your classes. Do you think my boyfriend could come to the next class with the film and the speaker on domestic violence?"

Damn, thought Julie, *a class on domestic abuse really isn't the place for casual visitors, or, worse yet, boyfriends.* It was a volatile topic, and Julie's reluctance was only thinly disguised. But she sighed in agreement, mentally crossing her fingers that Alicia's boyfriend wouldn't show.

Nineteen-year-old Shameela pulled down the steel shutters on her coffee cart parked at the entrance to the People's Pier, a recreational space on the Hudson River undergoing renovation. She was pleased; she had done well that day. Her brother said things would even get better when the Pier was finished and all the school children and their parents and teachers would be using the riverfront for games and whatnot. Shameela waited impatiently for him to arrive with the car so they could tow the cart back to their home in Brooklyn. Though it was a hard life, she was always dreaming and planning about the future. She would learn English, and her brother said she could go to a free school. Muhammed was searching for the right husband for her, someone honest and hardworking like himself, but one who would let her study. Her children would go to school and speak English so well they would teach her. Startled by footsteps in the dark behind her, Shameela turned around. Not Muhammed, as he always called to her so as not to frighten her in that dark patch of park. A man talking softly to her as you would to attract a stray cat came right up to her and put his hand firmly on her arm. He kept talking softly, leading her away into the darkness. Shameela understood nothing he said—maybe he was telling her not to scream, or that he had a knife or a gun. Who knew? She did not know the English word for it, but when he was through, she knew what had been done to her. She cowered by the cart, where her brother found her. He took her to nearby St. Vincent's Hospital where they did a rape kit, gave her a new set of clothes, and called the local precinct. They secured her clothing for DNA evidence and took her story through Muhammed's translation. "An old man, more years than my father . . . a beard? Like a scholar's but not so long; I will never forget his face," Shameela told the police through her brother. "Do not ask me any more!" Her brother wrapped his arm around her. "I will not let this ruin your life," he promised. "No one will ever know of this."

✿ Chapter Four

And there was such a commotion at the door and a bursting in of hooligans that neither could the teacher teach nor the students learn

—*Teaching Rhetoric in Rome*, St. Augustine, Teaching Rhetoric in Rome,
  c. 354 CE

Burnt alive! The man's body was charred to a crisp, from his neck to the bottom of his feet. He was lying face down on the hospital bed, breathing heavily into an oxygen mask. With a guilty start, Julie scolded herself as the image of the barbecued ribs at the anthropology department's annual Fourth of July party involuntarily flashed through her mind. She hoped the students could get past this opening scene, which was both horrifying and mesmerizing.

Today's film, *Provoked*, a reversal of the more typical case of wife murder, documented the true story of an Indian woman in England who had burned her husband alive provoked by his many years of abuse. Convicted and imprisoned for manslaughter, her case had been taken up by an Indian woman's group that sought to overturn her conviction with a "battered wife" defense, claiming she had murdered her husband as a form of self-defense because of his longtime abuse. In a new trial the British court decided for the first time that provocation could indeed be used as a legal defense in wife-abuse cases. An American court later made a similar decision. These significant legal precedents gave abused wives—especially vulnerable immigrant women—who killed their husbands a powerful tool to fight back in court.

When the film ended, Julie looked around the room to assess the students' reactions. She was relieved to see that the chair next to Loretta and Alicia was empty; thank goodness the boyfriend hadn't shown up. Or perhaps Alicia had changed her mind about asking him.

Julie began the post film discussion by contextualizing domestic violence as an issue of gender power and powerlessness that occurs in almost all cultures and at all levels of society. "Domestic violence is influenced by culture, but it is *not* just about culture, and certainly not just about *other* cultures," she stressed. "As I noted in our last class, domestic violence is rooted in the *intersection* of culture and power. So to fight domestic violence we must know about power relations, as these form part of the specific cultural context in which the violence occurs." Julie then nodded to a young woman in the front row who joined her at the lectern. "With this in mind," Julie continued, "let me introduce our speaker, Ruma Chopra, a volunteer with Badi Bahen, an American organization that provides help for South Asian immigrant women who are victims of domestic violence."

Before the speaker could begin, Jimmy Warren raised his hand from the back of the room. "Will this be on the midterm?" he asked, obviously debating with himself whether it was worth taking notes.

"You bet," Julie answered, while the young speaker smiled in understanding. "But more than that," Julie said, "it's vitally important information if you're planning to work in law enforcement or social-service fields. And it might even be useful to women you know personally who are victims of abuse and don't know where to get help." As she said this, Julie saw Loretta and Alicia look anxiously toward the classroom door. "So, I'll now let Ms. Chopra tell us something about the work of her organization and why it is so necessary among today's South Asian immigrant communities."

Many students looked surprised as they took in Ruma's elegant, contemporary appearance. Slightly built, with a stylish, short haircut, wearing fashionable blue jeans and boots, and an Indian *kurta*, Julie knew that Ruma hardly fit the students' image of a social worker, a term most of them associated with dowdy, middle-aged women. Ruma began by inviting the students to interrupt her talk with questions and added that she would leave time for a discussion afterward. "I know that Professor Norman has explained some of the cultural background of gender roles in India," she began, "so I'd like to talk specifically about our organization and its services.

"Badi Bahen, which means Big Sister, began in the mid-1990s," Ruma began. "Like other Indian feminist women's organizations existing at that time, our aim was to challenge the male-dominated culture that Indian men brought from their homeland to the United States. But our aim was also to be of particular service to women in the South Asian immigrant community. Male domination is not just an academic issue; it results in very specific kinds of behaviors that oppress women, violate their rights, and often result in physical abuse or even murder. A significant part of that abuse takes place in the home, thus our term *domestic violence.*

"While domestic violence occurs in all sorts of communities, it is often hidden from public view. This is particularly true of South Asian immigrant communities. Before the 1980s, all community organizations were led by men. Most of these groups actively opposed publicizing domestic violence because they feared it would undermine the positive image of Indian immigrants as a model minority: hardworking, educated, successful people with strong family values. And indeed it's true that these very family values *have* been central to the success that Indian immigrants have achieved here.

"But basic to Indian family relationships is a gendered division of labor and role expectations, which often works against the rights and interests of women. Men dominate both the household and the community, while women mostly play domestic roles and care for the children. Immigrant women, especially, also play a central role in maintaining and transmitting Indian culture to the next generation.

"It's not all about gender, of course," Ruma continued. "In South Asian culture, as in many traditional cultures, gender intersects with other characteristics, such as age, in allocating power. Seniority, for example, is a status that involves control: parents are expected to exercise control over children, and youth are expected to defer to older relatives. Seniority and gender may in fact come together in the abuse and violence against women, as when a husband's parents participate in, or even initiate, abuse against his wife.

"A key difficulty in addressing domestic violence in Indian communities is the importance Indian culture places on family solidarity and the fear of scandal. These factors foster great secrecy about domestic violence, and its victims generally experience such shame and self-blame that they will not seek outside help when they are abused. Before our women's organizations emerged, South Asian victims of abuse didn't have the assertiveness—or the resources—to seek out social services or the police. Some of those who wanted to speak up didn't know English or didn't speak it well, and translators were not readily available. And even in those American agencies that did have good intentions, there was a lack of cultural sensitivity that undermined their effectiveness with South Asian women."

A hand went up. "Could you give an example of what you mean by a lack of cultural sensitivity, please?"

"Indeed I can," said Ruma. "For example, American social service agencies generally advise battered women that the first thing they must do is get out of the situation, leave the abuser, go to a shelter, take refuge with other family members, whatever. That might work for an American woman, but in the Indian community, a woman who left her husband would be severely criticized. Not only would her husband and his family condemn her, but even her *own* friends and family might disapprove of her behavior and possibly refuse to help her, as well. And remember, many of these women have no family members nearby to whom they can turn and may have no close friends here either. In fact, their only social network here might *all* be on the husband's side, and these people would hardly be inclined to take the wife's part in a domestic conflict.

"Unlike in American culture, where the individual is the center of the universe, in Indian culture the kinship group, the family, the community, in short, the collective, is the core of a harmonious society. In fact, a marriage is really viewed as much as a union between two families as it is between two individuals. And culturally, it is women who are held responsible for maintaining this family harmony and solidarity and who are blamed if anything goes wrong. This means women are almost always the ones who must compromise when conflicts occur. Too often that means giving in, subordinating their own desires and rights to control by others in the family, even if it results in years of psychological and physical abuse.

"Although American women also commonly experience self-blame and the pressure to be the compromisers, and perhaps even some shame, American culture is much more permissive than Indian culture about revealing personal problems to others and seeking help from outsiders. Indian cultural inhibitions against washing the family's dirty laundry in public are very strong and severely limit an abused woman's ability to change her situation. This is particularly true of the new bride or young wife, who is the lowest person on the totem pole, so to speak.

"There are other problems also; for example, who will care for a woman's children if she leaves her home? What will happen to her immigration status, which is so often dependent on that of her husband? One form of wife abuse among immigrants is the husband's threat to have his wife deported back to India if she doesn't toe the line or if she reports his abuse to authorities."

"Well, couldn't that help the woman?" another student asked. "She could return to India to live with her own family instead of staying here with her abuser. Maybe she could get a divorce and start all over in India or even here, with somebody else. And an American court would probably give her the custody of the children anyway, wouldn't they?"

These questions made Ruma realize yet again how hard it was to convey the important influence of culture on behavior and how cultures were different from each other. "It's just not that easy," Ruma began slowly. "First, whether the Indian woman is sent away by her husband or initiates the marital breakup, she brings great shame on both herself and her own natal family, not just on her husband's family. And then, though divorce is not viewed as negatively as it once was, it's still a stigma in Indian culture, even for Indians living abroad. Think back to the United States maybe fifty years ago. And compare today's Indian divorce rate of around 4 percent to the American divorce rate of over 50 percent. In addition, although in America a high percentage of divorced women, like divorced men, remarry, this is much rarer in Indian culture and would prove especially difficult for women. In arranging a marriage for their son, an Indian family would put a divorced woman way down on their list. A woman's divorce would also negatively affect the marriage chances for other members of her family, particularly her sisters. On the other hand, there is now a matrimonial Web site for remarriages, so that's a real indication that things are changing, however slowly."

"But," the same student persisted, "Indians are supposed to be so educated; so many Indian women are doctors, right? A divorced woman could probably get a good job and forget about remarrying altogether."

Again Ruma considered her response. "Some Indian women in America do get divorced," she explained, "and some do remain single, but this is not the *norm*. Even many professional Indian women find it hard to disregard the cultural ideal that only prizes marriage and motherhood. Indian woman who remain single are not thought of as complete adult persons; this also is a point of contrast with contemporary American society. While Indian culture *does* change as it adjusts to America and its own process of modernization, the hold of traditional Indian gender roles remains very strong."

Jimmy Warren now raised his hand again. "What's the big deal about violence against women?" he asked. "Women also commit violence against men, like in the film we just saw. It was the husband who got barbecued in that one." A few of the male students laughed, but not for very long.

"You guys are so gross," a female student countered. "The whole point of the film was how much abuse the woman took before she got so angry and depressed she couldn't take it any more. That's not what happens to men. That's why it's called 'battered-wife syndrome,' not 'battered-husband syndrome.'"

"Maybe," Jimmy spouted back, "but look at what happened to Lorena Bobbit's husband. She snipped the tip off his family jewels and tossed it out the window. That's even worse maybe than being barbecued." Several of the male students and even some of the women stifled a laugh.

Julie wanted to acknowledge Jimmy's valid point and jumped in with a rephrasing of his comment. "Actually you're right, Jimmy; there are some cases where Indian—and American—wives have killed their husbands, as we saw in this film. But the important point, even in these cases, is that this scenario grows out of the same cycle of isolation and psychological, physical, and often sexual abuse as the much more common cases where a husband or one of his relatives kills his wife. This cycle is predictable to professionals who deal with domestic violence, but that doesn't help an immigrant wife with few or no resources. They become so unbalanced they feel they have no recourse except to kill their husbands, themselves, or even, more tragically, their children."

Ruma supported Julie's comment with some additional examples before adding, "It was the growing number of these cases that spurred us to form an organization that would offer concrete help, specifically to South Asian victims of domestic abuse before they got to the murderous or suicidal stage. We wanted to assist women to seek outside help from organizations such as ours, and hardly any such groups existed back then."

Julie called on a young woman in the front row. "But with all that you've said about women's dependency on their husbands and their husband's families and the strong shame against speaking out," the student questioned, "maybe exposing the issue of domestic abuse actually harms some women and the Indian community, too."

"We certainly considered that point, " Ruma agreed, "but the high response to our battered-women's hotline and the increasing numbers of women who sought our services convinced us that we are doing the right thing. We reach out with targeted public-relations efforts and cultural events and lectures like this one. We want to raise the consciousness of men, too, so they can understand how important *they* are in this issue. Our aim is to raise their awareness about how domestic violence destroys not just families but whole communities."

"Sounds kinda like feminazis to me," Jimmy Warren said audibly, pointedly glaring at Martha Gleber.

Ruma acknowledged that she had heard similar and even worse accusations from the Indian community. "Many men, especially those who considered themselves community leaders, were shocked at our exposing this problem to outsiders. But we persevered, and today many more women are coming forward to tell their stories publicly. That gives other women the courage to act to resist their abuse. Now they know they are not alone."

After a few more questions, Julie turned to Ruma and pointed to her watch, indicating the class time was up. She thanked the speaker, who then clustered with about half a dozen students at the open classroom door, ready to take up Julie's offer of coffee in the faculty dining room. Loretta, Alicia, Andrea, and Ruma were introducing themselves to each other and to others in the coffee group, including Joey Bukowski, an older, solid family man who worked for RCN Cable and was one of Julie's favorite students; Martha Gleber of course; and, surprisingly, Jimmy Warren.

Joey, always the gentleman, winked at Martha as he started to open the classroom door and bow her out, when suddenly there was a loud thud and Martha was thrown back against him, forcing him sideways into the wall. Joey yanked Martha away from a flying chair propelled from the hallway into the classroom through the now fully opened door. Striding into the room, yelling at the top of his lungs, was "a very angry young man indeed," as Julie later described him to security. He looked older than the typical student, and, although he was slight in build, he had spectacularly muscled arms and chest and a very surly look on his face. Julie stood back and gaped in horror, stifling an insane impulse to laugh at the intruder's ridiculous outfit—some punk rocker T-shirt, baggy pants whose crotch hung practically to his knees, and unlaced sneakers, which prompted Julie to think that he'd never learned to actually tie his shoelaces.

"Who's the teacher in this bullshit class?" the young man was yelling, "with this crap she's telling my girlfriend, write this, write that, put everything in your 'journal,'" he drew out the word sarcastically with a menacing look on his face. "Tell the teacher how your boyfriend abuses you, slaps you around! What about how you spend some guy's bread then think you're too good for him because you go to *college*," another sarcastically drawn out word accompanied by a mocking shifting of his shoulders. Joey pushed the women back behind him and put out his arms, palms turned out pacifically. He was tall and slender and didn't look very threatening. But as a long-time practitioner in *hsing yi chuan*, a form of Chinese martial arts geared to survival and protecting people,

Joey was not only well muscled but psychologically prepared for defense and well disciplined, never losing his cool.

"Hey, bro," he said in a low voice, "what's your beef here? This is a school; you don't threaten teachers. Back off."

Alicia, a heavy load of books in her arms, tears starting from her eyes, tapped Joey on the back. "It's okay, he's my friend. I'll take care of it." Before Joey could remonstrate and warn her back, the intruder leaped forward, fisting Alicia's books down through her encircling arms so that they thumped to the floor, spines breaking open and pages bent.

"Don't 'bro' me," the assailant spat, swinging an arm at Joey, who quickly stepped in front of Alicia to confront the other man. "You some faggoty guy taking this class where all they do is tear men down, with all this gender crap . . ." He got no further before Joey caught his outstretched arm, twisted it in some peculiar fashion, flipped him backward, and had him down on the ground with his knees straddling the guy's stomach, all in the flash of an eye.

Four cell phones in the cluster behind Joey were dialing the several numbers Julie was calling out: security, dean of students, human resources, and the anthropology office. Joey seemed perfectly calm sitting on the boyfriend and pinioning his arms above his head. Alicia timidly knelt down by her boyfriend and turned to Joey. "He's not really a bad person. He's trying to do good. He got his GED, and he got a job; he's just got a temper sometimes. He doesn't mean anything by it. I better go home with him now."

"Get off me," the boyfriend yelled at Joey, trying to twist from under his weight. "You want it to end, we'll end it here, but she's going home with me like she says."

"Mmm, not just yet, friend," Joey said calmly. "You know the line 'help is on the way.' Security'll be here any minute, and this becomes a police matter, out of our hands. I don't know how you got in here, and I feel sorry for Alicia, but you got yourself in some trick bag." As two security officers came toward the classroom, Joey explained the situation to them, relaxing his grip on the young man but remaining wary as he raised himself off the floor. "Someone's got to press charges here if you want the police to arrest this guy," one of the guards said, "Otherwise all we can do if he doesn't have a college ID is toss him out."

Alicia looked pleadingly at Julie and said, "I invited him here." She looked at the witnesses to the scene in embarrassment. "He wasn't really coming on his own. I guess I didn't get the right lesson from the film and the lecture, but do you think you could let it go this one time?" Julie sighed deeply, and Loretta drew Alicia back and practically hissed in her ear with concern, "This is the time to stop it. Press the charges while we're all here to support you."

"I can't do that right now," Alicia replied sadly but with determination. "I appreciate your help, but I don't want the police involved. They hate guys like Tony—they're just looking to bust them for something."

Unfortunately often true, Julie agreed silently. "I'll leave it up to you, Alicia," Julie replied. "I hope you know that your behavior is not at fault here. Maybe another time we can meet in my office and talk about these issues."

Alicia walked off with her boyfriend, the security guards shrugged, and Julie thanked Joey for his assistance, adding in an awed voice, "You gotta tell me how you did that!"

Joey laughed. "Are we still on for that coffee?"

"You bet," came a chorus from behind him. Joey opened the door more widely and once again waved Martha on. "Alright, alright, I get it Joey," she grinned as she grandly marched through.

Detective Danielle Ortega organized her material on the Halloween rape, satisfied that forensics reports, the vic's remarkably composed videotaped and written statement, and her official report and notes were all congruent. Surprisingly, a rape connected with the annual Chelsea Halloween block party was a first in the ten years Danielle had been at the precinct. She'd thought the event would become a happy hunting ground for costumed kiddie molesters and whatnot, but it'd never happened. So the desk sergeant's 3 A.M. call for Danielle to come downstairs to handle an alleged rape was a surprise on a quiet night. The victim, a thirtyish social worker who sat dejectedly in the metal precinct chair hugging her sweater and jacket around her body, was familiar with the whole rape-kit drill from her work and, though obviously upset, was extremely coherent and cooperative. She was wearing an Indian sari with a heavy cotton petticoat underneath and a ripped blouse, bra, and underwear, which she had kept on in case they held some forensic evidence. She told Danielle that around 9 P.M., while strolling through the Halloween block party, she was engaged in conversation by a white male, fifties, a little heavy-set, with a small pointed beard, casually but respectably dressed. He talked about several Asian festivals he had seen while he did pro bono work as a physician on his vacations, and she saw no reason to reject his invitation to walk to Buffie's Café on Chelsea Piers to continue their chat over coffee. He was a little full of himself, and she found some of his suggestive remarks about the pretty Asian nurses who had assisted him distasteful, but his conversation was interesting. At one point she went to the ladies' room; it was then he must have put something like a roofie in her drink. She felt dizzy and suggested they leave. They started off the Pier but he must have veered off with her to an isolated spot. When she woke up, her clothes were disheveled and ripped. She noticed a condom nearby, which she had, with remarkable presence of mind, picked up in a tissue. She had drawn her clothes around her as best she could and made her way to the Chelsea precinct. She told Danielle that she would certainly try to identify the rapist from photos or work with a police artist; she'd never forget his face. And could they inform her ASAP of the HIV results?

Chapter Five

Julie rushed out of her apartment, shouting, "Hold it," as the elevator door was about to close. Her young neighbor, Adriana, in the elevator with her mother, pressed the open button, allowing Julie to step inside. "Ooh, you look beautiful, Julie," Adriana said admiringly. "Where are you going in your Indian clothes?"

"I'm celebrating Diwali with some friends," Julie answered. "It's kind of like the Indian New Year." Actually, Julie amended her explanation to herself, Diwali was more than just the beginning of a new year; it was a religious holiday, a festival of lights that symbolized the victory of good over evil, a story told and enacted in street performances all over India. Diwali celebrated the victory of Rama over the demon Ravana, and Rama's return to become the king of Ayodhya. Merchants started new account books on the day after Diwali, and families bought new clothes, and perhaps a gold or silver object for their homes. They also exchanged small gifts and sweets with friends and neighbors. People cleaned their apartments from top to bottom on the days before Diwali. They set up household shrines devoted to Lakshmi, the goddess of wealth, lighting *diva*, little clay lamps filled with *ghee*, or clarified butter, in her honor. On Diwali night, family members performed a Lakshmi *puja*.

Julie would spend the day celebrating Diwali at the South Street Seaport, where the festival presented the public face of the Indian community in America, attracting both tourists and Indians from the tri-state area. In the evening she was having dinner at her friend Indira's home in Queens. Indira, her husband, and her two sons and their wives had all prospered in their adopted land, yet they still managed to hold on to much of their Indian culture. "You must come to my house for dinner," Indira had told Julie. "You will meet all my children and also my grandchildren. My brother and his wife have come all the way from Texas to stay with us for a week. Even though his wife is American, she is very fond of Indian culture and even enjoys our Indian cooking. We will all be together for the first time in over two years, so it is a big occasion for us."

Julie meandered by the Seaport's various food stalls, clothing displays, and Indian musical performances that took place on a stage erected in the center of the Seaport's plank-floored mall and on nearby side streets. The only thing missing were the fireworks, essential to Diwali celebrations in India, but now illegal in New York as being too dangerous to make an exception even for cultural diversity. As an anthropologist Julie appreciated how the Indian community used the public Diwali performances to draw their American-born children into traditional music and dance lessons. This helped maintain their culture and reinforce their children's identities as Indians in the face of the strong assimilationist tendencies that assailed every immigrant group in America.

Just yesterday Julie had heard on the news that the Indian community had succeeded in their adroit lobbying to have the U.S. Senate pass a resolution acknowledging the significance of Diwali to "the Indian diaspora." There was even talk of issuing a special United States stamp to honor Diwali. New York's City Council was also honoring Diwali this year, with a round of speeches at City Hall by the mayor, city council president, and local representatives of the Queens districts with large Indian populations. One of her favorite politicians, the young congressman Anthony Weiner, had addressed a large Diwali crowd in Corona, where he drew rousing applause for his line that "Today, even Jewish kids from Brooklyn are Hindus." The Indian community had even persuaded the city council to dispense with alternate-side-of-the-street parking for the holiday, the most important official acknowledgement of the power and positive image of an ethnic group. It put the Hindus right up there with the Catholics, Jews, Muslims, and African Americans, whose most important holidays were recognized in this way. *The Big Apple expanding its multicultural tent under which all could fit*, Julie thought happily.

Julie now consulted her Long Island Railroad schedule and alerted Indira on her cell phone to her arrival time. She relaxed on the train to Bayside, a section of Queens whose Indian population was mainly composed of Sikhs and immigrants from Guyana and Trinidad, rather than from India, as well as immigrants from many other Asian nations. Julie waited on the corner near the station that Indira had suggested, observing the multicultural crowd with interest. At the sound of a car horn, Indira's station wagon drew up by the curb near Julie, who quickly jumped in.

"Thanks so much for inviting me," Julie said, a comment Indira waved off. "It is my pleasure, Julie. This is a wonderful occasion for you to meet my family. My children live in New Jersey and don't come to New York so often. You know how it is, busy busy with working at the hospital and bringing up the children—not easy to get away. Not like India where the *ayah* picked up our children from school, and the *bai* did the housework. Still, who's complaining? We have all done so well here, and we are most grateful for the opportunities America has offered us."

Julie had met Indira at a conference on gender and health in the Indian immigrant community. Primarily a doctor who administered social services for outpatients requiring follow-up care after recovering from an illness, Indira was also called in when Indian women showed serious bruises that the attending doctors thought might be related to domestic abuse. Not that there were too many of these cases. Indira herself knew that most abused Indian wives were extremely reluctant to report their injuries to hospital staff. They were even more reluctant to admit that these attacks came from a husband, or some other family member—a husband's brother or father.

Indira's spacious three-bedroom apartment was in an upscale row of townhouses in a neighborhood that looked like a small town. Her apartment door held a small terra cotta sculpture of Lord Ganesh, the god of auspicious beginnings, welcoming visitors and bringing good luck to a household or the inauguration of any new venture. Although Indira had received good medical training in India and her husband had been an Army engineer, they had immigrated to America in the 1980s mainly for the sake of their two sons, who they thought would have better employment opportunities here. In India, technical and medical universities and jobs in those fields were incredibly competitive, with literally thousands of applicants for very few places. And indeed, Indira and her family had made the American dream come true. Her sons' Indian high school educations had put them far ahead of American students, and both had gone on to become physicians. Indira had arranged their marriages with excellent girls from India, one also a doctor and the other, with her Indian university MBA, a highly paid financial officer with a multinational corporation headquartered in New York.

Indira introduced Julie to a cluster of family members and walked her over to the heavily laden buffet table, which held a delicious-looking assortment of Indian dishes.

"I'm still a vegetarian," Indira explained to Julie, "but I make meat dishes for the children. We must accommodate ourselves to some new customs, but we still enjoy many of our traditional dishes too. Please eat. I hope you don't find the food too spicy."

One of Indira's daughters-in-law was bringing plates and glasses from the kitchen to the table, and Julie was not shy in sampling each of the tasty dishes. She marveled at how Indira, like many Indian immigrant women she knew, could shine in her profession and at the same time succeed in retaining many of India's traditions among her family. Julie recognized the difficulties and dedication this involved, especially with the constant pull of America's much more permissive popular culture for the younger generation.

When Julie complimented Indira on the food, her friend confessed in a whisper, "I have only made the *palak panir* and *gobi-alu.* There is a special Indian shop on Hillside Avenue where I buy the other things. When I first came here, I made all our traditional meals myself, but since the children have gone out on their own, I've taken a few short cuts."

"Don't apologize," said Julie. "My idea of dinner is shuffling through my take-out menus and deciding if I want Indian, Italian, or Vietnamese." Everybody laughed, and one of the daughters-in-law chuckled complicitly, admitting "We also do more takeout these days. In New Jersey now there are so many quality Indian groceries it is not necessary to make everything oneself. It is too much to have a profession and spend so much time in cooking." Julie appreciated the young woman's attempt to make her feel comfortable and was emboldened to ask how readily most Indian wives, accustomed to servants in India, were able to adjust to their new American domestic and child-care routines.

Shavani, the elder daughter-in-law, considered her response thoughtfully. "First, Julie, you know that even here in America many Indian brides live with their husband's parents in an extended family. So the mother-in-law is usually more than happy to take over all the food preparation and cooking, sometimes because she feels only she can cook to suit her husband and son. And most mothers-in-law also welcome taking care of the grandchildren in their own, old-fashioned way. If the wife works, that is a big help, but it can cause a lot of tension, too. I'm sure from your fieldwork in India you know this already." With an affectionate look in Indira's direction, the younger daughter-in-law, Rohini, added, "But we have been very lucky in our mother-in-law, but we do not live with her . . . so she is lucky, too, isn't it?" Here she gave Indira a big smile and clasped her hand warmly.

"You *are* lucky," agreed Julie, observing that both Indira's daughters-in-law did seem genuinely friendly with her. Of course Indira wasn't the typical mother-in-law either, not the kind one read about and whom Julie knew from personal experience could often be overbearing and critical of the younger women in a household. Part of Julie's current interest was to discover whether this relationship had changed much as Indians settled in America. She had read recently that the Indian city of Agra had instituted *sas-bahu* workshops for mothers- and daughters-in-law to discuss some of the conflicts in their relationships. Julie now asked Indira's daughters-in-law what they thought of that idea.

"I'm amazed," Indira called in from the kitchen. "That sounds more like a Western notion of talking things over that I wouldn't have thought would take hold in India. But it might work here, though," she added, looking toward her daughters-in-law and laughing. "Should we join such a group, perhaps? I could always learn how to be a better mother-in-law."

"Don't let Indira's modesty fool you," interjected her husband, Yogesh. "She is a super mother-in-law, and mother and wife as well. In India, there were so many servants to help around the house, but here we were on our own. It was a big adjustment at first, but Indira did wonders . . . " *And how much did you help?* Julie asked herself. She knew that even the best Indian husbands—with few exceptions—rarely stepped foot inside a kitchen or picked up a dust rag. *But maybe that's changing too*, she thought. *It's something I'll have to investigate with activity charts if I can get some men to participate.*

Julie was enjoying herself tremendously, but it'd been a long day. A glance at her watch told her that Indira had only a few minutes to drive her to the railway station if she were to catch the next Manhattan train and make it home before midnight.

"I'd better go, Indira," Julie said, making her farewells and receiving warm good-byes and hopes to see her again in return. As she and

Indira got into the car, her friend warned her, "Please be very careful going home. There are so many *badmashes* about. You are quite brave. I can't think that Rohini and Shavani would dream of taking a train so late at night. Especially the subway. I do hope you'll take a taxi from Penn Station."

Penn Station and the subways will be jammed this time of night, Julie knew. That was not where the danger lay. But she didn't want to alarm Indira, so she just called out, "Not to worry, I'll be fine," as she ran for the platform and the train she heard in the distance.

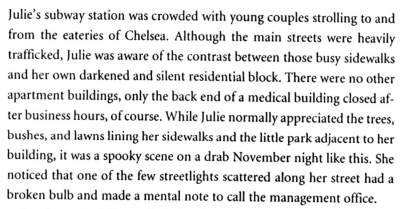

Julie's subway station was crowded with young couples strolling to and from the eateries of Chelsea. Although the main streets were heavily trafficked, Julie was aware of the contrast between those busy sidewalks and her own darkened and silent residential block. There were no other apartment buildings, only the back end of a medical building closed after business hours, of course. While Julie normally appreciated the trees, bushes, and lawns lining her sidewalks and the little park adjacent to her building, it was a spooky scene on a drab November night like this. She noticed that one of the few streetlights scattered along her street had a broken bulb and made a mental note to call the management office.

Involuntarily, Julie recalled a brief article she'd read in the police blotter section of her neighborhood newspaper about a rape that occurred on Halloween night on the nearby Chelsea Piers. She looked carefully behind her and quickened her stride to the building's entrance, hurriedly pulling her keys out of her coat pocket. Looking carefully behind her, she pressed the button for the automatic door to open. While the elderly and disabled residents heartily approved of the new automatic doors, Julie disliked the fact that once you pressed the open button, the doors couldn't be manually reshut. So anyone following you in . . . *Oh, let's not go that route!* With great relief she entered her building alone and made sure the doors closed tightly behind her.

✿ Chapter Six

The next day, Julie juggled her mailbox key with one hand, the other overloaded as usual with papers she had taken home to grade. Once upstairs, she sat back on her couch and rifled through her mail, mostly junk—*Oh, the wasted trees!*—but she was intrigued by one large, square formal envelope from her friend Shakuntala. Slitting it open, she found an elegant card with a hand-painted border of Indian paisley designs surrounding a silvered Lord Ganesh, the elephant-headed deity that had made a successful transition to America. Opening the card, Julie found an invitation with embossed red writing, the auspicious color for brides, announcing a wedding to be held in Mumbai in December. Shakuntala's brief note stated that her neighbor, Mrs. Khattar, was most happy to have Julie's presence at her daughter Anjeli's wedding. If Julie could come a few days earlier, she could also attend the engagement ceremony, nowadays held only days before the wedding. "*There will also be a* Ladies Sangeet," Shakuntala wrote. "*You will enjoy how we ladies all sing songs, some of them very bawdy, making fun of the bridegroom's side. Anjeli is a beautiful and lovely girl, and she has no relatives in America, so you will be like her older sister. It is very important that you come. Let me know when you have made your reservations.*"

That Julie would certainly do. After grading some papers, she would call the airlines later in the evening when the lines weren't as busy, though she still expected some logistical logjams.

After dinner and the evening news, Julie sat down at the kitchen counter, pulled out a legal pad, sharpened a pencil, and geared herself psychologically to make her travel plans for India. Recent news reports and her own previous trips told her that she was in for a cattle-car experience in coach: nonexistent leg room; long hours in a cramped seat punctuated by thuds from the passenger in front of her leaning his seat back; broken movie audio (not that Julie ever watched the fatuous airline films); long lavatory waits; fewer pillows and blankets—the list went on and on.

Apparently the major airlines had decided that economy-class fliers were not loyal fans of any one airline but *el cheapos* who chose strictly by price and therefore didn't deserve pampering. A recent newspaper article had leaked an airline executive's e-mail to his staff about a pissed-off customer: "We don't owe him anything. He flies us only when we're low bid. Let him tell his colleagues not to fly us; he'll be back when we save him a dollar." Julie ruefully acknowledged that this particular shoe fit. First class was out of the question financially, and even the "lie-flat" seats and personal video screens in business class didn't compensate for the price differential between that and the economy seats. *Maybe when I'm promoted to associate professor. . . .* She could have gone online to save a few bucks, but experience had taught her that this was more time-consuming than contacting airlines directly by phone in the off hours. "Let the games begin," she muttered grimly to herself.

Normally Julie followed the rule of three—call three airlines, three car rental agencies, three hotels, whatever, and then strike a rational balance between price and amenities. But she hoped that JetStar Airlines' advertised special would allow her to close the deal in one shot. She got off to a bad start with an airline representative who sounded like a seventeen-year-old rap wannabe. "Please slow down, I'm taking notes here," Julie implored. This earned her the exaggeratedly slow-mo response, "This is Marvin, your Winter Wonderland discount package representative at JetStar airlines; Let's rock and roll." Julie listened carefully to the options, divested Marvin of any notion that she wanted the "full monty" with the rental car, hotel, and sightseeing package, which he sourly agreed was okay, and was able to move him to the new security procedures where he was back to rocket speed. "Two hours before takeoff, no sharp instruments like penknives or toothbrushes"—A *toothbrush is a sharp instrument?* Julie thought incredulously, but Marvin was chugging along too fast to interrupt now—"no liquids except in see-through bottles, but lighters are now allowed on board, you'll be wanded before entering the waiting room area, and your shoes will, I repeat *will,* be examined."

"Right," said Julie, hanging up with a promise to think about it, adding "and we're not happy 'til you're not happy," but Marvin was way ahead of her and had already hung up, presumably to wait on a more affluent victim.

Julie now considered and immediately rejected Russia's Aeroflot. It had the cheapest fare, but with two stops in mid-winter Russia, combined with her lack of confidence in their maintenance of the planes, she decided against it. *Hmm, maybe Emirate Airlines is worth a try.* They had some cheap flights, the shortest layovers, and their route usually precluded storm delays. But the issues of security and of stops in the Middle East gave her pause. True, these days the Emirates were totally global, cosmopolitan, and even alluring to Western tourists, with fabulous new airports, shopping malls, resorts, and moderate religious aura, but still. . . . Nope, she decided, Air India was probably the logical choice after all. Their midmorning arrival in Mumbai was convenient, although she knew that her return trip to New York would leave at an ungodly hour in the middle of the night. But they had low economy fares, and since she was traveling a bit before the Christmas rush, maybe she wouldn't have a full plane and could stretch across a couple of seats and catch some z's.

With her travel dates fixed, Julie contemplated the unpleasant task of informing her department chair, Walter, that she would have to give her final exam in the last class meeting before the official end of the semester three days before the holiday break. The university frowned on this truncation of the official semester, and Julie herself was reluctant to do it, but the wedding festivities Shakuntala had arranged for her to attend were too important to her research to miss.

First, however, she would make sure that her trusted colleague Kwame could proctor her final exam so she'd have some good news to tell Walter along with the bad..

"Of course I will proctor your exam," Kwame told Julie when she caught up with him in the cafeteria. He scolded her for even hesitating to ask him. "You know nothing is more important in our African culture than friends and relations." Kwame was from Ghana and was always lending assistance not only to Julie but to a far-flung network of colleagues, visitors from home, and family members whose needs he never measured by Western standards of strictly balanced reciprocity.

Julie had frequently encountered the pressures these kinds of cultural demands put on people as many of her students were from immigrant societies. They repeatedly had to come late or miss class because they were meeting their relatives at the airport or had other, similar obligations. Just last week a student had come early to class to tell Julie that "I am here" and to request she mark him present in the roll book. "Now, I must go," he said. "My brother and his family are coming from my native place to visit, and I must meet them when they arrive."

"But," Julie sputtered, "then you won't be here, so how can I mark you present?" "But I am here," the student replied earnestly, "but now I must go." And so saying, he took his leave. As an anthropologist and, she hoped, a caring teacher, Julie was more than sensitive to these requests. Yet at the same time, she felt it was not a good precedent to accede to them. What made one student's excuse more acceptable than another's? It was a brainteaser she didn't need. After she finished her meeting with Kwame, she ruminated, not for the first time, on how important it was to have the support of good friends and colleagues. Americans liked to think of themselves as totally independent folks, but actually things worked here pretty much as they did in India, where one good turn led to another.

Despite having lined up Kwame, Julie dreaded seeing Walter. She was not disappointed. Glenda alerted her that Walter was "very busy" working on some Middle States data in his office, but after buzzing him on the intercom Julie was informed that "the chair could spare a few minutes." In general, Walter was unsympathetic to travel plans that disturbed department routine. As Julie seated herself opposite Walter, who, as usual, had barricaded himself behind his desk, she remembered a proverb she had learned in India: *If you live in the river, do not fight with the crocodile.* So she put on a serious yet pleasant expression as though whatever problem she was going to present to Walter could readily be resolved. She explained her need to leave New York before the semester officially ended and the importance of the wedding festivities to her research. There was a dead silence.

Finally Walter spoke. "You know, Julie, I feel as if I must remind you that your full-time job here includes finals week, graduation ceremonies, and the like." A *low blow,* Julie thought. *I'm one of the few faculty who always shows up capped and gowned to the max.* But instead she said, choosing her words carefully, "That's a wee bit unfair, Walter; you know I never miss a graduation or a class; in fact, I won't be missing this one; Kwame has agreed to proctor my finals-week exam." More silence.

"Well, yes," said Walter, "but what about your Middle States committee meeting that week?" *You mean Muddle States,* Julie thought sourly, adding to herself, *Hey, Walter, that's why you get full released time as chair.*

"It's only the first meeting, Walter," Julie replied, "and if things get really hot, maybe we can arrange a conference call." *When pigs fly,* she chortled inwardly, thinking of the eleven-hour time difference between India and New York, her paying guest room without a phone in Mumbai, and the fact that she would not, repeat *not*, be taking her cumbersome Middle States folder with her. But no need for Walter to know all that.

"Anyway," Julie continued, "it was a sadly flawed decision on their part, don't you think, to schedule a meeting during the last week of class? It's not very considerate to the student rep on the committee, who will have her finals to study for." *Gotcha!*

Walter made a tactical retreat, forced to accept that Julie had all her ducks in a row and was going, going, gone. "Do what you feel you must do, Julie," Walter intoned, "but I hope this holiday trip won't hold up the new book you've been working on. It will—ultimately—be so important for your promotion to associate professor." *Got me there,* Julie winced.

"Not at all," Julie picked up the ball. "This is a research trip, Walter, not a holiday. I'll be working on my laptop the whole time I'm away."

"That's alright then, I suppose," Walter yielded ungraciously. Then, pausing, he added, "But I've been hearing a lot recently about terrorist attacks in India, especially in Bombay—*Julie noted again that Walter refused to use any of the new names for places in countries he knew by their old colonial names, and she'd stopped correcting him about Mumbai.* "Just a few days ago I read about a terrorist attack on those two fancy tourist hotels; a lot of people died, including Americans and Europeans. I know you don't stay in such fancy places, but still . . . you know," Walter paused thoughtfully. "I think you should leave your roll book with Glenda while you're gone."

✿ Chapter Seven

Winging her way over the Middle Eastern deserts at dawn was always Julie's favorite part of the otherwise long and tedious journey to Mumbai. As she lifted the window shade to admire the rising sun, her seatmate on the aisle, a young American woman dressed in a North Indian *shalwar-kameez*, stirred and opened her eyes. Julie had envied her ability to fall asleep before the plane even took off and returned the young woman's broad smile.

"Look at that gorgeous sunrise," she exclaimed enthusiastically to Julie. "I just can't wait to get to India. I'm so excited."

"Is this your first trip?" Julie asked.

"It is. I'm marrying an Indian man from New Jersey, and I'm going to meet his family for the first time. We're going to have a traditional Indian engagement party and spend a few weeks meeting all his relatives. Then we're going to have a big Indian wedding at the Maharaj Hotel.

I've heard that's the best hotel in Bombay—oops—I must remember to call it Mumbai. So elegant. It's the place where all the movie stars and models stay, right?"

"Indeed it is," Julie said. "The sea lounge in the Maharaj is my favorite place for a morning coffee. The rooms are awfully expensive, though, so I've never actually stayed there. By the way, my name's Julie."

"Oh, hi, Julie, mine is Grace."

"Where will you be staying in Mumbai?"

"Oh, we'll be staying at the Maharaj. My fiancé left for India a week before me to get everything set up. What bad luck, just as my plane gets in, he'll be tied up in a business meeting. But he's sending his cousin with his car and driver—imagine that, a driver!—to meet me at the airport."

"The airport is always a bit chaotic," said Julie. "I hope they'll have no trouble finding you."

"I don't think so; he gave them my photo so they could recognize me, and on this flight there aren't that many foreigners. I've got two huge suitcases; I heard about these fabulous parties and all in Mumbai, and I did some shopping in New York for some really stunning Indian outfits. My fiancé owns a chain of upscale Indian clothing stores, and he knows all about the latest fashions. He said not to buy any jewelry; their family has their own jeweler here. Imagine, having your own jeweler! But, then, he's a big businessman in America, and I think his family here is pretty wealthy, too. After our wedding bash here, there'll be another big reception when we get back to New York."

"Where will you be living in America?" Julie asked.

"Oh, that's all figured out. We'll be living with his brother and his wife who have a big house in New Jersey. I love the idea of those big, close Indian families where everyone helps everyone and looks after each other. I think they call them *extended families*, is that right, Julie? I'm trying to get all the terms down pat; it's kind of complicated."

"You've got it exactly right, Grace," Julie agreed, though she wondered if "a big Indian family" would turn out to be quite what this somewhat unsophisticated young woman was expecting.

Grace started digging through her glitzy, oversized purse that seemed to contain enough stuff for a Julie-style two-week holiday. Finally she emerged with an envelope. "My fiancé—he's so handsome. Would you like to see his photo?"

Julie nodded and glanced at the color snapshot of a man scrunched down in the driver's seat of an open sports car. The sun was in his face, and he was wearing sunglasses, so the photo wasn't very clear, but Julie could see he was undoubtedly handsome—*if you like that type, which I don't*, she thought—in the typical Bollywood style of Hrithik Roshan, an Indian film star currently breaking hearts all over Mumbai and in the Indian diaspora as well.

"I wish you the best of luck," Julie said sincerely and then headed for the lavatory to freshen up before the crowd got there. It would not be long before they landed at Mumbai's Chhatrapati Shivaji International Airport.

Deplaning together, Julie could see that Grace was a little overwhelmed by the crowds, the kaleidoscope of color, the noise, and the general chaos, a common American response to traveling in India. Unlike what awaited most American travelers in the States, here huge families stood in clusters bearing garlands to welcome home their friends and relatives. Julie guided Grace through customs and baggage claim and helped her lift her two huge suitcases onto a wheeled cart.

"I'm going to run on ahead, Julie," Grace excused herself. "I don't want Dev's cousin to miss me. I hope I'll see you again sometime."

"You bet," said Julie, keeping an eye on the carousel for her bag, which appeared in less than a minute. She lifted it off and also headed for the parking lot, fending off the many beggars pleading for alms outside the terminal's door and the swarm of porters who tried to carry her bag. Julie saw Grace further along, rolling one of her bags behind her, holding on for dear life to her huge carry-all. Behind her a man grabbed her other suitcase off the cart, then pushed Grace along, apparently headed to an old beat-up car waiting in the terminal parking lot with its trunk lid open. Another man was standing outside the car by the passenger door. Julie called out to Grace, who turned around and gave her a big wave. Julie gave her a thumbs up and a broad smile. She saw the first man usher Grace, somewhat roughly, Julie thought, into the back seat of the car, and they headed out of the airport.

Julie looked after them feeling a little uneasy. The man who pulled the luggage along, and was apparently the driver, was wearing a washed out *lungi* and grimy *banian* that gave him the look of a *goonda* from an Indian film. While the other man was more respectably dressed, his flared pants and patterned Western style shirt looked like a throwback to the 1950s. *Strange cousin,* Julie thought. *I hope this turns out all right.*

Julie hailed a taxi and threw her bag in the back seat, diving in after it. She gave the driver her address, a residential block on Chowpatty Beach, forty-five-minute's drive straight south along a major boulevard. All the street names had been changed to reflect the new Indian nationalism, but Julie was by now familiar with the landmarks along the way. She let the driver know it, just to make sure he didn't take her on a circuitous route to increase his fare. First they passed through the *bastees*, where tin-roofed wooden and cement shacks huddled together, housing the thousands of peasants from India's villages that came to Mumbai every day seeking work. To an American the area appeared abjectly poor, but Julie knew that for many of the residents it was a big step up from the destitution of their native villages. Many of the bastee's inhabitants had steady jobs and some material comforts, such as electricity, the security of a daily meal, and the opportunity to send their children to school. Lately, though, Julie thought sadly, the rise of Hindu nationalism and the Shiv Sena Maharashtra movement had made life more difficult for these migrants, especially for Muslims and the people from the southern state of Tamil Nadu.

At Shivaji Park Julie directed the taxi driver to take the coastal road, which was just a little longer and one of her favorite drives. She glimpsed the Haji Ali mosque on its island off the beachfront of Breach Candy, and then the American Consulate. At Kemp's Corner, when the taxi turned inland toward Chowpatty, Julie knew she'd soon be "home," as she had come to think of the room she rented from Shakuntala's friend Shilpa each time she came to Mumbai for her fieldwork. She loved returning to India where nothing seemed to have changed, although she knew this wasn't true, of course. But in all the little details of Shilpa's neighborhood, things did seem just as they had been: the *paanwallah* stall on the beachfront; the Parsi tearoom around the corner; and the servants gathered outside the driveway of Shilpa's building, wolfing down their cold *chapattis* for breakfast or on their lunch break. The betel-nut stains on the walls of the entrance hadn't changed either. Squinting in just the right way, Julie saw them as Indian graffiti, though of course there was no artistic value or political intent, just the spittle from hundreds of mouths chewing betel nut, which stained everything red.

Julie had called Shilpa on her cell phone from the airport, so her friend was waiting for her with a big hug when she knocked at the apartment door. Lehri, Shilpa's servant for many years, immediately relieved Julie of her suitcase, which Julie thought easily weighed more than he did. But Julie had long ago given up trying to carry it herself and offered instead her profuse thanks.

On her previous trip, this expression of appreciation had led to an anthropological moment! Shilpa had, with some exasperation, let Julie know that her thank you's to all the people who served her were not necessary. "Enough with the 'thank you,'" Shilpa said. "These people get paid for this work; you will spoil them with your thank you."

Julie had reflected on that: could it be that the American norm of saying "thank you" in response to service said something about the American ideal—however contradicted in the reality—about the equality of people regardless of their job? With a system of hierarchy based on the opposite principle—caste defined people exactly in terms of what job they did—in India, a thank you for service was perhaps a cultural anomaly. Still, Julie offered Lehri a big smile and a warm thank you as he carried her suitcase into "Julie's room." She always gave him a nice cash gift when she left, knowing he had two daughters to marry off and could use all the money he could get for their dowries. Shilpa was lucky to have Lehri; many of the rural migrants to Mumbai now preferred to work in the factories springing up in the Mumbai suburbs. Those jobs paid much more than domestic service, and all over India men, and even women, now saw factory work as a way of earning enough to amass dowries for their daughters.

She then plopped down on the parlor couch, while Shilpa told Lehri to serve her some lunch of rice and *dal* and some hot chapattis.

"You must be exhausted, "Shilpa said. "But at least these days the Air India flights don't come in at such ungodly hours as they used to. Still, I'm sure you didn't sleep at all. Was the flight alright?"

"Same old, same old," said Julie, "packed to the gills, people arguing over who got tea served first, lavatories eventually out of water and paper towels, and children running up and down the aisles. But the main thing is, I'm here, home again."

Shilpa beamed. She'd come to think of Julie as a daughter, ever since the time six years ago when Julie had first rented the room that her own daughter, Mira, had occupied until she had married and moved to a posh suburb outside of New Delhi. Shilpa's husband had died a few years ago, and her two sons had moved out. One, a bachelor, was a computer engineer in Bangalore, India's Silicon Valley; the other, who managed a sports equipment factory that exported goods to the States, lived with his wife and two children in an upscale co-op apartment near the American Consulate. He and his wife had begged Shilpa to move in with them, but Shilpa had gotten too used to her old neighborhood and had no wish to begin making new friends elsewhere. As it was, they were very near and often left their children with Shilpa, who, of course, adored them and indulged their every whim.

After her husband's death, Shilpa had refurbished the boys' bedroom to accommodate Mira's visits with her children. Then she had come up with the idea of renting Mira's empty room to respectable and trustworthy paying guests recommended by friends. Mostly these were academics, like Julie, usually staying a few months or so. Shilpa found them congenial company, and of course with skyrocketing prices in Mumbai, the money came in handy as well.

"So, what is your program now, Julie?" Shilpa asked. "Nothing today for sure," Julie replied. "I'm beat from the plane ride, and starting tomorrow I have a jam-packed program for the month that I'm here. Shakuntala wangled me an invitation to Mrs. Khattar's daughter's wedding and to some of the prewedding festivities only two days from now. Tomorrow the *Sat Sang* meets, and I want to be wide awake for that."

Julie unpacked her bag, putting her clothes in the room's old-fashioned, commodious *almirah*, then walked out to the balcony. She stood for a few minutes gazing out over the Chowpatty beachfront, with its constant comings and goings of a huge, diverse swirl of people. Julie so enjoyed Mumbai's crowds; it made the city seem very much like New York, and she had felt right at home from her very first trip here, something many Indian people she met found surprising.

As Julie organized her books and papers, she congratulated herself again on having found Shilpa's place in Chowpatty. Not only did she have her own room, but also her own *bathroom* with hot water available almost all the time. And a Western toilet! Squatting on an Indian-style toilet was one of the few things Julie *did* have a hard time getting used to, even though she was in good physical shape.

Shilpa's building was also very conveniently located, with a bus to the shopping district of Colaba and the Gateway of India, the city's most famous landmark, right at the door. Taxis, buses, and sometimes even an elephant or two plied up and down the main thoroughfare. The building was owned by Gujeratis and thus was strictly vegetarian. That was fine with Julie, who was more than happy to share Shilpa's simple fare. For something more elaborate, she could hop a taxi or even walk to any number of good Indian restaurants for her favorite *chicken tikka* or *chicken masala*. By now Julie knew practically all the neighbors in the building: which ones had the evil eye and must be avoided when setting out for the day; which ones were not only rich but also respectable; which families fought all the time; and which ones thought they were "too good for everyone else." Although a Punjabi, Shilpa kept cordial relations with her Gujarati neighbors, but her fast friends were other Punjabi ladies, who, like her, had been living in Bombay—as they still called it—*We're too old to change*, they explained—for years. They had formed their own Sat Sang, or women's group, that held a *kirtan* every Tuesday and a *kitty party* every Friday afternoon, at which the women could simultaneously participate in religious devotions and enjoy a respectable social outlet. Julie had attended the group's meetings regularly, and the women were a valuable source of information for her doctoral dissertation research on urban-Indian marriage, family, and kinship relations.

After her simple but delicious lunch, Julie decided to nap for a few hours, hoping she'd still get a good night's sleep and then awaken the next morning fresh and energized for her day in the field. *So much to do, so little time!*

❀ Chapter Eight

Julie woke early, eager to start her day. She relaxed with her morning coffee, which she brewed in a little automatic pot in her room to save Lehri the trouble of attending to it. She turned on the TV for the morning English-language news program, sat back in her chair, and then leaned forward in some surprise as a picture of a woman's body lying on a roadside emerged on the screen, with a dramatic voice-over:

> *The body of a European woman was found yesterday evening in the brush in a secluded area of the Ahmedabad National Highway, north of Mumbai's international airport. The police surmise that the woman was killed by a hit-and-run driver or possibly was a robbery victim, as she was found with her knapsack but no money or identification. The police have not yet identified the body.*

Julie leaned closer and squinted at the TV screen, the image of Grace, her nice young seatmate on the plane, flashing through her mind. *Why on earth should I think that?* she chided herself. The picture was so grainy with the face partly turned away so you could hardly even see any individual features. So many European backpackers still came to India even though the rush of the 1960s was long gone, and such assaults were probably not that rare. *And certainly Grace wasn't carrying a backpack or even a knapsack.* Julie recalled her showy carry-on holdall very well. The newscaster then moved on to the political news, and Julie thought she'd better move on as well and get ready for the big day ahead of her.

Julie finished her coffee, gathered her notes into her favorite capacious mirror-embroidered Indian shoulder bag, waved good-bye to Lehri who was squatting in the kitchen drinking his morning *chai*, and waited for the elevator to creak its way up to the fifth floor. She spiritedly strode out to Walkeshwar Road to find a taxi to Colaba where the ladies' kirtan was meeting.

Namasteji, namasteji," the women cried out to each other as they gathered in the living room of Mrs. Puri's apartment. "Ah, our Julie is back with us. *Aap kaise hain?* How are you?"

"*Namaste,*" Julie returned their greetings. "Shilpaji asked me to send her regrets—her knee is really bothering her, and it is not possible for her to go out these days." Murmurings of sympathy followed, and then the women settled down on the floor to listen to the week's reading of the *Gita*, the Hindu holy book.

"What is our women's dharma?" Mrs. Puri, in her role of *guru*, dramatically asked the women surrounding her, holding up the Gita in her lap. "How in this fast-moving, materialistic world, where people think only of money and are becoming so greedy, can we find the time to carry out our devotions to God?"

"*Ha ji,* yes indeed, that is the right question," Mrs. Sahni cried out from the back. "The Gita says we must do our duty. How can we best know what that is and follow it in these days of *Kul Yug?*"

"Do you know these words?" Julie's neighbor whispered in her ear." Julie nodded affirmatively.

"We must help improve the life of the poor," Mrs. Nanda answered in her calm, confident voice. "We must help those who have less than we do."

"All very well to say," chimed in Mrs. Thappur, "but where do we find the time? Nowadays the servants are so bad, you have to watch them every minute; you can't even trust them to buy a fresh vegetable or get the best price. What do they care? It is not their money they are spending."

"That is true," said Mrs. Mohan. "We all would like to do social service, but everyone is so busy."

"Exactly right," interjected Mrs. Thappur again. "So much time I'm spending on my children, arranging their marriages, getting them settled, where is the time to do social work? After all, one's first duty is to one's family."

On this note there appeared to be a consensus, and the sweet voice of the group's lead singer, Mrs. Sondhi, began the first *bhajan*, accompanied by women playing the *dholak*, cymbals, and harmonium, an accordion-like instrument. Someone passed Julie a book of devotional songs, and she followed along, moved both by the music and by the evident sincerity on the women's faces. After completing the first bhajan, Mrs. Sondhi called out a page number and began a new song. The women all joined in on the chorus, and even Julie ventured to sing the Hindi words in a low voice. "Sing, sing," Mrs. Mehta jogged Julie's elbow. "Not to worry if you don't know all the words correctly." So Julie sang, lifted as always by the spirituality of the occasion. At the same time, she looked forward to rising from her cross-legged position on the floor and enjoying the tea and snacks that would follow.

After the last bhajan was sung, the women rose and gathered around the table laid out in Mrs. Puri's dining room. Each week the kirtan rotated among the women's houses, and to miss a turn was a serious breach of the rules. While the women treated the religious part of the occasion with the utmost seriousness, they also obviously took pleasure in the light gossip that accompanied their tea afterward. Much of the conversation turned to marriages: those that had taken place, those coming up, and those in the process of being arranged. In fact, one of the great advantages of the group was the opportunity for the women to meet a wide circle of friends of the same ethnicity and social status, within which successful marriages could be arranged.

In the States, Julie knew from her reading of Indian newspapers, many young, educated Indian men and women were utilizing Internet marriage sites on their own behalf, but in India, even in today's super-modern, globalized Mumbai, almost all marriages were still arranged by elders. The extended family was still very strong, and marriage continued to be the concern of families rather than just the individuals involved.

Julie's thoughts on marriage were interrupted as a little boy, who looked about four, dashed into the room among the women. "This is my little Jayanth," Mrs. Puri told the group, adding for Julie's benefit, "my eldest grandson," giving the boy a big hug.

"*Dadima,*" the child demanded of his grandmother. "I want an orange." Mrs. Puri plucked one from the bowl on the table and proceeded to peel off the skin, pull apart the segments, take off every last white string, and remove the pits out of each segment, before giving it to him. He then sat down on the floor and proceeded to eat it, piece by piece, dashing to the back of the house when he finished.

Julie thought fondly of her own nephew Kai, her sister's four-year-old. Getting the orange would have been preceded by a "please," and completed with "thank-you," the "magic words" in America, but then Kai would have been all over anyone who tried to peel the skin, pull off the strings, separate the sections, and remove the pits.

"I do that myself, Aunt Julie" was Kai's favorite sentence when he was with her. Julie pictured him pulling off the orange peel so that the juice splashed all over the table with half the pits finding their way to the floor. *And we would be so proud of that,* thought Julie. *We really believe that's the way children should grow up, polite, but fiercely independent.* One reason Julie loved anthropology was because it attuned her to every detail of human behavior—even something as small as eating an orange—and what it might reveal about culture.

Before Julie left the gathering, she reminded herself to speak with Mrs. Chatwal, who was in the process of arranging a marriage for her son. Mrs. Chatwal had seemed agreeable to Julie's request for an interview, and Julie approached her now to fix a time and place. "Is the arrangement for your son's marriage proceeding well?" Julie asked. Her impatience must have shown in her eager look and voice, for Mrs. Chatwal laughed in a friendly way.

"Don't be so much in a hurry, Julie. You Americans want everything done so quickly. You get married quickly and then just as quickly get divorced. Just like your going into Iraq, *juldi juldi,* and look what a mess you made. Here in India we treat marriage more seriously. We cannot learn by our mistakes and then just say, *sorry* and make it alright. If we make a mistake we have not only ruined the life of our son or daughter but we have spoiled the reputation of our family as well. So we must be very careful." Julie knew that what Mrs. Chatwal said was true and promised herself to be more patient. Setting an appointment with Mrs. Chatwal for the end of the week, Julie then took her leave.

Excited about the upcoming interview, in the taxi going home, Julie mulled over how her own views on arranged marriage had changed over the years. On her first field trip to Mumbai she had met many young, college-educated women who were happy to have their parents arrange their marriages, and initially she had found that unfathomable. But their arguments about how they were free to enjoy their youth without worrying about getting married, were quite persuasive. Julie recalled her own high school and college days, when the anxiety of the competition to "be popular" with the opposite sex was the most prominent feature of an American girl's teenage years, even for those like herself who envisioned a career. They were distracted from enjoying all sorts of activities that might label them nerds or geeks. And now, of course, Julie understood much better the huge risk that a young Indian couple would be taking if they married "for love," particularly if their families were irreconcilably opposed. In India every important resource in life—a job, a house, a social circle—was attained through family connections. Without those, a couple would be completely dependent on only one other person for personal happiness. And certainly, after many trips to India and through her research on the Indian diaspora in America, Julie knew or knew of many happy marriages that had been arranged.

And yet, the idea of marrying a stranger, someone she did not know and did not love, still seemed hard to swallow. It was as if you'd given up and were settling for second best. Lately, though, she'd become more skeptical of "romantic love." Of course she knew happily married "romantic love" couples in America, too, but increasingly, in her friendship circles, and even those of her mother, tempestuous failed marriages ruled. And her own experiences of falling in love hadn't ended particularly well either. Maybe she should just leave it that in different cultures, different things worked. *Or perhaps marriage as an ideal forces an awful lot of big feet into tiny glass slippers never meant for everyone.*

❀ Chapter Nine

As the result of the union of persons [through marriage] . . . two families are also united, and the boy and the girl come together not simply as individuals but as members of their families. The [marriage] not only transforms two persons, but it puts two groups into a new and vital relation with each other.

—William Archer, Songs for the Bride

Julie was enthusiastically looking forward to her interview with Mrs. Chatwal. Most of her data on arranged marriages in India were from parents who were marrying off their daughters. This interview on arranging a marriage for a son would add an important perspective to her research. In the old days, Julie knew, the boy would probably not even meet the girl before the marriage, but these days, after an initial chaperoned "bride viewing" by the family, the two young people might be allowed to meet unchaperoned a few times. Or, if the man lived in America, they might talk over the phone or exchange e-mails. But one important thing that had changed, at least in educated, upper-middle-class families, was that both the boy and the girl got a chance to say refuse the match, though the pressure was always greater on the girl to say yes if the match satisifed her parents.

Julie felt rather sorry for the parents of daughters because the real burden of a match always fell on them. Marrying off a daughter was a *religious* obligation, *kanya dan*, the gift of a virgin. Julie recalled her first field trip to India, which had taken her to a remote province in eastern India. There, a young man walking along the road had stopped to talk with her. "Are you a virgin?" he had asked. *Talk about culture shock!* She had had to ask him three times to repeat himself before he finally got it and rephrased his question: "Are you married?" Julie laughed as she thought about the contrast the encounter revealed between Indian and American assumptions about women.

And the gift of the bride was only the beginning for parents. Not only were a girl's parents obligated to marry her off, but the new relationship that ensued with the family of the groom actually involved further giving on various ritual and ceremonial occasions throughout their lives. Great financial expenditure, sometimes entailing substantial borrowing, was involved in a daughter's marriage: the bride's dowry; financial responsibility for the wedding festivities; and the presentation of gifts to all of the groom's immediate and extended family. Julie knew that the functions of a dowry were a subject of anthropological debate: Did it belong to the bride, as a substitute for the inheritance she did not receive in traditional India, or was it compensation to the boy's family for taking on a mouth to feed that didn't earn her keep? Or was it, as it functioned these days, a joint gift for the husband and wife to start their new life?

Sadly, the financial burden of daughters had resulted in the widespread practice of aborting fetuses after sonograms revealed them to be female. The Indian government had outlawed sonograms for this reason, but Julie knew that the practice continued, both in India and in the Indian diaspora. Thus, in spite of the demographic reality, which resulted in more males than females, the major cultural anxiety surrounding marriage in India focused on the shortage of "good boys," and gave families arranging marriages for their sons the upper hand.

Since the traditional Hindu practice was for a girl to live with her husband's family, finding a good boy from a respectable, financially secure family was paramount for a girl's parents. Once a daughter married, her own family had little leverage over how she was treated, especially if the girl married abroad, as many did these days. Indeed, traditionally, the family of the girl owed great deference to her husband's family. This unequal social status colored all the relationships between people on the boy's side and those on the girl's side. Maintaining this status inequity became more difficult if a girl "thought too much of herself," and the apparent willingness of a girl to defer to her in-laws and their kin was an important criterion in evaluating her as a bride. These relationships were modified in the diaspora but still carried unspoken weight.

As Julie mused and peered out her taxicab window, she noticed how much the traffic had grown even since her last year's visit to India. As the cab passed the latest "in" restaurant, the *Oriental,* which supposedly required reservations a month in advance on the weekends, she remembered her own experience a few years ago when she'd tried to eat there alone. The staff had been so disconcerted by her request for a table for one that she'd had to repeat, "Just me, just one," to at least three different people before they finally found her a small table, back by the kitchen doorway. *But be fair,* she chided herself. *Nobody in India goes out to eat by themselves.* Many Indians perceived this as yet another bizarre example of America's individualistic culture.

The Chatwals lived in one of the older skyscraper residences in Breach Candy, an established upper-middle-class neighborhood adjacent to the rocky shoreline of the Arabian Sea. As Julie's taxi pulled up to the driveway of Mrs. Chatwal's apartment block, the *chowkidar* opened the door for her and *salaamed,* leading her into the lobby. After ringing the intercom for Mrs. Chatwal's apartment, he ushered

Julie into the elevator—a somewhat nerve-racking experience in a city with frequent power cuts—and pressed the button for the top floor. At Julie's push of the bell, a servant opened the door and directed her into the living room. Mrs. Chatwal was seated on a sofa in front of the French doors that opened to a balcony with a magnificent view of the sea.

"Hey, Sushila, bring us the pastries and coffee," Mrs. Chatwal called into the kitchen as Julie settled herself on a chair opposite her hostess. Noticing Mrs. Chatwal's simple, but obviously expensive sari, Julie was glad she had selected her outfit carefully. She wore a conservative *shalwa-kameez* and had braided her hair into a neat, secure plait that was extended almost to her waist by intertwining it with a colorful, hand-woven *paranda*. Julie could well imagine Mrs. Chatwal's disapproval of the popular Western fashion for sexy, free-flowing "big hair" and her distaste for the typical Western woman's gesture of constantly finger combing her hair out of her eyes. In fact, Mrs. Chatwal did immediately compliment Julie on her appearance. "A good *masala*, Julie, part Indian, part American. Not everyone from America is able to strike such a nice balance. Your hair is done very nicely. You know how auspicious long hair is in our Indian tradition."

"I do," Julie responded. "It's taken two years to grow, and when I return to New York, I'm having most of it cut off as a donation to Cancer Care."

"What a kind thing to do," Mrs. Chatwal smiled approvingly.

"I got that idea from a TV show on Indian women donating their hair to various temples," Julie explained. "Then the priests sell it for charity. I suppose it's spiritually benficial for them to give in such a way."

"Indeed," said Mrs. Chatwal. "A good example of how the ego must be restrained to further one's spiritual nature."

"Well, for some women it may not be *all* spiritually motivated," Julie politely corrected. "I've heard that some very poor women *sell* their hair to the temple, which resells it to hair merchants who process it and export it to the West. It's the latest fashion among celebrities who dye and style it for hair extensions."

"Really, "asked Mrs. Chatwal, with a faint smile. "So we Indians give up our hair to diminish our ego, and in the West people buy the hair to enlarge their ego. Well, no matter, the spiritual rewards of giving are not decreased because of how someone else uses our gift, *hai na?*"

Julie again sipped her coffee for a moment or two in silence. Mrs. Chatwal asked her about her family. "I have a twin sister who's a social worker," Julie stated, adding before Mrs. Chatwal could ask, "She has a little boy."

"Why, your parents must be very proud," said Mrs. Chatwal. "It is important that girls be educated. These are modern times," she continued; "Many girls are going into professions and whatnot. Why, I read just the other day that now girls in India can also work in gas stations and even in bars. What a change! In my day a girl who only entered a bar once would have ruined all her chances of getting married forever."

After a few minutes of inconsequential chatter, to Julie's pleasant surprise Mrs. Chatwal brought up the subject of the interview herself. "So, Julie, you want to know about our system of arranged marriages. And a very good system it is, I think."

Without commenting on Mrs. Chatwal's remark, Julie said, "Since most of the women I've talked with are arranging marriages for their daughters, I am particularly interested to hear about the marriage you are arranging for your son. I know you've been looking for a while. Have you found a suitable girl for him?"

"No, not yet," replied Mrs. Chatwal; "we're still keeping ourselves open to possibilities." What Mrs. Chatwal didn't say, but what Julie knew, was that keeping oneself open to possibilities meant being the center of a lot of attention. The mother of an eligible son like Mrs. Chatwal's would be besieged by the parents of daughters who offered hospitality, deference, and a sense of importance as they requested her presence to view their daughters. *That couldn't help but give a woman a feeling of power,* Julie reflected; few women would easily deprive themselves of the social swirl that centered on the mother of an eligible son.

From the many conversations at the Sat Sang, it was evident to Julie that Mrs. Chatwal prided herself on her family's respectability, hence the family background of any future daughter-in-law would be important to her. Mrs. Chatwal was a model Indian matron: sincere in her religious devotion but neither extreme nor priggish in her religious views; outspoken but not contentious; and modest and deferential to those above her by virtue of seniority and status but taking no nonsense from those below. She contributed her share to social conversation but rarely engaged in mean or idle gossip and never openly quarreled. Julie guessed these would be important qualities that she would look for in the family of any future daughter-in-law. Mrs. Chatwal had a practical intelligence and was quite pleasant, but Julie thought a new bride would need a lot of fortitude to live in this joint family.

Julie kept her thoughts to herself but expressed aloud some surprise that Mrs. Chatwal had not yet found a match for her son. "Oh, your son is so personable and well educated, and nice looking, too. I thought perhaps by now you might have found someone suitable."

"We had delayed seeking a match for Amit while he was in the Air Force," Mrs. Chatwal began. "Because he was stationed in such remote places, which girl would accompany him there? Now that he's left the military and joined my husband's business, things will be much easier. You know that's one of the advantages of our Sat Sang group—it is a good place for making contacts, no? We are almost all Punjabis there, so the community is the right one. Whatever modern ideas young people may have about everyone being equal, it is much more difficult for a family if the community doesn't match, isn't it?"

And if the class doesn't match also, Julie thought. She knew that family status and wealth were very important considerations in arranging a marriage. In fact, traditionally, these had been perhaps the most important criteria, and they still counted heavily. In the new urban milieu, judging these criteria was an inexact science at best; it included evaluations based on the clothes people wore; the schools to which they sent their children; the place where they lived and the furniture their homes contained; the kind of cars they—or rather their drivers—drove; the clubs, if any, they belonged to—a whole host of factors that added up to placement on a status hierarchy that was based on money. One advantage of belonging to the Sat Sang was that its weekly rotation gave a person a chance to see how other women lived and how they measured up—or didn't—on all these criteria.

Many of the women in the Sat Sang had daughters of the right age for Mrs. Chatwal's son, and some had already expressed an interest in a match. "I've met Mrs. Luthra's daughters," Julie said, "and all five are so pretty and well educated. Have you considered any of them?"

"Yes," Mrs. Chatwal replied, "they are pretty, and with good family values also. In fact Mrs. Luthra told me, 'You can have your pick for your son, whichever one of my daughters appeals to you most.'"

"Oh, why not?" Julie exclaimed enthusiastically. Mrs. Chatwal smiled indulgently and then made a little grimace indicating she did not share Julie's enthusiasm. After a short pause, she explained. "See, Julie, here is the problem. The family has so many daughters, how will they be able to provide nicely for any of them? We are not making any demands," a code word that Julie knew referred to dowry, "but still, with so many daughters to marry off, one wonders whether they will even be able to make a proper wedding. It's best if we marry our son to a girl who is the only daughter. Then the wedding will truly be a gala affair."

Julie inwardly rebelled against this consideration, but she acknowledged silently that this was her American culture talking. In any case, she was not quite convinced that Mrs. Chatwal had given her the whole story.

"Is there anything else standing in the way with the Luthras?" Julie asked in what she hoped was a casual tone.

Another pause, longer this time. "Yes," Mrs. Chatwal finally admitted, "there is. This family has one other daughter, already married and living in Mumbai. Mrs. Luthra is always complaining to me that the girl's in-laws don't let her visit her own family often enough. So it makes me wonder, will she be that kind of mother who always wants her daughter at her own home? This will prevent the girl from adjusting to our house. It is not a good thing." Mrs. Chatwal had obviously made up her mind to shut the door on the Luthras, and Julie decided not to pursue it further.

Julie fully understood this logic from Mrs. Chatwal's perspective. Ideally, an Indian bride's loyalty transferred to her husband's family, and her relationships with her own parents and siblings became subordinate. A girl's willingness to orient herself toward this ideal was an important factor in evaluating her value as a potential daughter-in-law, especially when she would be living in a joint family as Mrs. Chatwal anticipated. Being a mother-in-law meant exercising control—it was one of the privileges that came with the territory.

Julie tried to recall some of the other marriageable daughters Mrs. Chatwal had mentioned to her last year. Mrs. Kaul's daughter had seemed an excellent prospect. The Kauls were a very highly regarded family from Mrs. Chatwal's native place in Punjab and owned a big auto parts business in Mumbai. The girl, an only daughter, fair and slim, and well educated, had a brother studying in the United States. But now all Mrs. Chatwal's talk of Mrs. Kaul's daughter as a match had died down. "What happened to the Kaul daughter as a prospect?" Julie asked. "You never mention her any more. She is so pretty and so educated; what did you find wrong?"

"She is too educated," Mrs. Chatwal replied immediately. "We've decided against it. My husband's father saw the girl on the bus one day and thought her forward. A girl who roams about the city by herself is not the girl for our family."

But Julie knew that, again, Mrs. Chatwal was not telling all. The Chatwals were more than equal to the Kauls in wealth, but in the traditional, very subtle status hierarchy of North India, the Kaul lineage was somewhat more distinguished than the Chatwal's. This disadvantaged the Chatwals because traditionally, while greater *wealth* on the girl's side was no drawback, it was the *boy's* family that should have the higher *social* status. That too made sense from the Indian perspective, Julie understood. If the bride's family, like the Kauls, enjoyed a slightly higher social status than the groom's family, as in the Chatwal's case, the bride might think herself too good for them, and this would cause no end of problems. So Julie interpreted Mrs. Chatwal's phrase "too educated" as her code for a girl who might be too independent, too modern, and too unwilling to take a subordinate place in her husband's joint household.

Julie leaned forward as Mrs. Chatwal began talking again. "Another girl seemed a possibility at first, the daughter of a client of my husband's. When this client learned that we were looking for a match for our son, he told Mr. Chatwal, 'Look no further, we have a daughter.' He invited us for dinner to see the girl, but I told my husband, 'No, let's do tea only; it's less of a commitment, it doesn't obligate us so much to choose the girl.' The girl was studying for her exams, but she came out to say hello to us."

"And what did you think?" Julie asked with curiosity. "Well, Mr. Chatwal liked the family and was impressed with his client's business accomplishments and reputation. But I didn't like the girl's looks. She was quite fat and wore glasses. I told my husband, 'Say we are deciding to postpone the boy's marriage indefinitely.'" Julie understood that Mrs. Chatwal thought they could do a lot better for their son.

What a soap opera! Julie knew "fat" was out and had even heard that many young Indian girls were going on diets, something she was sure was unheard of in Mrs. Chatwal's day. In fact, she had read recently that Punjabi women were the most obese in India, a statistic undoubtedly related to the traditional North Indian view that "health—meaning plumpness—was wealth." When some of the older women in the Sat Sang commented to Julie that she looked "pulled down," Julie knew they meant "too thin," hence, unhealthy. *But in America,* people said, *you can never be too thin, or too rich!*

Julie's impatience to hear a happy ending to the story contrasted with Mrs. Chatwal's apparent ability to wait all the time in the world in order to make a satisfactory choice. "I hope this conversation has been helpful to you in your work, Julie. You can be sure I will let you know how things turn out."

Julie was truly grateful for Mrs. Chatwal's candor and helpfulness, and on a more personal level was enjoying the suspense and looking forward to hearing the eventual outcome. She gathered up her purse and notes and started to take her leave. "Thank you so much for making the time to speak with me, Mrs. Chatwal. I really appreciate it."

"Not at all, my dear," returned her hostess, walking her to the door. "I hope to see you next week at the kirtan. Remember, be patient; I think you Americans have a saying, 'Act in haste, repent in leisure,' isn't it?"

"We do indeed, and it's good advice," Julie said. "I guess that's why so many couples in America now live together before they get married."

Mrs. Chatwal looked aghast, although even in India the custom was catching on a little, though only among the most independent, professional women. "Ai, *bap re,* not here," Mrs. Chatwal said, narrowing her eyes. *Maybe not now,* Julie thought, *and not for Mrs. Chatwal's crowd, but change is coming, ready or not.*

Chapter Ten

Getting ready for Anjeli Khattar's wedding, Julie considered her appearance in the slightly peeling full-length mirror. She had chosen a loose yellow silk shalwar-kameez that was flattering to her slim figure, with a *dupatta* in a matching print. Her long, dark hair was twisted into a French braid that hung halfway down her back.

Shilpa knocked lightly on the bedroom door to see how close Julie was to being ready. As Julie came out, there was a knock on the front door, which Lehri opened to admit Shakuntala. Shakuntala and Shilpa hugged each other warmly as Shakuntala announced that her car was downstairs to take Julie to Anjeli's wedding. "We'll be on our way as soon as I've looked Julie over and approved her dress," Shakuntala asserted. Shilpa laughed; Shakuntala was a little overbearing, but her gibes were mostly in good fun and were meant well, though she also meant every word. An important part of a woman's reputation derived from her appearance, which needed to be appropriate to her various social statuses and which also reflected on her family and friends. At a wedding, where everyone came under scrutiny, appearance was crucial. Since Shakuntala was bringing Julie, Julie's appearance would reflect on Shakuntala, and as Julie and Shakuntala were both guests from the bride's side, their appearance would also reflect on Anjeli's family.

Shakuntala stepped back and viewed Julie with a critical eye. "Lovely outfit; it suits you," she said, nodding, observing Julie's long legs lightly outlined by the silk folds of the shalwar, while the gauzy dupatta only suggested the slim but well-formed figure beneath the kameez. "But why don't you wear a sari, Julie; today is the perfect occasion for it."

"Oh, Shakuntala," Julie sighed, "you know I feel so awkward in them. I've tried so many times to wear a sari, and I'm always afraid the *pallu* will come down and the whole thing will unravel. I've had bad dreams about that happening in public with everyone bursting into laughter."

"Nonsense," said Shakuntala kindly. "A sari suits your figure very well. We can pin up the *pallu*, and you'll be fine."

"No dice, Shakuntala. I know we're not doing any real walking today, but a sari is just too uncomfortable for me. I have to take such mincing short steps that I would feel as hobbled as those long-ago Chinese women with bound feet."

Shakuntala continued to examine Julie from head to toe, nodding her head rapidly side to side with approval in that unique Indian way. "*Bahut accha hai*; very good," she said, looking at Julie's painted toes in high heeled sequined sandals that exactly matched the color of her outfit.

Just then Shakuntala threw out her arms in despair as she noticed Julie's lack of jewelry. "This won't do at all," said Shakuntala. "We are representing the Khattar's side in this wedding, and we must all show our best. Your earrings and necklace will do," she said, fingering the gold hoops in Julie's ears and the gold chain with the dancing Shiva charm around her neck, "but you must wear some proper bangles." With that, Shakuntala removed the multicolored glass bangles from Julie's wrist and replaced them with two of the many gold bangles that adorned her own.

"That's better," Shakuntala scolded, "when it comes time for your own wedding, I see I will have to be there to make sure you are dressed properly." Julie thought of herself as decked out like Lady Astor's pet horse whenever she wore such an array of jewelry, but on some things there was no saying no to Shakuntala.

Julie also knew that wearing jewelry, especially bangles, was auspicious, and practically a requirement for any woman who was not a widow. When a woman's husband died, the first thing she did was remove her bangles. Traditionally widows were expected to spend the remainder of their lives in self-imposed penance, living simply, without luxuries like jewelry; fine, colorful clothes; and rich, spicy foods. In the past, Julie knew, very devout widows even committed *sati*, throwing themselves on their husband's funeral pyres. That didn't happen any more, with the exception of a few sensational cases in the rural areas, but the ritual symbolized how inauspicious it was for a wife to outlive her husband. Widows rarely remarried in India, though it was perfectly acceptable, indeed encouraged, for widowers to do so, especially if they had no children. The treatment of widows was one Hindu custom that really angered Julie. She remembered the anthropological maxim not to judge other cultures if you wanted to understand them, but that didn't mean you had to agree with or like everything you found there. Julie well remembered that when her father had died of a sudden heart attack in China, where her mother was teaching for a semester, it had been a big help for her mom, during and after her period of grief, to eventually carry on with her normal activities.

But here, too, changes were coming, especially among Indians in the diaspora. In fact, she was delighted to see in a recent Indian film—an essential clue to understanding the directions of contemporary culture—an entertaining subtext about a widow who was the object of an elderly neighbor's flirtation. Sometimes change was unambiguously considered progress, Julie decided, and this was one change she hoped would catch on. So Julie resigned herself to allowing Shakuntala to have her way with the gold bangles. Now, as Shilpa and Shakuntala looked Julie over one last time, they both surprised themselves by asking together, "Speaking of marriage, why is such a pretty, intelligent girl like you not married yet?"

Julie had been asked this question many times in India. She knew her friends were asking out of genuine, even maternal, concern, and given their culture, the question made perfect sense, and was even an urgent one.

"I guess I just haven't found Mr. Right yet," Julie replied, thinking, *Well, that's the short form.* "Maybe I'll meet someone at the wedding," she added, only half jokingly. "You're always saying that Indian weddings are a great place for matchmaking."

Shakuntala and Shilpa shook their heads in mock dismay, chiding Julie for joking about such a serious matter. Waving good-bye to Shilpa, Julie and Shakuntala took the lift downstairs and settled into Shakuntala's car. As they drove off, Julie asked Shakuntala about the boy she had interviewed for Amrita in New York. "Anything moving toward a match there?" Before Shakuntala could answer, Julie chided herself, *He's a man, not a boy; for heaven's sake, he is almost thirty and a PhD engineer! Well,* she cheered herself up, thinking of her choice of words, *I guess I am really seeing things from my informants' point of view.*

"No," Shakuntala said, "we've decided to drop him as a prospect because his immigration status was too chancy. Without his green card, it would take too much time to settle the affair. And now Amrita isn't sure she wants to marry in the States after all. 'Mummy,' she says, 'now they

have everything in India.' And I'm thinking along the same lines myself," Shakuntala continued. "Now our children have good opportunities here, not like when Indians first started going to States. We have all
the name-brand fashions, the shopping malls, even cheerleaders for our
cricket teams. So many Indian people are now returning to India. Why
the necessity to go abroad? Let's see after Anjeli has been there a while
and gives a report back; we can wait a little longer. Amrita is in Delhi
now, at a friend's wedding. I hope you will see her when she returns next
week. She also is very grateful for your help and advice."

Julie nodded her head and changed the subject. "Tell me more about
this wedding we're going to. I met many of Anjeli's relatives and even
some of Kumar's relations at the engagement and the ladies Sangeet, but
there will be lots of other guests there, and I don't want to say the wrong
things to the wrong people."

"Not to worry," said Shakuntala. "You know Anjeli's parents—they
are neighbors to my parents, and they are lovely people. I'm sure it will
be a gala affair, but, frankly, though Anjeli's family is very good, their
financial position has gone down somewhat lately. I think they're in a
bit over their heads for this wedding—five-star hotel, all this and that,
but you know how it is, the youngest daughter, they want to do their
best. And the gifts also—you know we can't say *dowry*, that is illegal in
India—and the Khattars were happy to give, though the boy's family
seemed a little greedy. What to do? Anjeli was determined to marry a
boy in America, and her parents wanted to comply with her wishes."

"You'd think that dowry business might have died out some with the
Indians living abroad," Julie mused aloud, "but it still seems to loom as
a large issue, though it's taken different turns. Sometimes it seems to be
a kind of leverage over a girl's family, especially if she will be living in
America, where she is less able to reach out to her own family if things
turn sour. Perhaps giving in to dowry demands makes a girl's parents
feel more hopeful that their daughter will be well treated when she is so
far away."

"You have a point there, Julie. It's important to get things off on the right foot," Shakuntala replied. "That is why we agree on the dowry before the commitment is made to the marriage. Sometimes even when the boy doesn't care about the dowry, his parents may insist. It's part of their prestige, you see, and if the boy has unmarried sisters, it's a meaningful financial gain that they can use for their own daughters' dowries."

Julie and Shakuntala halted their conversation as the car approached the wedding venue. Julie made sure her little notebook was at the top of her purse where she could easily reach it and readied her camera for the extensive photo-taking that played a strategic part in her ethnographic research, both for data gathering and recall. Luckily for her, Anjeli's parents had readily agreed to her photographing the wedding ceremonies, and Julie hoped some of her pictures would be vivid enough to use in her planned book for both ethnographic and pure visual effect.

"Oh, look, "said Shakuntala, "here comes the *bharat*." Heading their way was a prooocession led by the groom riding a colorfully decorated white horse, his face covered by a veil of flowers, followed by a small boy of about ten. Behind him a brass band accompanied a crowd of the groom's family and friends, yelling, clapping, and dancing. Traditions had changed, Julie realized. In the past, when most weddings had taken place at the girl's house, only men had formed the bharat procession. But now, in Mumbai at least, the wedding itself was more likely to be at a top hotel than at the girl's home, and women as well as men walked in the bharat procession.

"Fabulous!" Julie exclaimed. "No Mumbai traffic jam will stop the groom arriving on a white horse! I don't think that could happen in New York—though maybe in New Jersey," she amended. In Mumbai, during the wedding season, it was a common sight, however, and all traffic gave way.

After the groom's party entered the hotel, Julie and Shakuntala moved into the reception area, where they were treated to the plaintive sounds of Indian classical music played on the *shehnai* by three musicians in traditional dress. Julie ran through the symbolic meanings of each step of the wedding ritual in her mind and made some brief and hopefully discreet notations, knowing she would need to fill in the gaps when she returned to her room.

First the priest formally introduced the members of Anjeli's and Kumar's family to each other. Julie tried to keep track of who was introduced to whom, as the priest called out the names from a list prepared beforehand. As the family members greeted each other, those from Anjeli's side presented a small gift to the relative from Kumar's family. Then a man, who Shakuntala explained belonged to Kumar's family, began a recitation of a poem that he explained had been written especially for this occasion. "He is praising the members of both Kumar's and Anjeli's families and wishing them success in the marriage."

Julie snapped off photographs as Anjeli's brother escorted Kumar inside the hotel where the marriage ceremony would take place, while Anjeli was led by her maternal uncle. Kumar and Anjeli both proceeded to the flower-covered *mandap*, an open canopy where the formal ceremony was conducted according to ancient Vedic rites. Anjeli's uncle then blessed the couple and gave them a cash gift. Anjeli and Kumar seated themselves on two throne-like chairs, with Kumar to Anjeli's left, as directed by the Hindu priest sitting on the floor in front of them. The couple then placed garlands on each other as the priest recited Sanskrit verses from the Vedas.

"See," Shakuntala told Julie, "we have adjusted to modern times, holding the wedding in a hotel on a weekend instead of in the girl's village, under the stars at an auspicious hour as determined by the astrologers. After all, who would come out at 2 A.M. to attend a wedding nowadays! But the important things don't change."

How true, thought Julie, as she gazed awestruck at Anjeli, radiant in her elaborate makeup and traditional red bridal sari symbolizing fertility, carefully wrapped to conceal the contours of her sexual charms. Much of the wedding symbolism, Julie knew, simultaneously centered on both fertility and sexual restraint, suggesting the bride's central role in reproduction and carrying on the purity of her husband's family's bloodline.

This was also reflected in Anjeli's tightly and painstakingly coiffed chignon, woven through with flowers. The large, exquisitely worked gold and jeweled forehead ornament hanging from her hair and the large gold nose ring she wore both symbolized a woman's attachment to her husband and his family. Gold shimmered from every part of her body, from her abundant gold bangles to the layers of ornate gold and jeweled necklaces. Such abundance of gold was not only auspicious, like the *bindi*—the dot that Anjeli wore on her forehead symbolizing her married status—but also represented the wealth of her family. Later, when the couple went back to the groom's home after the wedding, or, these days, more likely on their honeymoon, Anjeli would wear clothes given to her by Kumar's family. Her hands were painted with *mehndi*, or henna, a vegetable-dye decoration worn by all brides and considered essential to the auspiciousness of the occasion. Indeed, henna parties, which took place just before the wedding, were now even de rigueur in America, and mehndi painting was even enthusiastically adopted by hip young Americans.

Kumar wore the traditional Punjabi dress and turban of a Punjabi groom, including *kaintha*, traditional beads that hung around his neck. *A handsome guy*, thought Julie, *and a good match for Anjeli's beauty.* As the marriage ritual continued, Shakuntala remained at Julie's side to explain the different elements of the ceremony. "It is very hard for outsiders to follow our Hindu rituals," she whispered, to which Julie responded that it would be impossible without her help.

"And I guess I'm not the only one in the dark. See?" Julie waved a small booklet she had picked up from a pile near the reception entrance. "These little cards explain what's going on." In fact, Julie thought, comprehending the full, complicated symbolism of the multilayered Vedic ritual was probably beyond all but the experts; even most of the Indian guests would not understand the priest's prayers in Sanskrit. In fact, most of his instructions to the ritual's participants were in the vernacular language of the guests, in this case Hindi, the most widely spoken language of North India. Julie knew that in Indian diaspora marriages Hindu priests often had to give the instructions in English as the bride and groom were from different language communities, another reminder of how immigrant culture had adapted to new circumstances. Julie was relieved to see a number of Indian guests also referring to the wedding card explaining the ritual, as she was. While this was not her first Indian wedding, each was a little different, and this was certainly the most ceremonially elaborate Julie had attended.

After Anjeli's family welcomed and honored Kumar, Anjeli offered him a mixture of yogurt and honey, which he tasted with a prayer that he might imbibe its sweetness and purity. The kanya dan followed, with Anjeli's father offering his daughter to Kumar, who affirmed his acceptance. This religiously ordained "gift of a virgin" was the heart of the Hindu marriage sacrament. It transferred the auspiciousness of the bride to her husband's family through the ritual exchanges of the marriage ceremony. Kumar then presented Anjeli with a beautifully woven gold-bordered sari, symbolizing her new role as his bride. He then prayed that, wearing her finery, she would live long in prosperity and grow old together with him.

Julie carefully observed the priest as he prepared and worshipped *agni*, the holy fire, the eternal witness to an Indian marriage. As the priest recited some Sanskrit blessings, Kumar took Anjeli's hand, and they declared their devotion to each other and prayed for their future happiness. The priest tied the end of Kumar's scarf to the pallu of Anjeli's sari, signifying their union, and Kumar led Anjeli in taking seven steps around the fire. Then they reversed the circle, with Anjeli leading Kumar. Each step symbolized the principle duties of the couple to ensure a happy, prosperous, peaceful, healthy life, blessed with children and lifelong companionship.

Julie took several photographs as Anjeli's brother helped Anjeli place her foot on a rock, while Kumar enjoined her to be firm like a rock, resisting all enemies. Anjeli repeated a prayer that she would have the strength to loosen her ties to her own family and bond with her husband's family, that she would never be apart from her husband, that he would have a long life, and that the members of his family would flourish in happiness and prosperity. Anjeli and Kumar again exchanged garlands and seated themselves, this time with Anjeli to Kumar's left. They raised their eyes to each other, symbolizing the creation of an everlasting bond between them, and offered a prayer to God.

"See, now they feed each other sweets to symbolize the binding of their hearts and minds, and now Kumar is applying *sindoor* in the parting of Anjeli's hair," Shakuntala whispered. Julie knew that this vermillion powder symbolized the blood union and was the unmistakable mark of a married woman. As the ritual neared its end, the priest sprinkled holy water on the newly married couple. Shakuntala put flower petals in Julie's hand, and they joined the other guests in showering the couple with flowers and wishes of good fortune and a long and healthy life. "Anjeli and Kumar look so happy; they really suit each other," Julie said to Shakuntala. Then, blowing her breath through her fingers three times in the old Russian superstition to guard against the evil eye, she added to herself, *I hope they'll be as happy a year from now.*

🌸 Chapter Eleven

After the wedding ceremony concluded, Julie joined Shakuntala at the buffet table, which was laid out with a huge number of dishes. The quality of the food was a critical factor in the way the guests evaluated a wedding and talked about it afterward, so nothing had been spared. The modern catering included many nonvegetarian plates, such as *seekh kebab*, the minced spicy lamb rolls that Julie loved; chicken *pakoras*, and baked fish. Most of the dishes, however—the *paneer tikkis*, vegetable pakoras, *chat*, *papris, panipuris, channa masala*, and *samosas*, were vegetarian. Set out at one end of the table was a huge variety of Indian sweets: *gulab jamin, ras goolah*, and many others, not all of which Julie recognized but which she knew were made of pure milk, sugar, and ghee, adding loads of calories to any meal. But Julie couldn't resist and just filled her plate.

"Very nice," said Shakuntala to Julie. "Still, not like the old days, when weddings lasted a week and food was distributed to the whole village. My mummy still talks about her own wedding, where there was a whole bullock cart filled with *chutneys*." Julie also recalled conversations with Shilpa in which her friend had nostalgically enumerated the quality of each and every dish at the wedding of some third cousin or other that had taken place over fifty years ago.

Shakuntala stayed by Julie's side as they greeted Anjeli's parents. "We're so happy to have you here," Mrs. Khattar said. "It will greatly relieve our anxiety about Anjeli being in the States. It's a great comfort and consolation to us, knowing that she will have a friend there and that you can telephone and even see her. You live near them in Queens, no?"

"Not exactly," Julie demurred, "but a very short subway ride away."

"Oh, that is so good," Mrs. Khattar continued. "Anjeli is so young, and I'm afraid she has been too sheltered, even living in Mumbai. She has not become acquainted with the ways of the world, like your girls in the States. Our girls require a lot of advising and guiding. It will be good to have someone from our side there to help her."

Julie reflected on the irony: the young bride would be surrounded by her husband and his family but would need Julie as a friend to look out for her. Julie was not sure she was entirely comfortable with this responsibility, but such was the spirit of the new engaged anthropology. Gone were the days of Boas and Malinowski, when anthropologists would never take sides in any community they were studying, fearing it would affect people's behavior and "pollute" their data collection. But in an Indian family, people did take sides, and Julie was placed on the side of the bride. *And who could blame people for using all the resources they had to protect their family's interests?* she thought to herself.

And so, Julie nodded her head in agreement with Anjeli's mother, who was obviously torn between her deeply felt hope that Anjeli and Kumar would be deliriously happy and her knowledge from experience that life was a series of bumps. Many Indian brides were not adequately prepared for the disappointments or even the real difficulties that awaited them.

"Anjeli and Kumar are deeply attached to each other," Anjeli's mother continued. "We were very happy that Kumar was so taken with Anjeli on their first meeting. Of course Kumar is more mature and understands how to handle some of the problems that do arise in all families. To be frank, Kumar's parents preferred to delay the marriage, but Kumar himself insisted it take place now. It is good that his parents will not be accompanying them to America, though they will surely visit at some future time. And perhaps even stay." Mrs. Khatta pursed her lips thoughtfully. "Who knows? All this is in God's hands. We can only do our best to make our daughter happy."

"You can depend on Julie," Shakuntala said reassuringly. They complimented Anjeli's mother on the wedding, Shakuntala declaring, "You have outdone yourself, *bhenji*; this is a fabulous affair." She then took Julie's arm and moved away from the buffet table to greet Anjeli and Kumar. Julie handed Anjeli her wedding present, a gift certificate from an upscale housewares boutique. She congratulated them both and expressed her hopes to see them soon in New York.

When they had moved on, Shakuntala said to Julie, "I'm sure things will go smoothly. Kumar is well placed in America: he is a vice president of a bank and has lived in the States for a long time. His uncle is there also, a very successful businessman, who lives in New Jersey; you must have met him at the engagement party. Some other relatives are there also; Kumar's parents have been to America many times, and they are a very modern type."

Julie nodded sagely; though she knew Shakuntala was implying something, Julie could only interpret her friend literally. She did caution her on one point. "You know, Shakuntala, in America, everyone in a bank above the level of teller is called a vice president. And after the banking meltdown last year, a lot of banks are in real trouble." Shakuntala laughingly dismissed Julie's skepticism. "It is we people who are supposed to be suspicious, Julie. This was a good arrangement; the go-between was the uncle of Anjeli's mother who lives in the same native place as Kumar's grandparents. All these people are well-known to each other; that's always a good thing. And see, how good-looking Kumar is, very fair, *na?* Handsome like a Bollywood movie star." *Well, that part is true,* Julie thought, *and could go a long way toward building the love that did grow in so many arranged marriages.*

An older couple then appeared at their side, and Shakuntala and Julie greeted Kumar's parents with a polite namaste, after which Shakuntala wandered off to meet some friends, promising to find Julie again so they could take their leave together. Like so many Punjabis of their age, Kumar's parents were both somewhat corpulent, an appearance that formerly signaled material prosperity but which was less approved of these days when people understood more clearly the connection between the rich Punjabi diet and diseases such as diabetes. Kumar's mother was wearing a deep purple sari with numerous pieces of gold jewelry and what Julie judged was too much makeup for a woman her age. She reminded Julie of the Indian proverb: *a crow that puts peacock feathers in its tail remains a crow all the same.*

Kumar's father was neatly dressed in a business suit. As he leaned toward her to make his namaste, Julie could smell the alcohol on his breath. No alcohol was served at the wedding, but it was readily available at the hotel bar. Julie wondered if a few drinks weren't perhaps partly responsible for his somewhat suggestive demeanor, looking her over in a way that made her feel uneasy. "And where are you from?" he inquired.

"From New York."

"And your family, have they come with you to India?"

"No, I'm actually here on my own. I'm an anthropologist doing research in Mumbai."

"Anthropologist?" Kumar's father raised his eyebrows.

"Yes," Julie replied to the unspoken question, "I'm a professor at NUNY in New York."

"Ah, NUNY, that is a public university, isn't it?" Kumar's mother interrupted in a condescending tone. "Our son, you know, has his MBA from Columbia University, a much better school, I believe. And our daughter is finishing her college in India," Mrs. Kapoor continued. "When she completes her degree, she will join Kumar and Anjeli in America."

Mr. Kapoor added to his wife's remark, "It is good for girls to have a profession, but they must never lose sight of what's most important . . ." and again his wife interrupted.

"Yes, in India we still think a girl must get married and have children and take care of her husband and his family. I know you Americans think that is not so important." Julie wondered if Mrs. Kapoor held to that principle equally for her own daughter as for her daughter-in-law. She thought perhaps not.

Rather than comment directly, Julie just smiled and veered off to what seemed like safer ground. "What a gala wedding, isn't it? Anjeli is so beautiful and such a lovely person, and her family also are such fine people."

"Yes, well, perhaps that is so," Kumar's mother nodded somewhat reluctantly. "Kumar was quite determined on Anjeli as his choice," implying that she was not *their* choice. "Our boy is at the top of his profession, you know; he is rising fast at his bank, and he is also an American citizen. This is a big attraction, but Anjeli also made up her mind so quickly that we had no chance to see the many other families who were interested in us meeting their daughters.

"But life in America is not as easy as people think," Kumar's mother continued, her mind on a path she had clearly thought about before. "Our son has to work very hard, and Anjeli must take proper care of him. There are no servants in America to do all the housework and such, as we have here. It will be better when we join them in America." *Better for whom?* Julie couldn't help thinking. And she took note of Mrs. Kapoor's expressed intention to join the couple. That probably explained Mrs. Kapoor's wish for a daughter-in-law from India. The expectation was that such a girl would be far more obedient and malleable than an Indian girl brought up in America or, heaven forbid, an American girl.

Julie noticed the emphasis Mrs. Kapoor put on the good qualities of her son, while her comments on Anjeli's positive qualities were expressed almost stingily. *Not too different from home,* Julie thought. *Every boy's mother thinks no girl is good enough for her son.* Still, after her interview with Mrs. Chatwal, her many conversations with Shakuntala, and her years of fieldwork, Julie understood very well the concerns of both the parents of the groom and the bride about their children's marriage, though these concerns reflected very different perspectives. New brides in India were between a rock and a hard place, Julie calculated. Their marriage vows stressed the separation of a woman from her natal kin yet at the same time defined her presence in her husband's home as a potential threat to the unity and solidarity of *his* family, which she now must consider her own. Most young brides started out eager to please their husband's family, especially if they lived jointly, but they also yearned for the intimacy with their husbands that characterized marital affection in the West.

"Yes," Mr. Kapoor appended. "I am retiring from my business. I have my elder brother in America. We have visited America before, but perhaps this time we will stay for good, along with our daughter when she completes her college. We shall see."

Julie forced herself to smile, but she was starting to feel the effects of the long day, and her feet were killing her from standing for several hours in her high heels. She politely said good-bye to Kumar's parents, congratulating them again on their son's marriage. Having been briefly reintroduced to Kumar's uncle from New Jersey with his wife and daughters, Julie surmised that she'd met all the close relatives now and could make her exit. She looked around for Shakuntala; if her friend wasn't ready to leave, Julie would just take a taxi.

As Julie twisted her head to search the crowd, a good-looking man, a little older than she, sharply dressed in a designer suit, came up close to her and introduced himself with a formal namaste. "I'm Sukhdev Kohli, one of Kumar's cousins. You look like you need assistance. May I be of help?"

"I'm just looking for my friend to tell her I must go," Julie replied politely. "It's been a wonderful wedding, but I've been here only a few days and still have some jet lag."

As Julie spoke, she thought. *This guy looks so familiar. Have I met him before?* With his sophisticated appearance and air of self-confidence, he wasn't someone you'd forget easily. On the other hand, he showed no signs of recognizing her, so perhaps she was mistaken. "Yes," he agreed, "the long flight can be quite exhausting."

"And Air India planes are always so chaotic," Julie assented. "So many families with small children. It's impossible to rest at all. At least I had good luck with my seatmate, a lovely young American woman on her first trip to India. I always enjoy speaking with people who are new to your fascinating country, and it helps pass the time on a long plane ride. She had a very romantic tale to tell, coming to India to meet her fiancé and arrange for a real Indian wedding."

Julie was too tired to notice that Kohli's eyes narrowed, and he frowned slightly as he looked at her more intently. "Indeed, you're right," he agreed. "India for most foreigners is a land of pure romance." But he was furiously thinking, *Could it have been Grace that this woman met on the plane?* Noticing Julie continuing to swivel her head for her friend, he asked with an expression of concern that, to Julie's fleeting glance, did not reach his eyes, "Are you feeling all right? Please, allow me to drive you home. Where are you staying?"

"Oh, thank you, that's very kind, but it's not necessary. My friend drove me here, but if she is not ready to leave, I can easily get a taxi as I'm only down Marine Drive to Chowpatty." As the man insisted, Julie tried again to think where she might know him, but the image wouldn't jell, and she gave it up. Just then Shakuntala appeared at her side. "Ah, Julie, I've been looking for you. You've met Mr. Kohli, I see. Turning to the man, Shakuntala asked in a friendly voice, "*Kaisi hai, bhai sahib,* we haven't met in a long time, since Mrs. Sahni's daughter's wedding, This is my friend, Julie Norman, a professor of anthropology at NUNY in New York City."

"Yes, we have met. I was just offering Professor Norman a ride home—I think she is feeling the crush too much."

"Julie, this is Sukhdev Kohli, Kumar's cousin. He has several fabulous Indian clothing shops in Queens and also on that famous Oak Tree Road in Edison, New Jersey. All the celebrities buy their clothing there. You might have even worn some garments from his store." As Julie shook Kohli's extended hand more formally, his palm felt as cool as a snake's skin.

"You're from New York! What a coincidence," he said. "Please, take one of my cards. You must come to my shop. You will look beautiful in our Indian fashions—nothing but the most up-to-date styles." Julie nodded and smiled as she slipped his card into her purse. *Maybe I've seen him on one of the Indian news channels,* she thought as she scanned her memory once more, *but maybe I haven't, and it's not important. Right now all I want is to get home, rest a bit, and get to work.* She said goodbye, thanked Mr. Kohli again for offering a ride, and allowed Shakuntala to guide her toward the hotel's exit. She didn't see Mr. Kohli remove

✿ Chapter Twelve

Julie looked placidly out the window of the Air India jet descending toward JFK, as most of the other passengers ignored the flight attendants' injunction to remain seated until the plane had stopped completely and jostled in the aisles opening the overhead compartments to retrieve their luggage. Almost the last person off the aircraft, Julie sauntered jauntily through the terminal to the baggage carousel, laughingly recalling the chaos of the flight. Someone had dropped a custard tart, which someone else had stepped on, leading to an argument between the flight attendant and the passenger about who was responsible for cleaning it up. A large group of Christian evangelicals returning from some mission to convert the natives had extended their blessings to all the passengers throughout the ride and had loudly debated whether the Lord would want them to choose Cokes or Sprites and whether He would want them to watch the violent Rambo-type film being shown on the overhead screen.

Too restless to sleep or work on her notes by the end of the trip, Julie had tortured herself watching a tediously detailed infomercial film about—what else—shopping! It featured an Indian woman so fair that Julie was not even sure she was Indian, an increasingly common image in Indian advertising. *Mm*, she thought, *the symbolism of skin color in*

traditional and modern India might make a good subject for an article.
. . . The woman was choosing fittings and cabinets for her new kitchen,
lovingly stroking one sample after another with a look of what Julie
called "consumer ecstasy" on her face. This was followed by a shopping
spree of pots, pans, rice cookers, blenders, and all the other accessories
needed to cook Indian food in America. Perhaps those items had now
become part of the new dowries being demanded, replacing the motor
scooters and tape recorders of old, as more women married Indian men
living abroad. With India's economic upturn due to globalization, the
country's new consumerism had apparently transported itself to Indian
immigrant communities as well; that, too, was a topic she'd have to
include in her book.

While Julie waited for her bags to appear, she fished out her cell
phone and dialed her mother's number, the first thing she did on her
return trips from India. Not that she'd ever catch her mother at this
midday hour. It was early mornings or *fahgeddaboutit.* Her mom was
up with the sun, had early classes, on the run all day either teaching
or at the library or the gym. She always made time for "truth, beauty,
and social justice," though. Her latest effort was collecting shoes to give
to homeless shelters, inspired by a poem by a Puerto Rican poet who
viewed the unequal distribution in the world of the shod and the shoe-
less as symbolic of the unfair distribution of wealth. She almost never
chatted on the phone, and her answering machine gave emphatic instructions to *Be brief.* In the evening she only answered the phone if she
heard the voice of Julie, her sister, or a few good friends, and her conversations were always short—for long gossip sessions she'd say, "That's
what café's and restaurants are for." Actually that suited Julie fine as she
herself rarely used the phone for purely social chatter.

"Mommie dearest," Julie cooed into the receiver, clamped between
ear and shoulder as she slung one of her bags off the carousel. "Since you
don't have a cell phone, I didn't expect to catch you but just wanted to let
you know I'm home. Great trip, call you soon." It amused Julie that her

mother could schlep off solo to China or Indonesia, dragging her luggage onto trains or buses in the most out-of-the-way places, but she wouldn't learn the simplest thing about modern electronics. In new time zones she'd have hotel clerks reset her digital watch, she "didn't do" faxes; she dismissed blackberries as something you ate with sour cream; and she had resolved to be the last person on the planet to cling to a videotape machine instead of a DVD player. She did use a computer for her writing, of course, and sent marvelously funny e-mails on her travels, but, in the end, she was just an analogic person adrift in a digital world.

"Home again," Julie sang to herself as she opened the door to her apartment. Before she could even get her bags in, Chairman Miaow was purring in the hallway. Welcoming her adored pet with a squeeze that elicited a protesting squeak, Julie sighed at the two Trader Joe's shopping bags where Pauli had dumped her accumulated mail. Her windowsill garden was burgeoning; Pauli had been faithful as usual about watering her plants. His welcome note was propped on her refrigerator, telling her to call him when she returned, but "not too early tomorrow, *bubbe*; I'm trying out a new club on East Houston St. and hope to be home wery wery late. . . ." Julie laughed. How could you not love a gay Italian from Bay Ridge who called his women friends "bubbe" and never lost hope that every visit to a club or Caribbean cruise would produce his knight in shining armor, irresistibly drawn to him by his fabulous dance moves perfected as a professional—if intermittent—performer. Of course, he'd always had a day job, which was where Julie had met him. He'd started an aerobics dance class at her gym, using pop and Broadway music of the 1940s and 1950s, which drew a faithful crowd of his "ladies," of whom Julie was one. She'd become his confidant, the recipient of frequent "perils of Pauli," as she called them. "I tell you, Julie, it's a jungle out there," he'd complained to her last year. "That audition for the chorus of the Met's new opera *War and Peace,* was murder. The good news is, I got the job—but I told them if I was going to lead Napoleon's white horse they'd either have to drug me or the horse—and I'll be making livable equity pay for a couple of weeks. The bad news is," he'd added theatrically, throwing out his left hand where he'd always worn a gold band, "Lennie and I have split, and I'm almost homeless, so, please, if you know of an apartment . . ."

It so happened Julie did: her mom's friend Irena wanted to move from her small co-op in Sheepshead Bay. Though she loved the nearby ocean and the European atmosphere of the neighborhood, the super was a thug and wouldn't make any repairs without a bribe. Irena was afraid of complaining about him and had found another apartment, "practically in the country in Queens," and was willing to sell her place for what she had paid. The maintenance was low, and Pauli was confident that his weightlifting brother-in-law could take on any super ever born. He now owed Julie "his life."

"Forget your life," she'd told him, "but when I go on my field trips, come stay in my apartment and take care of Chairman Miaow and my plants. My mom only gets up here every few days, and the Chairman doesn't like three-day-old kibbles and a nasty litter box." Pauli was thrilled "A Manhattan vacation a couple of times a year . . . Ain't we got fun?" he had crooned.

Julie had allowed herself some complacency as she started unpacking and organizing her stuff in her the apartment, one of the more spacious one-bedroom layouts on the twelfth floor. "High enough for sun but not so high that you won't be able to walk up the stairs when the elevators quit," a friendly senior citizen wearing a Che Guevara T-shirt had trilled from the lobby bench as she'd watched Julie moving in. "Which letter?" she asked.

"F," Julie had replied distractedly as she guided the moving men into the elevator.

"Ooh, the one with the big closets! Aren't you lucky? Mostly nice neighbors on that floor too. A lovely couple, the Fitzgeralds, two little girls to die for—Charlotte and Waverly. Such names they give them these days. And on the other side the Russells—she's from Brazil, he's a teacher. Two lovely children also; don't worry, no noise, all very well-behaved. The Nachmans, near the incinerator, they never say hello. Don't take it personally—they never say hello to anyone, including themselves. They'd get divorced, but neither one will give up the apartment. It's not like it was when these buildings were first put up by the union in the sixties. Then this area was all warehouses; who wanted to live here? Now Chelsea is so chic, and with so many young families, they built a playground last year. Who could have imagined it? Some of the *alta cockers* don't like the changes, but I love it—adds life to the building."

Much as Julie wanted to hear more—it occurred to her that someone should do an anthropological study of this housing complex (*Hmm, maybe I could interest one of my graduate students; it would be a nice update from Herbert Gans's study of Levittown done so many years ago*) she needed to keep on top of the move. The moving men still had a few minutes of struggle ahead of them getting the couch into the elevator.

"I'm Julie; so nice meeting you," she'd said to the woman whom she now thought of as an informant—*I mean interlocutor,* she reminded herself. "I hope to see you again."

"You will, dear, you will. I'm always in the lobby."

Julie felt like she was back in the field. "Jeannie," as her new friend had introduced herself, was going to become an interesting and useful link to the culture of her new community. She liked that idea. Her mother's co-op, bought way back when it had been affordable, had upscaled; these days the tenants were mostly a collection of stiffs in power suits carrying laptop bags who wouldn't smile unless they were billing for it. "They're constantly trying to get on the co-op board to protect their investment," her mom would sneer. "They're obsessed with the lobby decoration and doormen's uniforms; they want them to look like generals in an operetta. We've already had a knock-down-drag-out on the board about whether the doormen can rest on stools during night shift duty." *No need to say whose side her mother took on that one.*

Not that her own co-op board didn't provide a lot of laughs. One candidate actually listed a bipolar mood disorder as one of his qualifications, claiming it would give him a unique perspective on co-op business. But her board had the imagination to give out raffle tickets as motivation for attendance at the co-op meetings, and Julie had won some paid laundry cards, a lovely, useless "rich person's" watch with only four gold dots on the face, and a bag of birdseed that she exchanged for a bag of kitty litter won by a neighbor who didn't have a cat. *Maybe I could try that kind of motivation in my classes,* she thought only half-jokingly. It wasn't so far-fetched; she'd actually read recently that the city's got-rocks mayor had suggested paying public school kids for attending their classes! Out of his own pocket? She didn't think so.

Julie now changed into comfortable sweats and sorted quickly through the mail. Some bills, academic correspondence, back copies of her *Nations* and *NYRBs* to savor over her morning cappuccinos, and a ton of junk mail that she could dump unopened. But a handwritten note from Pauli caught her attention. It listed her phone messages and ended with a starred item: *In the last two weeks you were away, some guy kept calling and leaving messages about wanting to see you. He seemed to know who you were,* Pauli wrote, *but he never left his name. It got a little weird after a while, and I just thought you should know.*

Chapter Thirteen

A brother inherits his father's wealth, a daughter is sent to a distant land. The bridegroom is the sailor, and the bride crosses the water.

—*Indian wedding song*

"Anjeli, you are the wife for me. I'm going to tell my parents to stop looking."

Anjeli remembered these words as she gazed off the balcony of the hotel where they would spend their "honeymoon," unfortunately only one night as Kumar had to return tomorrow to the States. She had known this would be a short trip. On his previous visit, several months ago, he had stayed nearly two weeks, seeing the many girls his parents had lined up for him. She knew she had not been his parents' first choice—they were after a family with more money—but Kumar had stood his ground. In the short time they were allowed to talk together privately, Kumar had told her this with great feeling.

Anjeli had felt the same. Her parents were willing to agree to the match, despite the rumors suggesting that Kumar's family was a little "money-minded" and the fact that they came from the business class rather than the professional class that Anjeli's parents had hoped for. Her parents had done what had to be done. Though they had no trusted friends or relations in America to look into things, they had investigated Kumar, his parents, and his close relations as best they could through their connections in Punjab and Mumbai. They had acceded, though somewhat reluctantly, to his parents' demands for what they thought were excessive gifts; and they had put on a wedding that Anjeli knew was well beyond their means. As their youngest daughter whose happiness was their main concern, Anjeli's parents could not resist her choice, and they hoped that their willingness to meet his parents' demands would mean a happier life for Anjeli.

A beautiful full moon cast its light on the sand and the placid water outside the balcony of the hotel they had chosen at Juhu Beach, near Mumbai's international airport. "Come inside, Anjeli," Kumar cajoled as he joined her on the balcony, putting his arm around her waist. *He's so handsome,* she thought. *I am indeed a lucky girl.* She was eager and yet anxious, hardly prepared for what she believed to be the most important moment of her life. She hoped it would be perfect, as in the Bollywood films that were the basis of most of what she knew about romance. Like most well-brought-up Indian girls, Anjeli had no experience with intimate dating, though in the modern way she did socialize in public places with her college friends of both sexes, a major change, she knew, from her parents' generation. In those days, her mother had confided, just having a cup of tea with a boy in the college canteen could erupt into the most shameful scandal.

As Anjeli accompanied Kumar inside, he moved her toward the bed and undressed her. She was hoping for some tender and gentle words, maybe whispers about how important this moment was for him also, but he was silent. In what she had desired as the meeting of her soul with that of the man with whom she would spend the rest of her life, she instead experienced only the physical demands. Though she made no protest, these were not very satisfying for her, and were even painful. Kumar then promptly fell asleep.

The next morning they had had to rush to meet their parents at the international airport, where Kumar's flight left for New York. Anjeli had hoped she and Kumar would have a chance to talk, but he seemed distant from last night's experience, quite casual, even, with no sense of how important the experience might be for her.

"Come on, come on, Anjeli, these European airlines don't operate on Indian Standard Time. And we must leave sufficient time for our parents to say good-bye to me in the traditional Indian style," he added, a little sarcastically.

"I wish you didn't have to go so soon," Anjeli said wistfully.

"Me neither," Kumar replied, "but all the arrangements for your green card have been made, and since we also had a civil marriage ceremony you'll be able to join me in a few weeks. My parents have decided you should spend the remaining time with them in Delhi and fly from there to New York. I hope that's okay. After arguing with them about my choosing you, I didn't want to get in another wrangle over what is, after all, only a couple of weeks. And they'll be spending the next few days in Mumbai with our relatives here, so you'll have some quality time to say good-bye to your family and friends."

"Stay in Delhi with your parents!" Anjeli was aghast. "You didn't tell me that! I thought it was agreed that I would stay in Mumbai with my parents until I left for the States."

"You're probably right," Kumar said, distractedly checking the room to make sure they had not left anything behind. "But now they've decided, and I really don't want to fight over such a small thing. Soon you'll be with me in New York, and we'll have all the time we want together. I'll call you and arrange things for when you come. Meanwhile my father can make sure that all the papers from this side are properly taken care of."

Anjeli nodded. *What else can I do?* she thought. *I must make the best of it. Now I am not my father's daughter but belong to another house.*

The few days in Mumbai flew by, and soon it was time for Anjeli to say good-bye to her parents. They had promised to come to Delhi to see her off to the States, and looking forward to their visit helped Anjeli feel better. But she had only been in Delhi two weeks when her father-in-law informed her that her temporary green card had come through and that she would leave for New York the next day. "Kumar has already taken care of the tickets; he will meet you at the JFK airport."

"But this is so soon," Anjeli protested. "My parents will have no time to come to Delhi to see me off."

"It is not your convenience that counts now," countered Kumar's mother. "You are a married woman, and it is your husband whose wishes come first. You can call your parents and say good-bye over the phone."

And so she did. Anjeli could tell how disappointed her parents were, and also how hard they tried to hide their distress and put a happy face on things. "Just think, Anjeli," her mother said, "so soon you will be with your husband in New York. That is the important thing. On Kumar's next vacation, surely you will come back to India; who knows, we may even be able to go to the States for a visit. And we'll be sure to write you every week, and you please write us as well. And don't forget, you have that Professor Julie's phone number; be sure to keep up with her. She seemed like a very nice person, and she is a good friend of Shakuntala Auntie."

Once she knew she had no choice, Anjeli was in a fierce rush to leave Delhi and Kumar's parents. She had packed all her wedding saris in a separate suitcase and put the gold jewelry that her parents had given her in her carry-all purse to take on the plane with her. At the last minute, however, Kumar's mother called the servant to take the suitcase to her bedroom. "Leave this here," she insisted. "No need for such fancy things in New York." Then she had opened Anjeli's purse, which was lying on the hall table, and removed much of the jewelry. "We'll keep this safe for you here," she said. "New York is not a secure place to keep so much gold. When we come we will bring it with us."

The flight was long, and Anjeli was tired. She couldn't sleep for the excitement and tried to put all the conflicts with her in-laws out of her head as she anticipated Kumar's meeting her at the airport and dreamed about their life together in America. She tried to freshen up in the lavatory before landing and was among the last to deplane, holding tightly to her purse, which contained her papers but hardly any money, and now only a few pieces of gold jewelry in addition to the bangles and gold chain she was wearing. Anjeli followed the directions to the customs line and then moved on to the baggage terminal, where she eagerly looked outside the doors for Kumar before the baggage carousel started to move. Unlike India, here the airport seemed so impersonal. There were few groups of friends and relatives meeting the passengers with the warmth and gaiety of the family reunions she was used to. Anjeli's suitcases were too heavy for her to lift off the conveyer belt, but a kind passenger, seeing her distress, obtained a cart for her and lifted her suitcases on to it. When she exited the baggage-claim area, Kumar was nowhere to be seen. Those waiting for passengers were mostly men in black chauffeur's uniforms holding up signs with various names on them.

Anjeli felt so disappointed she was almost ready to cry. And then she saw him, rushing to meet her, full of apologies about heavy traffic and concerned inquiries about her flight. "Sorry, sorry, Anjeli, I got held up. We'll have to get you a cell phone. I hope you didn't think I wasn't coming. Let me take the cart, and we'll go outside and get a taxi, and we'll be home in a very short time."

They waited in the long line for a taxi. Kumar shouted angrily at an Indian couple who tried to break into the line. "These newcomers think they are still in India," he said contemptuously. "They don't know about taking their turn in a queue."

"Never mind; now we're together, a little more delay is not so important," Anjeli said, trying to calm him down. When their turn finally came, the driver, who was a Sikh, helped Kumar lift the suitcases into the trunk, and Anjeli gratefully entered the taxi and leaned back, letting Kumar take charge. He gave their address to the driver, who asked no questions and seemed very familiar with the address.

As the taxi moved swiftly onto the highway, Anjeli looked out of the window, trying to order all her conflicting emotions and looking with interest at her first glimpses of America. "This is much different than the route from Mumbai airport," she said with a smile. "So clean and orderly." Kumar smiled back, and before she knew it, the taxi had exited the highway and was traveling on city streets. The neighborhood they were passing through seemed rundown to her, small apartment buildings with lots of signs in Asian languages she couldn't understand and small groceries and shops that almost reminded her of Mumbai.

"Here we are," said Kumar as the taxi pulled up in front of a ten-story apartment building. He helped the driver unload the suitcases, unlocked the door to the lobby, and pulled the suitcases into the building with Anjeli following. The lobby was not very clean, and the elevator, which took them to their sixth-floor apartment, was littered with plastic bags and discarded coffee containers. Kumar unlocked the three locks on their apartment door and ushered her in, following with her suitcases. The apartment seemed tiny and dingy to Anjeli, nothing like the spacious apartment she had lived in with her parents on Marine Drive, with its expansive view of the Arabian Sea. *But to be fair, there are no bastees and no beggars, either,* Anjeli admonished herself, *and the sidewalks are not cracked apart, and the traffic moves along without the continual blasting of horns.* As Anjeli inspected the place where she was to start her new life, she saw a small living room-cum-dining alcove, two cramped bedrooms, and a tiny bathroom and kitchen. The view was to the front, but at this time of the year, on a dank, late January day, when the trees had lost all their leaves and there was only dirty slush on the streets, there was nothing much to look at.

"Sorry for the mess," Kumar said, as he saw the disappointed look on Anjeli's face. "I haven't had time to fix up the place." The double bed in the larger bedroom had only been hastily made, and the living room contained just a few pieces of shabby furniture, with a formica dining table and four wooden chairs shoved off into the alcove. "I've been so busy working since I've been back from India, I haven't really had time to do things properly. We can do a take-out dinner tonight, and tomorrow we can shop for groceries and get things in order. That will give me a good chance to show you the neighborhood."

Anjeli was too tired to do much besides nod her head. "It doesn't matter; what is important is that we are together. I can have a lot of fun fixing up this place."

After a cold, unappetizing take-out dinner delivered from a neighboring Indian restaurant, all Anjeli wanted to do was take a bath and go to sleep. She straightened out the bed linens, changed into her nightgown, and started to crawl into bed. "Not so fast, my lovely," Kumar joked, quoting a line from some American film that was lost on Anjeli. "We haven't seen each other for far too long. This can be our real honeymoon." Kumar lay down on the bed beside her, and when Anjeli didn't respond to his attempts to caress her body, he said, "Don't be shy, Anjeli; we are now husband and wife. I've been waiting many weeks for you."

"I'm just tired, Kumar. I didn't sleep at all on the plane," Anjeli responded, too exhausted to even pretend to be enthusiastic. He seemed not to hear her protests and persisted so that she finally just gave in. After satisfying himself, he turned on his side without a word and fell asleep, just as he had on their honeymoon.

Never mind, Anjeli scolded herself. *"We've got to give ourselves time to get to know one another.* Trying to be optimistic about their adventure tomorrow, and totally worn out, she fell asleep herself.

Awaking the next morning to the smell of coffee, Anjeli looked lazily around for Kumar and found him in the kitchen. "See, Anjeli, this is America. Here husbands even make coffee for their wives," he said with a smile. "After breakfast I'll take you to Jackson Heights where you can buy all the Indian food—and anything else from India—that your heart desires. You will not even know you have left Mumbai."

"It's only two blocks to the subway," Kumar told Anjeli as they left the building, "and then the subway ride is quite short."

"Maybe we can save for a car," Anjeli said tentatively, as they waited in the bitter cold of the elevated line for the subway train to arrive. In Mumbai everyone she knew took taxis or had a car with a driver, but Kumar seemed quite used to this inconvenience, and she didn't want to start off their marriage as a complaining wife. "A car," Kumar replied jokingly, "so you think you married a millionaire? You'll find out America is not like in the films; it's a tough country, and you have to work like a dog to succeed." Kumar seemed to be getting upset, and Anjeli was sorry she had spoken. Luckily, just then the train pulled into the station and put a stop to the conversation. *I must be more careful what I say in the future,* Anjeli thought. *I don't seem to know what makes him angry.*

When they reached their stop, Kumar pointed out the several small Indian groceries that did indeed seem to carry every kind of Indian food. There were also many shops with gold jewelry and Indian clothing, and an eyebrow-threading salon that also advertised henna tattoos. There was even a paanwallah. Several shops sold religious items, and Indian DVD films and music CDs blared from numerous doorways that also advertised performances of Indian music and dance. The many travel agents made it clear that trips to India were frequent, and the number of shops selling phone cards reminded her that she must call her parents soon. Anjeli felt a great comfort in these familiar things and lingered to look, especially at the clothing and jewelry shops. Kumar's next words broke into her optimistic mood. "Things are very costly here, Anjeli. So don't think of buying. But *look* all you want. Here we call it 'window shopping,'" he said with a smile. "The best kind—no money to be paid out."

Steering Anjeli by the hand, they entered a sweet shop whose glass cases were filled with a huge selection of all the confections and pastries Anjeli enjoyed in India. "Let's celebrate and buy some sweets, Kumar; it will be nice for our tea this afternoon."

"You pick, Anjeli," Kumar agreed, "but see how expensive they are? Just select one or two that appeal to you most; we still have to do the grocery shopping." When they had made their purchase, Kumar led her back to the large supermarket on the main street. Here again she was pleasantly surprised to see the enormous array of Indian foodstuffs, every kind of fruit, even mangoes—*from Mexico true, surely not as good as the Alfonsos from India, but still*—and bags of Basmati rice and wheat flour, ten different kinds of dal, and all the vegetables she would need to cook the special Indian meals she hoped Kumar would like. Not just eggplant and cauliflower, but also American vegetables like green beans and mushrooms that looked like buttons and other things she had never cooked before. *Being so long in America Kumar probably would also like some American food* Anjeli thought. She would enjoy experimenting with American-style meals—*Not beef, of course, but with chicken and lamb and goat meat,* which was stored in big freezer tubs. They waited in a long line, and then Kumar checked over every item on the bill carefully before he handed over his credit card to the cashier.

"You have to be very careful about spending in the States. Food is much more expensive here than in India," Kumar told Anjeli when she expressed surprise at how much the bill amounted to. Actually, Anjeli realized, she had little idea of how much things cost in India. The servants always did the shopping under her mother's supervision, or occasionally her father went to the markets himself. Still, it was both unexpected and disappointing to see how careful she would need to be about money. Kumar's parents had definitely given her parents the sense that Kumar earned a very good salary and was on his way up the ladder of income and promotion, but now she wondered if they had told the truth. *Never mind,* she thought, reminding herself of the Indian saying, *"Spread your feet only as wide as your bedsheets." I will keep a close watch on the expenses and show Kumar what a good wife I can be by helping him save money.*

Arms laden with bags of groceries, they walked back to the subway. The trip home seemed longer to Anjeli. It was getting colder, and even the short walk to their building seemed more tiresome. She was eager to get home.

As they entered their lobby, a rowdy group of young people blocked their way to the elevator. They all seemed to be wearing jeans raggedy at the bottom with big holes in the knees and heavy boots like her uncle in the Army had worn. One boy wore a T-shirt with a picture of a skull and crossbones—*How inauspicious,* thought Anjeli. *Why would anyone want to attract such bad luck?* When he saw Anjeli staring at him, he called out with pride, "This is the Punisher. He kills his enemies; he's my man!" The boys and girls all had tattoos on their arms and necks, with silver pins in their ears and noses and even in their lips and eyebrows. Some of the boys wore their hair in long matted locks, which reminded Anjeli of the *saddhus* who roamed Mumbai, especially on festival days, demanding alms. *Could these people be saddhus?* She would have to ask Kumar when they got upstairs. Three of the boys had shaved heads except for a ridge of hair down the center that had been jelled and stuck up like a coxcomb. *So unbelievably ugly. What girl would be attracted to such a man?* Both the boys and girls had dyed their hair all sorts of colors—

pink, yellow, orange, and violet. Two of the girls wore black lipstick and black nail polish, and heavy blue eye shadow stood out on their very pale faces. Anjeli had seen punk rock music on TV in Mumbai—*Maybe they are punk rockers*, she thought, but she hadn't expected to see such people in the lobby of her own home and couldn't help staring.

The gang was pushing and shoving each other around, and when Kumar and Anjeli came through the lobby, they turned in their direction. One boy with a red ridge of hair was holding a rope leash tied to an ugly brown-and-white spotted dog with a snout like a pig. The dog, almost as large as a small pony, bared a mouthful of huge teeth at Kumar and Anjeli as its owner welcomed the couple in a sarcastic tone that belied his words and was obviously meant to intimidate them. "Hi, we're your neighbors. Welcome to America, lady; haven't seen you here before." Kumar pushed Anjeli away from the dog toward the elevator and roughly made a passageway for himself. By time they reached their floor, he was furious and as soon as he was inside the apartment shouted at her, "See, this is what we have to put up with. These people are trash. You make sure you don't give them any encouragement."

"I was not encouraging them, Kumar; there is no need to shout at me. Come, let us try to forget it and have our tea." Kumar calmed down a little, but his foul mood continued through the dinner Anjeli had tried to make extra special. He kept fuming about the kind of people that lived in the building, from the awful young people in the lobby to the neighbors on their floor. "You stay away from these people, Anjeli; they are crude, and some of those boys are even dangerous. And don't get friendly with that Gita who lives next door. She's a wild girl, and I want you to stay away from her." Anjeli tried to lighten his mood by telling him in a cheery voice some of the things she had in mind to do to the apartment to make it more attractive. "Yes, yes, all costing money. Let's talk of it tomorrow. After you clean the apartment up, it will look much nicer." With that, he plunked himself in front of the television set and watched TV until very late, long after Anjeli had already gone to bed.

🌸 Chapter Fourteen

If a wife obeys her husband she will be exalted in heaven.

—*The Laws of Manu*

Anjeli felt like a prisoner in her own home. Almost the only people she ever spoke to were the postal carrier and Gita, the friendly young woman next door, whom Kumar continually criticized. "She's not a good girl, Anjeli; do not become her friend. You should see the people she has coming and going at all odd hours. They look like some Mumbai goondas." Though Gita had invited Anjeli over many times for tea, Anjeli did not yet have the courage to disobey Kumar in this matter. Julie had also left several phone messages for Anjeli to call her, but Kumar had not encouraged her to return the calls. "I would rather you don't see that Julie person, Anjeli. Why isn't she married, raising a family, instead of roaming about all over India? These American women are too independent; they don't have our Indian values about family. Nothing good can come of such a friendship."

Anjeli felt bad about not calling Julie back, but she didn't want to upset Kumar and didn't want to start off their marriage with secrets.

She did share his concern about the gang of young toughs who hung out in the lobby and in front of the building. She was very afraid of the ugly dog that was always barking and looked very fierce. "It *is* fierce," Kumar had told her once when she had encountered them coming home from the grocery and practically threw herself into the apartment panting with fear. "Don't mess with them, for your own good." They *did* intimidate her, and she *did* try to pass them by as if she hadn't heard their jeers. Anjeli knew Kumar was just trying to protect her, but how could he put Gita into the same category as that vicious gang? How could she learn about life in America if she had nobody to talk to except Kumar? And she hadn't seen much of him in the two months they had been here. Each day he left for work early in the morning after a meager breakfast and a rushed cup of coffee. *No leisurely bed tea for us,* she thought sadly, remembering her carefree life in Mumbai in her parents' apartment. Kumar's conversation consisted mainly of a list of domestic chores he gave her to finish—the apartment was so open to dust, it seemed no matter how many times she cleaned and vacuumed, the same dust was there the next day. Kumar scared her with his constant warnings about not leaving the building because the streets outside were so unsafe. Except for the local grocery store, the only place he allowed her to go by herself that gave her any pleasure was the public library, a few streets away.

So different from Mumbai, where the streets were always crowded with people; lots of shops, open so early in the morning until late at night; cafés and tea parlors on every corner; performers of every kind, one man with a dancing monkey that she especially liked and always extracted a few rupees to put in his cap; all the festivals where everyone dressed in their best and strolled the beachfront at Marine Drive and purchased from cajoling vendors the most delicious snacks wrapped up in newspaper. She even missed the rushing traffic on Marine Drive with its noisy, belching diesel buses that never stopped running except for the very middle of the night. And most of all she missed the freedom: of hanging out with her friends on the Maidan or going for a coffee and sitting for all hours, talking and laughing, roaming one of the fabulous new shopping malls that Anjeli heard were even better than those in America. Anjeli realized the irony. Here she was in America, the country to which so many young women came out of a longing for more freedom and independence—she admitted to herself that was indeed a large part of her own willingness to give up her life in India, surrounded by loving parents and friends—to marry a boy from America, and now she was feeling so claustrophobic and isolated, she almost could not bear it.

Several times when she had asked Kumar if he would like to invite someone from his office over to dinner, he said curtly that there was no one in the office he wanted to be friends with. And except for one short note from her parents soon after she'd arrived, Anjeli had had no word from home either. She had written her parents one letter but did not even know if they'd received it. This afternoon she promised herself that she would write her parents again and try to put a good face on her life here with Kumar.

Sitting down at the dining table—the ugly, rickety formica table that was the first thing Anjeli promised herself she'd replace as soon as they got some extra money—she started to write . . . *Dear Mummy and Daddy* . . . but she was too miserable to go on with it. She didn't want to call her parents and have them hear the misery in her voice, and, in any case, the phone had no long-distance access, and Kumar never offered her his cell phone. *But I'm sure he calls his parents whenever he likes,* Anjeli thought somewhat bitterly. One day when she was feeling particularly homesick, she had timidly asked Kumar about calling her parents or sister in India, but he again complained about the expense—even though she knew that phone calls abroad had become much cheaper than in the past—so she was reluctant to ask him again. The only computer was in Kumar's office, so she could not use e-mail either.

Every evening Anjeli took a bath before Kumar returned home and put on one of her prettiest saris. She tried to prepare some of the dishes he said were his favorites from the groceries they shopped for together in Jackson Heights. Tonight she would make an extra effort to make it a pleasant evening. *But his moods are so unpredictable,* she sighed, and he was often so angry when he came home that they would wind up silently eating the food that she had so painstakingly cooked. But she would keep trying. She enjoyed cooking, and as she worked in the kitchen, she gradually lost her dismal mood and became happy in anticipation of spending a tranquil domestic evening with her husband. Perhaps they could talk about their new life together. She would not complain, but maybe if she could explain to him how lonely she felt all day, they could plan some excursions.

Kumar was late again. Of course, Anjeli would never eat dinner before he came home, no matter how late he was, and she was more worried than annoyed. When she heard the key in the lock, she eagerly rushed to the door, determined to hide her anxiety and to make it a perfect evening.

"Hello Kumar," she said, warmly. "I was worried about you; you're so late getting home."

"Are you keeping tabs on me, Anjeli? I don't need that kind of grief. It's bad enough at the office where everyone spies on everyone else to make sure they are doing their work."

"Please Kumar, I wasn't spying; don't get angry. I know you work so hard, and I just get worried. But tonight I've prepared your very favorite dishes, and I thought we could have a nice long talk over dinner." Hardly hearing her, Kumar strode through the apartment to the cabinet where they kept their small supply of liquor. "No food yet, Anjeli, please. It's been a really tough day, and I'm going to have a drink first. We can have food later."

"But, Kumar," she protested. "I've cooked a special dinner—the lamb *biryani* you like so much. It will not taste very good if we have to wait too long to eat it."

"That's too bad, then. And why are you wearing that sari? That pink color is awful on you. I've told you before I can't stand it. Put on something else." As he said that, he poured himself a drink from a scotch bottle that Anjeli noticed was already half empty. Repressing any comment, she went into their bedroom to change her sari.

When she had changed into a sari Kumar had complimented her on in the past, she was pleased to hear him say, "Much better, Anjeli. You are a beautiful girl, and you must wear the clothes that best show off your beauty. In this sari I will be afraid to take you out; everyone will think you are a Bollywood movie star."

Anjeli smiled and sat next to Kumar on the sofa, trying to ignore the fact that he had refilled his glass. Kumar didn't drink that often and only rarely got drunk, although when he did Anjeli realized she was just a little afraid of him. She had noticed when she had stayed with his parents in Delhi that his father seemed to drink a lot, and then everyone but his wife tiptoed around him for fear of raising his temper. Her own parents never drank alcohol, although she knew that many people in their class, the men at least, did. Kumar had actually teased her about the fact that no alcohol had been served at their wedding. At his parents' house, when Kumar's father caught Anjeli's look of slight dismay as he reached for the bottle of Johnny Walker, he had said to her, "There's nothing wrong with drinking, Anjeli; wait until you get to America. There everyone drinks; that's the culture there. You'll find that out soon enough." Anjeli had bit back a response and retired to her room in abject silence, praying for Kumar to call her very soon to America.

"Whatever you say, Kumar. While you have your drink, maybe we could just sit and talk for a little. Is there something happening at work that is distressing you? Please tell me. Maybe I can help in some way."

Kumar's mood changed immediately. "Help? How can you help?" he blurted out angrily. "What do you know about life here, about having to work like a dog for people who don't appreciate you and hold you back from promotion just because you're Indian? I have more skills and degrees than most of the jerks in my office, but I'm still not being moved up."

"Maybe you could talk to your boss, Kumar, explain to him how you feel."

"Talk to the boss? The boss is the problem! He's the one that's holding up my promotion. And now, with all the mortgage fallout, the bank is talking of serious downsizing. I might lose my job." Anjeli did not know what to say. In truth, she *had* no experience of being out in the world, of having to hold a job, of working to support herself or a family, of having to put up with people who treated her badly because she was Indian. In a way, Kumar was protecting her from all that. Like he protected her from that awful gang that hung out by their building, and she *was* so grateful for that. She was particularly frightened by the boy with the dog. He was very bold and always came very close to her when he spoke. He seemed almost demented, even dangerous, leering at her with his eerie gray eyes. One of her dreams was that she and Kumar could save enough money to move to a different place, maybe even a small house somewhere. That was one of the things she wanted to talk with Kumar about, if she could get him in a good mood.

As the liquor began to take hold, Kumar calmed down a little. "I'm sorry, I really apologize, Anjeli. I know none of this is your fault." Anjeli just nodded and smiled, apparently the right thing to do because Kumar then said, "Okay, let's eat that special dinner you cooked. And then we can watch a little TV, just relax. No more office talk, I promise you." As he ate, Anjeli waited on every bite for his approval, even though she knew the food had not improved with reheating. "Very nice, Anjeli, but not enough chilis and too much salt. When my mother comes here, she'll teach you how to really cook the Punjabi way."

"Your mother?" Anjeli could hardly whisper it. "Why do you want your mother to come here? Where is the room for her to stay? What is the need? She must not leave your father alone in Delhi; you know he's not in the best of health."

"Oh, my father will be coming also, don't worry. It will be nice companionship for you. In their company you can go out more during the day, and my mother can help you with the chores. Anyway, it won't happen for a while; there's lots of things they need to take care of in Delhi before they come."

After Anjeli cleared the dishes, Kumar sat himself on the sofa in front of the TV and patted the space beside him for her to join him there. Anjeli hated the American shows that Kumar seemed so fond of. This surprised her because in Mumbai she and her family had often watched American TV together. But here there seemed only to be shows where young girls in scanty clothes sang songs whose lyrics she couldn't understand and whose movements of breasts and hips were, to Anjeli's eyes, something that should not be shown in public. Only a year or so ago, she had read in the English papers that some celebrity attending an American football game had worn a costume that actually revealed one of her breasts and there was a big fuss and talk of lawsuits. The shows Kumar watched didn't seem much different from that, and—she couldn't help it—they disgusted her. *How can he have so little sensitivity to my feelings that he asks me to watch along with him!*

As she fussed in the kitchen Anjeli pondered the deep contradictions she had observed about life in America so far. On the one hand, Americans seemed so protective of their privacy; the Americans she had met in India or seen in films always talked about privacy, "giving me space," they said. She knew all children in America, even small babies, had a room for themselves, "my own room," they called it. So she understood why Americans were shocked when they saw how many people lived together in one house or apartment or shared a bedroom in India. The idea of sharing their space with so many other people was "unimaginable," as one American lady she had met expressed it. Yet on the TV shows Kumar watched, she had seen people talking about the most private—and often horrible—things that they had done or that had been done to them, sharing with an audience of strangers parts of themselves that Indian people would never reveal to anyone for fear of spoiling their family's reputation. And on the street, and on subway platforms, Anjeli saw men and women hugging and kissing each other, something she never saw, or dreamed of seeing, even in sophisticated, modern Mumbai. Once she had even seen a couple who looked Indian entwined with each other, kissing and intimately caressing on the street. It had caused her to blush, and when she called Kumar's attention to them, he had said dismissively, "Hey, Anjeli, this is America. People do that kind of thing, and no one minds." Anjeli thought of Julie, who studied different cultures; maybe this was something she could ask her about if they ever got a chance to meet.

As Anjeli mulled over these thoughts, Kumar, sensing that Anjeli was truly—and maybe rightly—upset by his behavior, stopped flipping the channels and turned off the set. He went into the kitchen and put his hands around her waist. He wore a serious expression, though there was a glint in his eyes. "Anjeli," he said gently, "I promise you, things will improve. We can start this weekend. On Sunday we'll go on a tour of New York, and I'll show you some sights." Anjeli replied enthusiastically, silently praying at the same time that the day her in-laws would invade their life would be far into the future so that she could build on the time she would have alone with Kumar. She was determined to enjoy the weekend, their first adventure, just the two of them, exploring the city.

Kumar wrapped his arms around Anjeli's shoulders and pulled her into the bedroom. There he held her tightly and kissed her so hard her lips hurt. When Kumar sensed her resistance to his embrace he chastised her. "Come, Anjeli, we're not in Kansas any more. You can forget all that convent upbringing of yours." Not unkindly, but a little roughly, he pushed her down on the bed and forced his way inside her.

Anjeli was determined to put the previous night out of her mind and to enjoy Kumar's promised Sunday outing. It was sunny and cold, but not freezing. Anjeli had not really brought enough warm clothing with her for a New York winter, something she thought Kumar might have warned her about. But she would not spoil the day with negative thoughts. She wore two sweaters over her shalwar kameez and a pair of woolen socks that she had wisely bought on one of their walks in Jackson Heights. "When he is in a good mood," she thought, "I will have him take me shopping for a warm coat."

"I'm going to take you on my special guided tour of New York," Kumar told Anjeli as they walked to the subway. I have bought a guidebook, *40 Perfect New York Days*, so we can see all the sights in New York properly, one by one."

By this time Anjeli was familiar with the No. 7 subway train, though she still couldn't imagine herself traveling by subway without Kumar by her side. At 42nd Street, they changed to something called "the shuttle," then to another train that took them even further downtown. Anjeli gazed in wonder at the great diversity of people riding the subway. *In that way,* she thought, *New York is very much like Mumbai.* She couldn't wait for the day when she had the knowledge and confidence to get around a little by herself.

They emerged from the subway at a place Kumar called Battery Park. After taking in the spectacular waterfront views, including the Statue of Liberty, Kumar told Anjeli that he would take her on New York's biggest bargain trip. "The Staten Island Ferry," he smiled, "the only free ride you'll ever get in America." The huge ferry terminal was an ugly building, nothing like Mumbai's grand Victoria Station, but the hall was much cleaner and less crowded. They boarded the ferry—no pushing and shoving here, Anjeli appreciated—that had just pulled into the dock and had wonderful fun on the short ride, braving the cold to stand on the open deck as Kumar pointed out the Statue of Liberty, Ellis Island, Governor's Island, and the awesome view of lower Manhattan's skyscrapers on the return trip. After docking, they strolled up several blocks to a beautiful glass building that Kumar told Anjeli was the World Financial Center, rebuilt after 9/11. They treated themselves to a hot chocolate among the indoor palm trees and window shopped some of the boutiques and art galleries. When they exited their subway stop in Queens, Anjeli said enthusiastically "That guidebook was right—this was a perfect day in New York. Thank you, Kumar. You have made me very happy."

Inside their apartment, Kumar pushed the answering machine on their phone, and Anjeli was pleased to hear Julie's voice. "Hi, Anjeli, it's Julie. Hope all is well. Why don't you give me a call when you have a chance? Maybe we can get together." Kumar erased the message without any comment, and Anjeli let it go, not wanting to spoil the day. She had some ideas she planned to bring up to Kumar over the next few weeks, and she was hoping he would go along with them. Today had been so pleasant, maybe this could be a turning point.

That evening over dinner, Anjeli began tentatively, "Kumar, I had a wonderful time on our city adventure today, and I look forward to doing that again. But you know, it is very lonely for me here during the week. I don't have any friends, and you are gone all day. I can't even go to the basement to do the laundry without you because I am afraid of those people with their dog who hang around here."

"Well, it's winter now, Anjeli, and it gets dark early. During the day you can do some grocery shopping in the neighborhood and go to the library. And this apartment needs lots of cleaning—it's so dusty all the time. When the light stays longer, it will be easier for you to go out."

"I can't spend all my time dusting the apartment, Kumar. It would make a big difference if I could see Gita sometimes. She works most of the week but is off on Thursdays, and even having a cup of tea with her would be a pleasant break for me. And I'd like to see Julie, too. It just isn't polite not to call her back. Maybe we could invite her over for dinner."

"I've told you I don't want you visiting Gita, Anjeli. While her parents work nights in the post office, she carouses around however she likes. She's a typical American *desi* girl who will give you wrong ideas about being independent, going here and there, roaming about all the places where you have no reason to be, spending my hard-earned money on nonsense. You can't be too careful with your reputation here—it's no different than India in that respect.

"Spend money?" Anjeli asked in bewilderment. "Where do I spend any money? You hardly give me enough for the few groceries I buy, and I haven't spent anything on myself. We haven't even bought the winter coat you promised me."

After a deep silence, Anjeli timidly continued, "What do you think about my getting a job, Kumar? Then at least I won't be wasting my time. It will give me something to do, and I can bring home a little extra money that we could use to fix up the apartment. Maybe we could buy some new furniture, even some small things to make the place look brighter. If I had a job, we wouldn't have to worry so much about money. Maybe I could find something part time; Julie might be able to help me find something at her college."

"Don't always keep arguing with me, Anjeli. Are you saying I can't support you? You seem to have plenty ideas of how to spend, but I don't think you have the first idea of how to earn."

"I could learn, Kumar."

"Enough, Anjeli. No more tonight! Maybe my parents should come sooner that will be some company for you at least."

That's not the kind of company I want, Anjeli thought with some anger. But she said, instead, "I want to be with people like us, Kumar, young people. I want us to go out and see this big new city like we did today. And I want some freedom to go out on my own, or with a friend, not always to be worried about what people will say about my roaming about." *And I don't care what Kumar says, I will have tea with Gita, whether he likes it or not!* she thought defiantly. *And I will call Julie! And maybe,* she thought, though less defiantly, *I will get a job.*

Chapter Fifteen

We look at man's life, and we cannot untangle this song. Rings and knots of joy and grief, all interlaced and locking.

—*William Buck*, translator, Ramayana

As Anjeli came close to her building, she saw the boy with the dog that had taunted her the previous week hanging out in front. Even though it was broad daylight, his leering at her made her afraid. She was sure he had followed her once or twice when she was grocery shopping in the neighborhood and she didn't know what to do about it. When she had mentioned it to Kumar, he scolded her as if she were somehow to blame. "These hooligans, they see you in those tight jeans, naturally they think you are easy. Can't you see that, Anjeli?" It would be terrible if Kumar got into a fight with this boy to protect her. *Kumar is a professional person. What does he know about getting in fist fights with such people?* The boy had his gang behind him, and she was sure they were taking some drugs. *Maybe I can call the police, anonymously, without telling Kumar.* But right now, she just wanted to get inside the building and shut the door before he could push his way in behind her.

Struggling with her shopping bags, Anjeli awkwardly fished around in her purse for her keys. It was a losing battle. She'd have to put down the bags. As she walked nearer to the door, the boy followed close behind her. "Hey, beautiful lady; can I help you take your stuff inside? Or better yet, give me your key, and I'll open the door for you."

"Please," Anjeli almost cried. "Please leave me alone."

"Oh, so you do know English, beautiful lady," he leered. "I love you," he added, making a kissing sound with his lips. "You need protection in this neighborhood, and I'm your man. Stay with me, and I'll make sure no one bothers you. Just me, I'd like to bother you. Would you like that, beautiful lady?"

Anjeli was becoming truly frightened. Just then, Gita appeared, and Anjeli sighed with relief. "F--- off, you creep," Gita shouted at him. "You bother us one more time, and I'll call the police."

"I'm not bothering you, you ugly bitch. I wouldn't touch you with a ten-foot pole," he shouted back, but he moved out on to the sidewalk, obviously not wanting to carry the encounter further.

Gita took out her key and spoke loudly to Anjeli intending the boy to hear. "Don't let him frighten you, Anjeli, he's just a creep. No girl would go near him unless he forced her." Throwing him a dirty look, Gita opened the door and pushed Anjeli into the building lobby and shut the door with a hard thump behind her.

"Oh, thank goodness you came along, Gita. I was really frightened. I think he's been following me home sometimes also."

"You can't back away from these creeps, Anjeli. This one is a little more than weird, though; maybe we *should* do something. Last year there was a rumor that he assaulted some girl on the street, but according to the neighborhood gossip, she was so scared of his gang she refused to press charges."

As Anjeli and Gita entered the lobby, they were glad to see the postman, who was just completing the mail delivery. Anjeli started to take out her mailbox key, but he intercepted her, handing her a few bills from her mailbox along with a blue air letter from India that she'd been longing to see. "Don't get too many of these anymore," the postman remarked. "You folks are about the only ones who use them. Nowadays I guess everyone uses e-mail, right?"

"You are right," responded Anjeli with a smile, "but some of us more traditional people still think only a handwritten letter will do. Though postage is getting so expensive even in India that the old letter writers there seem to be losing their customers."

"Yeah, my job'll be next, I suppose." With a rueful laugh he wheeled his bag out of the doorway.

As Anjeli and Gita headed into the elevator, Gita asked, "Is that letter good news, Anjeli? It's nice to see that look of happiness on your face."

Waving the airletter, Anjeli exclaimed, "Oh, it's a letter from my sister. She is usually such a good letter writer, but I haven't heard from her since I've been here. I hope everything is okay."

"I'm sure she's fine, Anjeli. Check with Kumar; he may have picked up some letters from home and forgotten—on purpose," this said with a sly wink, "to give them to you."

"You're too suspicious, Gita. Kumar would never keep my mail. He knows how I long to hear from my sister and my parents."

"You don't get it, Anjeli; that might be exactly why he'd keep your letters. But never mind—I don't want to spoil your joy. Hey, why don't you come for a coffee tomorrow afternoon, or a *chai* if you prefer. We can have a nice long gossip. If your in-laws ever come, you won't be allowed. I have some delicious *bhel puri* and some sweets from that Maharani sweet shop in Jackson Heights that you can help me eat."

"That will be lovely, Gita. I will see you tomorrow. *I just won't tell Kumar*, Anjeli thought. *It isn't fair for him to forbid me to see her. What harm can come from a neighborly visit?*

Anjeli put away her groceries impatiently, so eager to read her sister's letter. They had been like best friends, and she missed Priya terribly. Though Anjeli was thrilled when her parents had arranged

Priya's marriage, she was heartbroken to see her go off to Delhi. But Priya did write very often, even after the children were born and took up so much of her time. That's why it seemed strange to Anjeli that she hadn't heard from Priya since she had arrived in New York. *I hope nothing is the matter,* Anjeli worried, fingering the air letter's return address with great affection and then carefully opening the letter.

Dear Anjeli,

We are all quite anxious at not having heard from you in a long time. You haven't answered any of my letters. Perhaps Kumar doesn't like you to call, and we know everyone in America is so busy, busy, but we do long to hear from you. We know you are all right from Kumar's parents whom we see occasionally at various functions, but I want to hear from you, yourself, about your life in America. When your mother-in-law sees Mummy and Daddy, she only talks about the expenses of living in America and tries to wring some more money from them. Once when Kumar's father drank too much whiskey, he accused Daddy of not paying up all the dowry they promised for you. I don't envy you when Kumar's parents join you next week in America. Hopefully they will not stay long. Since his sister is finishing her college, maybe they will start arranging her marriage, perhaps even looking for a boy while they are in America.

All the family here are well, but please, please do write to us. We miss you a lot, and the children want to see their Aunty Anjeli.

Lots of Love,
Priya

Tears welled in Anjeli's eyes as she thought of her dear, loving sister. Her parents had not found it easy to arrange her marriage because Priya was a *manglik*, a Tuesday child, for whom it was not easy to find a compatible horoscope, and even modern Indian families closely followed the guidance of astrologers in the crucial matter of marital compatibility. But Priya had never become bitter and was quite resigned to wed whomever her parents chose because she knew that as long as she remained unmarried, Anjeli's marriage would not take place. What good fortune to find Prem! He was a wonderful husband and father, and Priya was adored by her husband's family as well as her own. Their wedding had not been as lavish as Anjeli's, but Prem's family appeared quite satisfied and had made no demands, refusing any but the most token symbolic gifts from Anjeli's parents.

Wiping away her tears, Anjeli's thoughts turned sad but also a little angry. Why hadn't Kumar told her his parents were coming so soon to stay with them? Anjeli knew she would have to confront him with the issue when he returned from work tonight. Then she chastised herself: *Don't confront; inquire, discuss, raise the question . . .* that was the advice of the women's magazines. It seemed like a never-ending job to make things run smoothly, but this was one discussion Kumar must have with her.

Anjeli felt cut off from everyone who was dear to her. Asking her beloved sister and mother for advice would break their hearts as they would blame themselves for making such a wrong choice of a husband for her. *Who can I talk to?* Kumar had relented on her visiting Gita— "But only in her home, no roaming about with her!"—but Anjeli herself wasn't sure if she wanted to confide in Gita yet. Though Gita was near her own age, Anjeli didn't know how much she gossiped with the older housewives on the floor. Briefly she thought of Julie, whom she felt would never betray her confidence, but she hadn't gotten really close to Julie yet and would feel a little uncomfortable discussing such personal things. And she must be very busy; Anjeli didn't want to "lean on" her—a new English expression she had learned that was inexplicable in an Indian context—and take up her time. It wasn't like India where she and her friends could call each other or meet at the spur of the moment. She recalled her disbelief when her friend who returned from a visit to America reported that Americans had to even make an appointment to see their own parents. *What could such an incredible comment mean, making an appointment to see family? Maybe sometime Gita or Julie can explain it to me.*

Kumar was late again as he had been so many nights recently. And these days he always had a drink before dinner. Tonight Anjeli must make sure he didn't have too much. She *had* to know about his parents' intention to come to America so soon and why he hadn't told her.

Anjeli sat restlessly on the couch waiting for Kumar, hoping he wouldn't be *too* late. She must have the time to discuss things properly. She had changed into a pretty shalwar-kameez, not too fancy, as she didn't want Kumar to think that she was trying to "dazzle" him into agreeing with her, something he had accused her of when she had once tried to make up the next day after an argument. Though she couldn't see how wanting to look nice for your husband was a wrong thing. To be fair, her in-laws' visit was not a complete surprise; Kumar had mentioned its possibility several times. She had just put off thinking about it, hoping maybe it wouldn't happen.

But what made her most angry, she realized, was that she had only received the news through her sister, in the letter the postman put into her hand. Could Gita be right? Was it possible that Kumar was hiding her letters, taking them from the mailbox and not passing them on to her? And what about her letters to them? Why had Priya said they hadn't heard from her? Kumar often took her letters along with his own to mail. Was it possible that he never sent them? *But one thing at a time,* Anjeli determined. *The main thing to find out is when his parents are coming.*

Kumar finally arrived home without any excuse for his lateness, settled himself on the couch, and picked up the TV remote. But before he could turn on the set, Anjeli joined him on the couch. "Kumar, could we please talk before you watch? I received some news from Priya today that was a big surprise to me. She wrote me that your parents are coming to America to visit us next week. Why did you not tell me about this?"

"I've told you a hundred times my parents will be coming to America, Anjeli; please don't pretend this is news to you."

"Yes, you have told me, Kumar, but not that they were coming so soon. In just one week, Priya said."

"Well, I didn't know myself exactly when they were coming, Anjeli. So please don't make a federal case out of this."

Just then the phone rang, and Kumar picked it up. Anjeli never answered the phone unless she was alone in the apartment. Kumar listened for a moment and then took the phone and went into the bedroom, closing the door behind him. After a few moments he came back and sat in the chair facing Anjeli. "That was my mother, Anjeli. My parents *will* be here next week. I have the flight information, and of course I'll have to take the day off from work to meet them at the airport. Please do whatever is necessary to get the apartment ready for them; we can go shopping this weekend to make sure there is enough food and all in the house."

When Anjeli did not respond, Kumar continued, "I know, Anjeli, that you don't like the idea of my parents living with us. I've known that from the beginning. But I hope I made it clear that your wishes are not of primary interest to me on this issue. My parents have done so much for me; they have sacrificed their own pleasures and scrimped and saved, denying themselves luxuries in order to send me to America. And they are very modern thinking. My father has never asked that you keep *purdah* in front of him. And my mother will take you around to meet all her friends as you're always saying you don't get out of the house enough. I'm here in America because of my parents, and Uncle Suresh also, whom I lived with for so many years when I first came here. You can't expect me to forget all my parents have done for me just because you don't want to trouble yourself to accommodate them and give up some of your own pleasures."

"Kumar, that is not fair," Anjeli replied in a neutral tone of voice. "I am not thinking of my own pleasures. I am thinking of us, how our being together will be affected by your parents' visit. Where will we get the extra money to provide a proper visit for them?"

"We'll manage somehow, Anjeli. And please don't keep using the word *visit*. I don't want you to delude yourself. This will be a long stay, perhaps even a permanent one. I will never ask my parents to leave my home no matter how much money it costs. Our parents depend on us, Anjeli. You know that is the Indian way, and I never want them to feel that I have failed them. Come, let's have dinner," he halted their conversation abruptly. "I've already missed the TV news, and I'm hungry."

Sitting down to dinner, seeing Kumar was enjoying the food, Anjeli hesitated a moment and then timidly ventured, "Kumar, what do you think about my getting a job?"

"A job?" he responded, looking up from his eating, "Why do you want a job? Didn't we have this discussion already? Now suddenly that my parents will be here, you again are talking about a job. Are you thinking that will be a good excuse to avoid being with them? Not very nice on your part, Anjeli. Why do you dislike them so much. What have they ever done to you?"

"Please, Kumar, don't take it that way. I was only thinking that it would be good to have some extra money. Maybe if I earned even a small salary, we could save to move out of this building. If your parents will stay permanently, a house would be so much more comfortable for them." *And maybe with a little savings we could also think about having a child,* she almost added. She knew Kumar was dead set against having a baby in his uncertain economic circumstances, though of course it would please his parents. Or at least she thought it would. Of her own feelings, she wasn't so sure. She had hoped that marrying a man living in the States would mean more romance and more adventure than her friends' marriages in India. Though that appeared to be a false hope so far, she was not in a rush to settle down with children.

"Well, some extra money wouldn't hurt, I'll agree to that," Kumar offered reluctantly. "But with a job you'll be tired all the time. Who will take care of the house, the cooking? These things will still need to be done. I don't want to hear constant complaints about how much you have to do."

"That won't be a problem, Kumar. I was thinking only a part-time job, maybe just two or three days a week. And in a way your mother being here will be good. She can help with the cooking; she will enjoy that, I think, and it will be useful for me to learn from her. I can call Julie about a job; I believe she will help me."

After Kumar left for work the next day, Anjeli called Julie at her office. "I'm so sorry I haven't returned your calls earlier, Professor Norman."

Here she was interrupted by Julie who said firmly but with a little laugh, "Please, call me Julie, Anjeli. I'm your friend, not your professor. And don't call me Julie Aunty, either. That makes me feel a hundred years old. I called because I was hoping we could get a chance to meet sometime. I'm eager to hear about how you are enjoying your life in America."

"Oh, everything is fine," Anjeli replied, then added hesitantly, "but I am calling you for some help. I would like to get a job. Kumar and I have talked it over, and he is in complete agreement."

Complete agreement, Julie thought skeptically, *I bet there's a little more ambivalence than that. They probably need the money, just a few more cases where the boy's family exaggerates his salary.* Aloud, she said, "Of course, Anjeli. I'll be happy to help. What kind of job are you thinking of?"

"Well, I thought maybe you would know about something at the college. Maybe a few days a week or something like that. I think Kumar would feel better knowing I am working in a place where I have a friend. And maybe later on I could even take some courses. I don't have any experience, but I have taken some computer classes. I wouldn't expect to get paid very much, but it could be a place to start."

"I'll get right on it, Anjeli, check around, see if anyone here needs an assistant in their office. I'll get back to you as soon as I hear anything, not to worry."

"Oh, thank you Prof . . . I mean, Julie, and I know Kumar will also appreciate it."

I bet he will, Julie thought, but said, "Give him my regards. I'll speak with you soon."

Anjeli was awed at Julie's confidence. *Nothing is too much for these American professional women,* she thought. And fleetingly added to herself, *Maybe someday I could be like that . . .*

After hanging up the phone, Julie strolled over to the university bulletin board, which advertised jobs, housing, bikes and cars for sale, upcoming actions on everything from the antiwar movement to animal rights, and a host of other fliers. She took down a few job notices that looked promising and later called some of the administrative department heads she knew personally, but everyone was looking for full-time people. Only one ad from a professor of philosophy looked like a possibility. Before getting Anjeli's hopes up, though, Julie thought she'd better check if the job was still available. When the office secretary assured her it was, Julie left her name, commenting that she was in the anthropology department and knew someone she could highly recommend for the position, if Professor Fleagle were able to keep it open for a few days.

"No problem," the secretary assured Julie. "Most folks these days want more hours; everyone's hurting for money."

"Great, I'll be back in touch." Julie called Anjeli during the day, when she knew Kumar would be at work and they could talk more freely. "I think I've got something that would suit you perfectly, Anjeli. If you want to apply, I'll be happy to write a letter of recommendation and speak to the professor in charge."

"Oh, Julie, that's so kind. I will call him immediately for an interview."

"Glad to help, Anjeli. Let me know how it all turns out."

❀ Chapter Sixteen

The washerman's donkey belongs neither at the house nor at the water tank.

—*Indian proverb*

When Anjeli rang Gita's bell, her neighbor opened the door immediately. "Come on in, Anjeli. I have some good Indian chai and not only bhel puri but for after some *kulfi falooda* from Maharani Sweets, none of that frozen stuff from the supermarket. We live right next door and should meet more often," Gita said.

If Kumar thinks we meet too often, we won't be meeting at all, Anjeli reflected. She knew Kumar was not above confronting Gita directly about spending too much time with Anjeli if he had a mind to.

In their mini-tour of Gita's apartment, Anjeli could see that it had a very different feeling from her own. Gita had decorated her own small bedroom with posters of the latest Indian movie stars and pop singers and also American hip-hop and rap artists and a photograph of DJ Rekha Malhotra, the queen of *bhangra*. The living room and dining room furniture was reminiscent of that in Anjeli's parents' apartment in

Mumbai, the end tables and bookcases filled with Indian crafts and the walls covered with prints and paintings of Hindu gods and goddesses, Lord Ganesh by the entrance among them.

Gita had laid the table with the melmac dishes that were so popular among an earlier generation of Indians but which were now totally passé, even in India. Anjeli had hopes of buying the fashionable Mikasa dinnerware she now saw in so many magazine advertisements. *When we have more money,* she sighed.

"Please sit down, Anjeli; the tea will be ready in a minute. And help yourself to the bhel puri. I get it in a special place. Even though I'm an *ABCD*, I'm addicted to Indian food."

"What is this ABCD, Gita? I thought I spoke excellent English when I was in India, but after coming to America, I think I hardly know English at all. At least the way people speak it here."

"Sue that fancy convent school you went to, Anjeli. They don't pre-pare you for what you need to know in America. But ABCD is an easy one; it means *American-born confused desi.*"

"Oh, you are born here! That is why you were so unafraid with that awful boy who keeps bothering us while I was scared to death."

"Being scared won't get you anywhere in America, Anjeli. Here self-confidence is everything. I'm not going to be like my parents, who came here without anything in the late 1980s when the American economy had tanked and my folks were glad to get any job they could."

"Where are your parents now, Gita? I don't see them at home very much."

"They both work for the post office, and at night they help out in an Indian grocery store. It's all about money for them, but I guess it needs to be. You have to admire these immigrants from India—from all over Asia, really. They work so hard for the sake of their children, for *their* ed-ucation, *their* success. At least with the post office my folks do have some economic security. If they can save enough, maybe they'll buy a grocery store or a gas station themselves. In India my father was a government clerk; you know those jobs pay nothing, and my mother, of course, didn't work, just stayed home with her children. My parents came to America so their future children would have better opportunities. In India it's all about who you know, and the competition for places in schools, even primary schools, is getting too tough, worse than America even."

"Yes, my sister tells me there is even a big crush for pre-K, so I can imagine the competition for middle and high school! Even personal connections don't guarantee anything anymore."

Nodding in agreement, Gita added, "And all those reserved places for the *scheduled castes* make it more difficult for middle-class people like us. Not that I'm saying they shouldn't have some benefits; we Hindus treated them so awful, just like the blacks are treated here. But still, more for them means less for us. Such sacrifices our parents had to make, I really appreciate what they've done for me. You can be sure I won't ever put them in some old people's home like these Americans do with their elderly parents."

"What a horrible thought," Anjeli responded with deeply felt emotion. "I can't imagine how people can do that. Some things about India I'm glad to get away from, but some of our Indian values are best and should be preserved."

"*Some*," Gita said thoughtfully, "but one custom I will never agree on with my parents is arranged marriage. Now that I'm almost finished with my master's degree, they're already bugging me to 'see'"—she air-quoted the word to give it its literal Indian meaning in this context— "some boys they have met in the Indian community here. You know, the second cousin of some aunt's sister-in-law who lives in New Jersey and is a computer engineer, or whatever. My parents will only look in a narrow group of boys: same caste, same community, same native place they came from, and the same families who knew their grandparents from half a century ago. What about the boys out there who aren't from my community? It may be that one of them would be the one I would love and want to marry. I want to have the choice.

"Some of my cousins in India, and even some desis I know here in America, they just sit resigned for months and even years, waiting for their parents to choose the guy *they'll* have to spend the rest of their life with. Marry a man you hardly know, a virtual stranger? How did you go along with it, Anjeli? Didn't you care who you married?"

"Of course I cared," Anjeli answered with quiet dignity. "That is why I was happy to let my parents find a boy for me. My marriage is too important to be arranged by such an inexperienced person as myself. Even in Mumbai, which has become so sophisticated, I never dated or was really alone with a boy. What could I ever know about who was the right boy for me? I know it's the fashion for some girls these days to meet boys on their own and marry for love, but I was happy for my parents' guidance in this matter.

"I had lots of fun with my friends, and some boys also," Anjeli continued, "but I didn't have to break out in spots worrying that some boy I wanted to date preferred some other girl in our group. Our parents want the best for us, don't they? So we can enjoy our lives and let them do the work and worrying."

"Okay, I grant you the last part of that perhaps," Gita admitted. "But I want to *love* the man I marry. How can I possibly do that if I don't know him personally? Maybe I won't even *like* him."

"If he is a good man, why should you not like him?" Anjeli retorted. "In the American way, the girl knows the boy so well, maybe even lives with him before they marry, so she wears a white gown at her weddings but in truth, where is the mystery and romance in getting married? In the Indian way our marriage really changes our lives, and we have all our married years ahead to get to know and love our husbands. That's much better, don't you think?"

"The truth is, Anjeli, I'm not sure what I think anymore—about a lot of things, where I can see both the Indian and American side. But not about this. Even if my parents gave me a chance to reject every boy they chose, it wouldn't work because they'd be staring down the wrong end of the telescope at a ridiculously narrow pool of possibles, just boys from our specific Indian community."

"But, Gita," Anjeli contended, "isn't it best when husband and wife come from the same community? If you marry outside your community, difficulties are sure to multiply. And there are lots of good, even Westernized, Indian boys from your own community, I'm sure, maybe even like you, an ABCD," Anjeli smiled at her friend. "Your parents might find someone like that in the matrimonial columns of the Indian newspapers. Or on one of those Internet marriage sites. These days very respectable people in India and all over the world are using the Internet to arrange matches. Yes, that way they might find you a very suitable boy."

"Oh, right," laughed Gita. "Can you imagine a truthful profile of me? It would have to say, 'Traditional Indian parents seek suitable match for chubby, dark, Indian girl, MA, meat-eating, independent-minded, loves to dance and go to clubs, no joint family living, no dowry demands met.' . . . I know how the matrimonial ads read nowadays: 'Professional girl with strong family values!' That's just another way of saying 'meek and obedient.' Not for me, thanks. Sita's not my role model, dutiful wife that she was. I'd rather be the Rani of Jhansi, riding out to defeat the British! That's my ideal of a real woman."

Anjeli laughed at Gita's remarks, and Gita laughed along with her, but then said more seriously, "I don't want to spend my life with a 'suitable boy.' I want a soulmate, a man I love, whatever that chemistry is, and who loves me back in the same way. For that we'd have to be on an equal footing. In an arranged marriage the boy already expects that he will have everything his own way, just like in India."

"Do you think, Gita, that you will recognize your soul mate when you meet him? Can you tell what love is?" Anjeli ventured boldly.

"Well, I thought I could, once," Gita began, distress clouding her face. "A boy at college, an ABCD from our own community even. I introduced him to my folks a few times, but we didn't want to make too much of our relationship or both sides would be pressuring us to get married. Anyway, it wound up going nowhere. Because I seemed so Americanized, he figured I'd do everything he wanted, and I don't have to tell what that was. So looking back, I'm not even sure that it *was* love. The chemistry seemed to be there, but more and more I didn't respect his character. It was hard, but I finally broke it off. My parents were kind of disappointed. They saw him as a suitable match, but of course, they don't really know *anything* about how these boys today feel.

"The boys have it so much easier than the girls. That's why so many boys agree to an arranged marriage, especially with a girl from India. No trouble to court the girl, you know your mother'll choose a 'homey' girl who'll keep a clean, comfortable house for you and put a good Indian dinner on the table every night. All the power and privileges that married men have in India. Parents will wait longer for their sons to get married, and when the boy finally goes along with his parents' choice, if that marriage doesn't go well, he's much freer to find his fun elsewhere, isn't he?"

"Oh, Gita, don't say that. See how good a match my parents found for me in Kumar? I had seen other boys and didn't like them, and my parents didn't force me. But when Kumar and I met, we knew right away we didn't want to look further. Kumar has told me this also. So I know our love for each other will grow stronger as we get to know each other better . . ." *I think, I hope . . .* Anjeli's voice trailed off.

Gita raised her eyebrows at Anjeli, who admitted silently to herself that she in fact did feel uncertain about the emotion upon which she was offering such firm opinions. Abruptly but politely Anjeli changed the subject. "Gita, I forgot to tell you, two important things are happening. As they say in America, one is the good news and one is the bad news."

"Let's hear the bad news first," said Gita smiling.

"Well, that's just a little joke, Gita—it's not such bad news. You remember that letter I received from my sister yesterday? She had met Kumar's parents in Delhi, and they told her they are coming to America. They called us last night." *Not really us,* Anjeli qualified inwardly, *but I don't have to tell Gita everything.* "They will be here next week."

"Well," said Gita, "that may not be the worst news you'll ever get. I mean you might fall under a bus tomorrow, but, yeah, I'd definitely put it in the 'bad news' category. You'd better hide all your gold jewelry and expensive saris; mothers-in-law have a habit of wanting to lock up the dowry and dole it out to the daughter-in-law when it suits them. God, Anjeli, can you imagine me living with a mother-in-law? I can barely live in this small space with my parents and my brother without us all tripping over each other."

"Well, I'm hoping it won't be for too long . . ."

Here Gita interrupted Anjeli. "It will be too long, even if it is just for a week. Take my word for it. Why do you think these mothers-in-law want their sons to marry a girl from India. It's so they have someone to boss around just as if their son was living in India. "

"You may be right, but I'll just have to adjust. They are Kumar's parents after all, and they have done a lot for him. But my second piece of news is really good. I'm going to try to get a job."

"Now that *is* good news," Gita said enthusiastically. "Tell me about it."

"You remember that NUNY professor I told you about, the one who came to my wedding? I called her, Kumar agreed, and she said she would help me. I have an interview this week. With some Professor Fleagle—he's in the philosophy department. And—you must never tell Kumar I said this . . ."

Here Gita pointed to herself with an exaggerated widening of her eyes, and said, "Me, tell Kumar anything about you? Never, Anjeli. My lips are sealed."

"It is perfect for me at just this time because even though it would be only a few days a week, it will keep some distance between me and Kumar's parents. And the money will be so handy, his parents can never criticize me for it. Maybe I can take some more courses also. At a university—what quarrel can they have with that?"

"Ah," Gita winked, "the university. You watch out for all those professors. We may think professors have their heads in the clouds, but they are just men all the same."

"Gita, you're shameless! Don't think such things. But look, I want you to have a set of my house keys," said Anjeli. "Now that I hope to be working and will be out of the apartment so much, it will be good to know that if I lock myself out, I can call on your help. Kumar's parents go here and there; they have a lot of friends, and I wouldn't want to have to wait in the hallway for them to come home."

"Absolutely, Anjeli. I'll keep them very safe, right on my own key ring."

Just then the door opened, and Gita waved hello to the young man who entered. "Anjeli, my younger brother, Anil; he calls himself Nil, you know, to pass as a regular American. Like no one will notice he's Indian, right?" Gita laughed.

"Hey, can it, Gita," Nil said, leaning over to see what snacks he had missed. "Yuck" he made a face at the remains of the bhel puri and the sweets. "How're you doing, Anjeli?" He offered his hand "Nice to meet you."

"Anjeli and I were just talking about arranged marriages, Anil. I was asking her to find someone for you." As Anjeli started to protest, Anil retorted, "Give me a break, Gita; you know there's no way I'd ever get into that."

"Oh, I think maybe you already have a girlfriend, Anil; you're just not telling us about it. And not even finished your first year of college yet! I bet she's American and can't cook all that delicious Indian food you love." Gita added sarcastically.

"I'd never tell you, anyway, big mouth," Anil snorted, "and you know I can't even stand the smell of Indian food. See ya, Anjeli." Anil strode into his room and shut the door firmly, as if he were shutting Gita, Anjeli, and his Indian upbringing just as firmly out of his life.

❀ Chapter Seventeen

Even if he is a stone, he is your husband; even if he is a weed, he is still your spouse.

—*Indian saying*

Thinking over last evening's argument with Kumar, Anjeli tried to bury her anger by busying herself in household chores. She reviewed her spice cabinet, making a list of the ingredients she needed to stock up on in her next shopping trip. She carefully oiled her pans to ready them for their next use, wiped down her already immaculate stove top and oven, and dried and put away the few dishes that remained in the sink drainer. She was startled when the phone rang and almost decided to let the machine get it; then she hoped it might be Kumar calling to make up their quarrel, unusual as that would be. And if it were Kumar calling, he would be angry to get the machine, wondering why Anjeli was not at home.

"Hello," Anjeli spoke tentatively.

"I want to speak with Kumar Kapoor. Is he there?" a woman's voice asked.

"I am sorry, Kumar is not here now," Anjeli replied. "He's at work."

"No, he's not," the woman contradicted. "I was just at the office, and he's not there. Who is this?"

"This is his wife," Anjeli continued timidly. "Who is this?"

"His wife! Not his sister? He told me he's living with his sister. He never told me he was married."

Before Anjeli could respond, she heard the phone clatter to the floor, followed by a new voice, coarse, angry, and male, which growled, "His wife! This bastard Kumar has a wife? That's not what he told my sister. For the last year he told her *they* were going to get married. Now she says that for the last coupla months he passes her by at work like he don't even know her, he don't answer his cell phone, and she don't know what's going on. I shoulda figured it was somethin' shady. Now I'm taking charge. You tell your rotten *husband*," he emphasized the word menacingly, "that Carol's brother Al is coming by your house to give him a message in person he won't be able to brush off so easy like he's brushing off my sister. And he better be prepared to play ball if he knows what's good for him." Before Anjeli could respond—not that she had any idea what she could say to such a puzzling, angry man—the caller slammed down the phone.

Anjeli felt real fear invade her whole being. *Who could this be trying to find Kumar and speaking in such a threatening way? Maybe it is a policeman? No, why would he mention a sister? Maybe someone in the building overhearing our loud quarrels is coming to cause us trouble or has called the landlord about us. What if we lose our apartment, especially now when Kumar's parents are coming? That would be a disaster. Should I leave the apartment? No, that could be a bigger disaster if the man comes back when Kumar is home and there is a real fight. Even a shooting!* She'd recently read about an Indian man who got so angry at a woman who rejected his advances that he went to her parents' apartment and shot her dead as she answered the door. True, those were Muslim immigrants, and this caller sounded like an American, but still, such things could happen.

Anjeli sat down, paralyzed by fear and resentment. Finally she resumed the mindless tasks she had set for herself; what else could she do? After what seemed like several hours, she heard a loud banging on the apartment door. "Open the door, or I'll bust it down," the voice in the hallway yelled. Anjeli hoped Mrs. Singh next door would hear the commotion, come out, and tell the man to stop or she would call the police. She'd been shocked to learn from Mrs. Singh that she drove a cab. It was beyond her imagining that any lady she knew in India could ever do such a thing. *What kind of place is this America that ladies have to drive a taxi?* Kumar had discouraged Anjeli from being too friendly with Mrs. Singh—they were low-class people, he told her—but Mrs. Singh, though a little rough in her ways, was very pleasant and helpful, and Anjeli was glad to have her as a neighbor. But several minutes passed without any intervention, and the thuds on the door continued along with the man's shouting. Finally, Anjeli thought she could safely put on the chain and open the door just a little to try to quiet the man down. "Just a minute, I will come to the door." Anjeli tried to speak calmly. The noise stopped, so she opened the door the few inches the chain allowed. A giant of a man stood outside, heavyset, with a thick eyebrow that crossed over his eyes without a space and a nasty set to his mouth, which seemed to be missing quite a few teeth. This particularly struck Anjeli since the beautiful white teeth of Americans was a thing known around the world.

"I cannot let you in without my husband being here," Anjeli said in what she hoped was a reasonable tone. "It is not our custom. But if you tell me your name and leave your telephone number I will give it to Kumar, and he will surely call you back."

"Not your custom, you moron! What world are you living in? You got a box of rocks for a brain?" the man spit out. Anjeli understood his literal words but couldn't quite figure out their meaning, so she just looked at him without responding, not that he waited for her to speak. "Are you as dumb as my dopey sister? Your husband's been leading her on for the past year, telling her to hold on to that crappy job, working for peanuts at that lousy bank until they can save money for a house! She can't even support herself—I gotta give her a few bucks all the time, but they were gonna buy a house! Total B.S. And now you say he's married to you. Well, you pass this message on to your husband"—here he leaned on the door to pencil some words on a piece of paper, his meaty forearm with a tattoo of a heart surrounding the name Frannie scrolled in colorful calligraphy. "You tell him that Carol Busario's brother, Al, came around, and here's my cell number 24/7. Now my sister and everyone at work knows he's dumped her, and she's not coming back to that crappy job anymore. And she don't have a pot to pee in, and it's gonna be up to lover boy to bridge the cash gap for a while if he don't wanna get burned." Anjeli listened closely but couldn't understand half the words the man was using: *Why "a pot to pee in"? What could that mean? "Get burned"? Is he going to set Kumar on fire?* Anjeli was so lost, but she was also too afraid to interrupt him or even close the door.

The man Al continued in an angry voice, "You tell that husband of yours we're gonna set up a little meeting. and he better be ready to pony up 5,000 good ole U.S. of A. dollars, not any of that monopoly money you towelheads use. If he don't call me to set it up, he better be very careful every time he crosses the street. And that goes for you too." Then the man dropped the piece of paper through the opening in the door, turned away, and clattered down the stairs.

Anjeli shook with a mixture of fear and anger. *Who is this man? Can he be making this all up? But if so, why pick on Kumar?* She would have to tell Kumar what happened when he came home. She hoped he wouldn't be late tonight, and, now that she thought of it, Anjeli didn't understand why the man said Kumar wasn't at work. She made herself a cup of tea; whenever she was upset her American coffee habit gave way to her life-long habit of drinking tea, which comforted by evoking home.

I must give Kumar the chance to explain, Anjeli thought. *It will be no good to yell at him.* If he lost his temper, he could get very mean. *But why should he be angry at me?* she wondered logically. *I have not done anything wrong. He cannot blame me for this.*

Anjeli forced herself to continue cleaning to pass the time until Kumar came home. To her surprise, she heard his key in the lock long before the hour he normally arrived. Steeling herself to be calm, Anjeli called from the kitchen, "Is that you, Kumar?"

"Who else would it be, Anjeli? Are you expecting someone else?" he answered in a hostile voice.

Anjeli came out to the living room and faced Kumar squarely, saying, "Kumar, we must talk. Something very bad happened today, and I don't know what to do. But I must tell you, and you must answer me with the truth."

"Okay, okay, just let me take off my coat." Kumar sat himself down on the sofa and glared at her, but Anjeli would not allow herself to be intimidated. "This afternoon I had a very frightening experience, Kumar. Some awful man called and said you weren't at work; then he came to the apartment, even though I told him you were not at home." Kumar's face looked grim and his frown grew deeper as Anjeli plowed on.

"He told me he was the brother of a girl you had promised to marry, some Carol, from your office. That she didn't know you have a wife; she thought your sister was living here. How is that possible, Kumar?"

Kumar jumped out of the chair and shouted at Anjeli angrily, "Stop harassing me, Anjeli. I get that all day at work. This was a girl I saw long before I came to India to meet you. This is all finished; that man was trying only to make trouble for me and to scare you."

"Don't shout at me, Kumar. This is not blame on me, but it is your doing. All the time you are at me that we have no money, but now I hear you are seeing this girl. Don't say it has ended: if it was ended before we married, why does she still work at your office and think I am your sister? Now this man wants you to give him $5,000 because out of shame this girl must leave her job. Where will you get $5,000? He threatened to hurt you, maybe set our apartment on fire. And don't tell me you were at work today; these people called and said you were not there."

"It's not my fault this stupid girl must leave her job. I have not been with her for months now. And where would I get money to spend on her? You see this lousy apartment; I've told you the job is in difficulty. Even if I had not married you, I could not afford to see this girl."

"It's very hard for me to believe you, Kumar. I don't know what to do. I am at your mercy here. I cannot leave. Where could I go? I have no friends, no money. You must make this right, Kumar. It is your duty to me."

"Don't tell me what my duty is, Anjeli," he shouted angrily. "Your place as an Indian wife is to trust and obey me. If you threaten me, I can also take action." Saying this, Kumar moved toward Anjeli and grabbed her wrist with one hand and raised his other hand as if to slap her face.

Never will I let him hit me, Anjeli determined grimly. She backed away and said in a steely voice, one she didn't even recognize as her own, one she had never heard come out of a woman's mouth in her own home, "You've hurt me—let go of my wrist. And don't ever think of hitting me, Kumar. If you do, I will call the police. This is America; the police will come, not like in India."

Kumar backed away and collapsed onto the sofa, covering his face with his hands. Anjeli began to cry. "I believe you if you say you stopped seeing her, Kumar. But one hears such stories—so many men come to India to marry when they have a girlfriend or even another wife back in America. What am I to think? This man was very scary. And why did he say you were not at work? Where were you, then, if not at work?"

"The truth is," said Kumar, "I didn't go to work. We have some real money problems, Anjeli. I started off for work, but I just couldn't face going to the office. I walked around all day, doing nothing, just thinking about the financial jam I'm in. Don't you think I'd like to move out of this lousy apartment, get a nice house somewhere, give you nice clothes? But I'm in way over my head. I've been borrowing money for a long time to send to my parents and help pay for Lakshmi's college. My father's business has been in trouble, and I can't say no to my parents. And now this man wants $5,000. Where am I to get so much money? Still, I will have to do something for him. These people don't fool around. I'm sorry you got involved in this, Anjeli. Don't cry. I'll get the money somehow. And I promise, I'll never raise my hand to you again."

🌸 Chapter Eighteen

As soon as Anjeli awakened, she felt this would be an auspicious day. Her job interview with Professor Fleagle was late enough that she would have time to be very careful about her appearance but early enough that she would be home in time to make Kumar some of his favorite dishes for dinner and rasgoolas, his favorite dessert. Maybe they could get out of the stuffy apartment for a walk afterward, and she could tell Kumar about her day. She just knew she would get the job, and she could allay his fears about her working. She would seek his advice about the best and safest way for her to travel to NUNY; he knew the subway system top to bottom and would appreciate being consulted about that.

Anjeli went out to the kitchen to make breakfast for Kumar. Usually he just rushed some coffee and toast, but today she would offer to make him one of those omelets he loved but hardly ever had time for. She greeted him cheerfully and set a cup of coffee before him. "Isn't it a beautiful day? We are really getting some nice spring weather now." Kumar seemed preoccupied and just stared moodily into his cup. Anjeli's optimism was a little dashed, but she persisted in her one-sided conversation. "I made my job interview for just noontime, "she continued placatingly. "Then I will not have to come home in the rush hour, do you think? If I get the job, we can celebrate at dinner."

"Why should you think you will get this job if it pays anything worthwhile?" Kumar replied sourly. "Did your important friend Professor Julie fix it up with this man so the job will be yours, guaranteed? Anyway, I will be home late, so don't make anything for dinner that will taste like cardboard by the time I eat it. I have special work to do at the bank tonight."

Disappointed by Kumar's sarcasm, Anjeli was nevertheless excited by the potential upturn in their prospects if—when, she corrected herself—she got this job. She was glad that Kumar had to leave ahead of her as she wanted to choose just the right clothes to wear for the interview, an outfit that would be professional and comfortable for an office but would not require expensive cleaning bills. She might not always have time to change her clothes before Kumar got home, so her attire must meet his standards of modesty, too. She didn't need unnecessary conflict about the job. Later, when his parents arrived, they would be in the house when she left for work, and she could expect them to loudly voice any disapproval they found with her appearance.

Saris were out anyway, as they would be ruined on the subway, especially in the nasty, rainy weather Kumar had said often lasted through April. And in the summer, Anjeli could just picture her mother-in-law checking the neckline of her *choli* and the drape of her pallu to make sure it covered her breasts properly and no skin showed at her waist. Even if Anjeli wore a shalwar-kameez, she could still imagine her mother-in-law following her into the office to see that her dupatta properly covered her. And she didn't need any tirades from Kumar to reject the summer fashions that young Americans and even desi girls wore to work or on the streets: pants tight around the rear and gripping the thighs; sheer, clinging blouses that might have long sleeves but dipped low in back or in front; tank tops only covered by tiny, long-sleeved "shrugs" presumably to provide warmth but merely emphasizing the breasts; and tight

swathes of fabric wrapped around the hips that seemed to serve no practical purpose except to announce "here are my big, round hips" to every
man in sight. When Anjeli had told Gita that these skintight garments
looked so uncomfortable as well as immodest, Gita had laughed. "Get
with the lycra revolution, Anjeli," she said, adding that all this clothing stretched every which way like a rubber clown face and was really
comfortable and practical. "No, no, never!" Anjeli had shooed Gita off
with her hands.

"You're a beautiful young girl," Gita had sighed in frustration. "Why
should you look like some dowdy old lady with long baggy skirts and
droopy shirts? You'll see, most of the other people in this professor's office will be part-time students, just about your age; you would fit right
in if you dressed like them."

"Oh, you," Anjeli had said, and hugged Gita warmly as together they
had sorted out from Anjeli's wardrobe several changes of modern style
shalwar-kameez, with the pants of medium fullness and the kameez
more like a long, Western style blouse than an oversize tunic that fell to
the knees. Some were of thin wool, which would not need much cleaning, and the others were of lightweight cotton that could be mixed and
matched and easily washed in the machine.

After checking herself in the mirror and patting her Metrocard in
the outside pocket of her stylish shoulder bag, Anjeli left for the subway
feeling confident and optimistic again. Kumar had explained the trains
she would need to take, and with Julie's directions she had no trouble
finding the NUNY main building where both Julie and Professor Fleagle
had their offices, though Julie had said they were in different departments and didn't know each other. Exactly at noon, Anjeli entered the
humanities department, which housed philosophy, foreign languages,
and speech, and asked for Professor Fleagle. She almost had to smile:
the young receptionist, leaning over a lower drawer in the file cabinet,
was dressed just as Gita had predicted, with tight-fitting layers of tank
tops over T-shirts over a tiny denim wrap that contracted as she stood

up. She greeted Anjeli in a friendly manner and waved her down a hallway to Professor Fleagle's office. Through his open doorway Anjeli saw
another casually dressed young woman standing over a cluttered desk,
laughing animatedly with the man who sat behind it. Anjeli was waved
in by the professor, whose eyes, she noticed, followed the lycra'd rear
end of the departing visitor till it was gone from sight.

   "Anjeli," Professor Fleagle began, getting up to shake her hand over
the desk, "you've started off well by being punctual." Then, resuming
his seat, he continued, "People may think of philosophers as slow,
deliberate thinkers, but in this office there's a lot going on, and we
often work on tight schedules. In addition to teaching, I have a grant
for convening several conferences a year, and I like them to go off like
clockwork. We sometimes have lunches or wine-and-cheese events
after the conference presentations, and one of your jobs would be to
coordinate those events. We need someone who won't get flustered or
lose their temper if things go wrong." Professor Fleagle winked, "Only
I am permitted to do that."

   Anjeli smiled, more to let the professor know that she understood
his remark as a joke than because she thought it funny; her resumé,
after all, stated that she had fluent, idiomatic English. She replied that
she was certain she could handle any of the aspects of the position to
which she was assigned, and if there were any assignments she did not
understand, she would clarify everything before the event got underway.
She responded to a few more questions from the professor with what
she thought were professional and well-phrased answers and was then
surprised to hear him comment approvingly on her apparel. "I am quite
familiar with the subcontinent, Anjeli," he told her, leaning forward
over his desk, "and I like the middle ground you have chosen between
Western dress and wholly traditional Eastern dress. My specialty is
Eastern philosophy, and I am well acquainted with much of Indian
religious painting and sculpture. My special expertise is in medieval
Tantric Hinduism and the sculptures of Konarak and Khajuraho, so I

am very familiar with Indian clothing and jewelry. You probably know
that there is a great continuity between ancient and modern times, and
these medieval images are significant expressions of Hindu philosophy.
Only after the British came was the sexual openness of Hinduism re-
pressed and censored, a sad example of Victorian hypocrisy overtaking
the sensual and much healthier Hindu culture. Have you ever been to
these temples? Your face reminds me of the beautiful sculptures of the
voluptuous Hindu goddesses represented there."

Anjeli flushed and did not answer his question about the temples,
places she had not visited but which were famous all over India, and especially with foreigners, for their erotic sculptures, photographs of which
she and her college friends had giggled and fantasized over for hours. She
did offer a "thank you" in response to his little speech, as she thought of
it, though in truth she didn't know quite what she was thanking him for.
A compliment on her outfit, she supposed. "My husband, who is a bank
manager downtown, also likes the American adaptation of traditional
dress," Anjeli offered tentatively. "He has been here much longer than
me. But I think even if he were to approve, I could not accustom myself
to American fashions." Anjeli paused as she noticed Professor Fleagle
raise his eyebrow somewhat skeptically, a look she and her friends used
to practice to gales of laughter in her convent school dormitory. She was
not sure how to interpret the gesture, whether her statement sounded
too submissive, puritanical, or critical to him, and she quickly amended
her statement by adding, "but in time I may feel differently."

"Fine, and I know you'll do splendidly here, Anjeli," Professor Fleagle
said, adding information about the grant-provided wage for her job
description and the flexible schedule of two to three days a week that
he hoped she could work. "There will be occasional late evenings," he
added, "but I will always let you know about these in advance, and
the grant provides for double the hourly rate in the evening as well as
guaranteed transportation home. Check with Kimmy at the desk for the
personnel forms, and can we say I'll see you at 11 A.M. on Monday?"

"Thank you so much, Professor Fleagle," Anjeli breathed sincerely.
"I truly appreciate your confidence in me." They shook hands again, a
custom that Anjeli had not quite gotten used to, especially between men
and women, though it seemed harmless enough. She knew a handshake
was an attempt to be both friendly and professional, so she could hardly
refuse her new boss's outstretched hand. Professor Fleagle then made a
namaste with a deep bow, perhaps, thought Anjeli, to impress her with
his understanding of Indian culture. She turned and left the room, gracefully she knew—*all those posture lessons at the convent*—but without a
lycra'd behind for the professor's eyes to linger on." *Oh, what do I care?
I won't tell Kumar every little detail the way I'll tell Gita. What is it the
Americans say, "What you don't know can't hurt you"?*

✿ Chapter Nineteen

In America there is work and no time. In India there is family and no space.

—*Indian saying*

Anjeli's in-laws had been in America two weeks, and things were worse even than she had thought possible. And Kumar had refused to defend her from his parents' criticisms. When their plane landed, the Kapoors had hardly come out of the baggage area with their suitcases before Kumar's mother had begun to carp at Anjeli, and even at Kumar. As soon as the Kapoors had gone through customs, Anjeli and Kumar had rushed up to meet them. Anjeli knew that Kumar was as anxious as she was that all would go well. Wanting to start things off correctly, they both bowed to his parents to touch their feet. Kumar's mother patted Anjeli's head as was usual to acknowledge the deference, but she did so with an unfriendly and distant look, managing to surveil her appearance from head to toe.

"What outfit are you wearing, Anjeli? These jeans and this sweater and all—you have become very American in a hurry. It doesn't look nice for your husband to have his wife dressed like that. And your hair—you are married now; you must not wear it loose like some fast girl. Kumar attempted to distract his mother by taking the cart with their suitcases and checking with her that they had everything. Simultaneously, Anjeli reached in her purse for a barrette she sometimes kept there and pulled her hair back. "That is much better, Anjeli. I know these desi girls wear their hair every which way, but we are a respectable family, and even here in America have our reputation to keep up," Mrs. Kapoor asserted.

Anjeli restrained herself from commenting and was disappointed that Kumar didn't speak up for her to his mother. *This is how it's going to be,* she sighed, somewhat resentfully. *I might as well get used to it.* Kumar's father stood aside as this was going on, and to Anjeli he looked already tipsy. *Probably too many free drinks on the plane.* His drinking worried her; while Kumar rarely got drunk, under strain he did reach for the liquor. Anjeli could see that having his parents with them would be a great strain indeed. Well, she would do her best to keep things harmonious as a good bahu should. Her fervent prayer was that they wouldn't stay too long. She knew that Kumar's mother was going to consult a doctor here about an eye problem; maybe if that were taken care of quickly, they would go home soon. But they also had to seek some matches for their daughter Lakshmi, and that would take time, Anjeli reassessed pessimistically. Certainly, with his parents here, she and Kumar would have no privacy at all. And when Kumar was at work it would be just her and her sas and father-in-law alone in the house, where she would be subject to their every whim. The respectful avoidance that traditionally held between father-in-law and daughter-in-law would be impossible to maintain in such a small apartment. There was no question of purdah, of course, but, still, it was best to keep a reserve between them. *Thank goodness I have my job,* Anjeli sighed. *At least that will take me away from the apartment for hours at a time.* Fortunately she understood that however much Kumar would insist she pay his parents the attention due them, he also was finding her salary very useful and would not ask her to leave her job. Maybe she would just show some goodwill by taking off a few days in the beginning, if she could.

When the taxi reached their apartment building, the driver helped Kumar lift the huge suitcases out of the trunk while Anjeli reached for the small carry-on bags. But Kumar's mother grabbed them first, holding them close to her body. *As if I were going to steal something,* Anjeli thought in annoyance. Which reminded her, *Have they brought my saris and jewelry as they said they would? I must ask Kumar about that.*

Kumar opened their apartment door and lugged the suitcases to the bigger bedroom, which Kumar had insisted they give to his parents. Anjeli had spent hours cleaning, making the bed with fresh linens, and even washing the windows 'til they sparkled. She had placed a vase full of fresh flowers on the second-hand dresser they had purchased especially for his mother's saris, which Anjeli supposed numbered over one hundred.

Unappreciative of Anjeli's efforts, Mrs. Kapoor immediately disparaged the small apartment as if her daughter-in-law were to blame for its inadequacy. "I hope you and Anjeli are planning to find another place," she frowned at Kumar, who pretended not to hear her. He solicitously urged his parents to rest while he and Anjeli prepared dinner. "Or perhaps you would prefer a cup of chai? You must be very tired after your long trip."

"No, no, don't trouble yourselves," Mrs. Kapoor replied, though Anjeli well knew that her efforts to trouble herself with her mother-in-law's comforts would be calculated to a fine degree and that her mother-in-law would not be shy in expressing herself whenever Anjeli fell short. Each incident would be interpreted as Anjeli's putting her own pleasure before her duties as a daughter-in-law.

Kumar's mother pushed her husband into the bedroom and shut the door, saying to Kumar, "A rest is a good idea. Your father is very tired, and I'm sure I could use a wash-up. We ate on the plane, but of course the food was very inferior. There is nothing like home-cooked food."

With his parents in the bedroom, Anjeli ventured a plea to Kumar. "Please, you must help me make things comfortable for your parents. You know much better than I how to please them."

"Don't worry so much, Anjeli. I know my mother can sound a bit harsh, but I'm sure after the fine meal you prepared and a good night's sleep things will look better in the morning." Kumar then collapsed on the sofa while Anjeli went into the kitchen to prepare the food. No sooner had she begun than Kumar's mother emerged from the bathroom, where Anjeli had made a point of leaving fresh soap and towels, saying, "Let Mr. Kapoor rest inside. But I think I will have that tea after all; in any case, it is too early for dinner."

Anjeli interupted her cooking and rushed to fetch the tea down from the cupboard. Though she and Kumar now enjoyed the American coffee habit, she did stock an ordinary tea for their occasional cup. But for the Kapoors she had purchased some top-quality Darjeeling that she hoped her mother-in-law would appreciate. Mrs. Kapoor eyed Anjeli watchfully as her daughter-in-law put the water on to boil and infused it with the Indian tea and some cardamom and cloves in the Indian fashion. "Well, at least you haven't gone over to the disgusting American habit of tea bags," was all she said.

They sat at the table, which Anjeli had spread with a new, embroidered cloth that was part of her dowry. After pouring the tea, Anjeli covered the pot with a tea cozy. "It is such a nuisance not having servants here; no amount of modern appliances can substitute," complained Mrs. Kapoor. "But I'm used to that. I've been to America and know their ways here. You will also have to adjust, Anjeli."

Then, ignoring Anjeli, Mrs. Kapoor turned to Kumar. "You look pulled down, Kumar. Has Anjeli been taking proper care of you? Are you eating properly?"

"Not to worry, Ma Anjeli takes very good care of me. You know how it is here—everyone is very busy. We don't have people to shop for us or vendors who come to the door with the vegetables as in India. But she is a good cook."

"Busy?" Mrs. Kapoor raised her eyebrows. "It is our lot in life to be busy, taking care of husband and family. Nothing must lead us to put pleasure before duty."

Certainly not my pleasure, Anjeli thought with irritation.

"Mummyji, why don't you rest now, I'll clean up the tea things and get the dinner ready." As her mother-in-law had shown no signs of helping to take the tea things back into the kitchen, Anjeli stood up and gathered them herself. While Mrs. Kapoor retreated into the bathroom again, Anjeli returned to the table to finish her tea, which had now become cold. "Shall I heat up the tea, Kumar? Would you like some more?"

"Thanks, Anjeli, I'm fine. I will also rest a bit. I've got to be back to work tomorrow—no more days off. But later we'll have to work out some plans for the coming months."

Months! Anjeli thought. *The only plans I'd like to make is for them to leave, within a week, not longer.* Involuntarily she uttered Kumar's last word aloud. "Months? I thought perhaps they were just coming for a few weeks. Are they really going to be with us for months?"

"You can count on it," he said soberly.

Since her in-laws had arrived, Anjeli could hardly wait for each morning that promised her a day out of the house at her NUNY job. It reminded her of her mother's kirtans, a legitimate place to escape to—where she could, to use one of Julie's favorite expressions, do well and do good at the same time. Professor Fleagle seemed happy with her work; occasionally, when they finished some difficult project, he would call a "time out" for half an hour over coffee or tea, just to chat with her. He had discovered that she was newly married, no children—"yet," she had added, feeling that she should express the conventional desire for a family, which, truthfully, at this moment she did not feel.

His reply was very American, she decided, and not meant to be offensive: "that's what condoms are for, my dear," he had remarked, and explained almost in the same breath how she could go on, with free tuition, to take a master's degree at NUNY while she held her job.

Professor Fleagle—"Call me Phil," he insisted, but Anjeli didn't have the nerve to do that yet—had been very understanding about rearranging her schedule for a few days after her in-laws' arrival, alluding in a vaguely mysterious way that he himself had "been there, done that" in an earlier life. One day, soon after their arrival, her mother-in-law had called the office to ask some silly domestic question, interrupting Anjeli as she sat with the professor at the computer working on a PowerPoint presentation. "I'm so embarrassed," she apologized afterward. "I have told my mother-in-law not to call here unless it is an emergency." It was kind of him to wave off her apology, but as she sat down again, she took the opportunity to move her chair a little further away from his knees.

As Anjeli and Mrs. Kapoor carried their heavy grocery bags into the kitchen, Kumar's father followed them with an angry scowl on his face. In his hand he held the portable phone, which included its own voice-mail access. "Listen to this," he said as he thrust the phone up to his wife's ear. He pressed the message button, and a deep, pleasant man's voice was heard: "Hello, Anjeli, this is Phil. Kimmy called about Thursday; she can't do her late day. Could you possibly fill in? Extra pay, of course. I'll drive you home; no problem. Please get back to me ASAP. Thanks."

"Phil," Kumar's father rounded on Anjeli. "I thought you worked for a professor. But now he is Phil, and you are Anjeli. Like friends, eh, maybe like lovers?" Anjeli was so outraged she could hardly speak. Looking her father-in-law directly in the eye, she said in measured words "I never call him Phil; he is always Professor Fleagle to me, and he calls every single person in his office and all the department heads and deans, too, by their first names. I have asked him not to call me at home unless it is very important," she added. *But we are seeing each other the day after tomorrow,* she realized. *What's the big rush to call me at home?*

Her mother-in-law was not so stupid. She had figured it out too. "Oh, you told *us* not to call you at the office unless it is an emergency but *he* can call you in your own home with two more days only until Thursday."

"A very important phone call, I think," Kumar's father smirked. "Let's see what Kumar has to say about this."

As he was speaking, Kumar walked in the door and asked with some wariness, "Ma, Pa, what is all the shouting about?" at the same time turning a questioning gaze on Anjeli. Before she could respond, Mrs. Kapoor repeated her verbal assault. "See, your wife is getting messages from some Phil. Who is this man that he calls himself Phil and rings up at your home? And asking Anjeli to stay late hours—for what I want to know!"

"Ma, it's not like you think. It's Anjeli's boss at the university. He sometimes needs to call her at home about a change in her hours or something." *But what is so important that he can't wait until she comes to the office?* Kumar wondered in annoyance with a small, nagging doubt. *And why say it's Phil? Pretty familiar for a professor.* To assuage his mother's anger he said emphatically to Anjeli, "I've asked you to tell the professor not to call you here, unless it is something really important. Haven't you explained that to him?"

"I have, Kumar, honestly, and I know he's somewhat informal, but you have to admit that he's also been very flexible about my hours. I don't like to anger him over such a small thing, but I will ask him again." Anjeli sighed despondently. *I have told him how troublesome that is, especially now that my in-laws are staying with us. And I can't possibly call him back now. I'll just have to wait until tomorrow and sneak over to Gita's on an excuse and call him from there.*

🌸 Chapter Twenty

It had technically been spring for a month already, but you'd never know it from the cold, dreary weather. Julie had cut short her usual Sunday run and enjoyed a hot bath, then settled cozily at her dining table with her first cappuccino of the day. She flicked through yesterday's mail, which she'd been too tired to sort through last night. *Ooh, goody, a bunch of articles from Shakuntala,* she saw, picking up a bulky manila envelope bearing attractive Indian flower and animal stamps. Usually she and Shakuntala just e-mailed each other, but when her friend came across Indian newspaper or Web site articles relevant to Julie's work, she would send them on.

Julie carefully slit the packet across the top with the chased silver letter opener her father had made for her out of an antique knife handle and a steel blade, putting aside the stamps for Alexander, her stamp-collecting teenage neighbor next door. She drew out a bundle of newspaper clippings and Web site cuttings and a two-page letter in Shakuntala's distinctive handwriting learned by all upper-class girls at their convent schools.

> *JULIE!!! You're not going to believe this! I'll just give you the short form—as you always say—of the news itself; then you can read the enclosed articles.*

The case also appeared in the New York Times, *so you can check their Web site and maybe find more in the Indian newspapers they sell in New York.*

Remember that chap, Sukhdev Kohli, you met at the end of Anjeli's wedding, a good-looking fellow who is her husband's cousin, the well-to-do garment-wallah from New York? Well, now with all the festivities over, we have time to read the newspapers again and watch television news, WHAT DO I SEE? Big Police Investigation! Sukhdev's name is all over the media about his American girlfriend being killed. One TV "clip," I think you say, from back when her body is discovered, just some days before Anjeli's wedding, announced that some European girl, "identity withheld pending investigation," is found in bushes off the airport road, "maybe killed in hit and run accident." Aha! But who walks on the airport road? Then, "could be a car-jacking or maybe robbery by taxi driver." The backpack they found with her was empty. Such things do happen in Mumbai frequently, true?

Sukhdev Kohli—which relative was that? Julie muttered to herself. Yeah! The guy who offered her a ride. She fished out her file of notes from her trip, and there was his business card. But what was his connection with a dead American woman? Then she remembered Grace, her seatmate on the plane, who had spoken of her fiancé, calling him Dev. That's why he had seemed familiar to her, the photo of the guy in the sports car. With even greater interest now, she returned to Shakuntala's letter:

So, how could we connect a dead backpacker girl with Kumar's cousin Sukhdev? How could he be marrying some American girl? We know he has a wife and two small children in America and sends money to his parents. Bas.

But now these goondas are caught, and they say he hired them to kill this girlfriend after she got off the plane to India. If that's true, he must have lied to get her to India, eh? Saying, "Come, come, you must meet my parents—we'll have a real Indian wedding here." You know how these American girls all love our exotic Indian festivities. So much luggage they found with one of the goondas, such beautiful saris and shalwar-kameez from New York. And American dollars in a thick envelope. How would these low types get such money? Newspapers say Sukhdev denies everything. What to think?

And then, suddenly, it is over. Fast-fast. How? Nobody knows. Just Sukhdev is gone from India, back in America. People here don't like that. Too many cases with rich men hurting wives and girlfriends and getting away with it. Remember last year when you were here, that rich boy—his father owns a big shoe factory—jealous of his Bollywood actress girlfriend, he shoots her in a bar in front of witnesses even. Two months later, he is acquitted. Corrupt police and judges, don't you think? Such a protest mob at police station, many people were injured.

Sukhdev's case twists back and forth like a snake. Maybe there is more in the U.S. papers. E-mail me what you think of all this. Anjeli's mother is so glad you are in New York to be a friend to her daughter (I think she doesn't hear so much from Anjeli as she would like, I hope everything is okay). She sends her best regards to you.

Affly yours,
Shaku

Julie slumped back in her chair. Putting her mug aside, she laid Shakuntala's articles out in chronological order and saw for herself the inconsistencies and confusions that Shakuntala had noted. Grace's body had been found by the airport police soon after her murder. Just after the discovery of her body, a tip led to the location of her luggage and the ultimate apprehension and arrest of the killers. The police soon discovered that the deceased girl was, as Julia dreaded to read, a twenty-three-year-old New Yorker named Grace Roberts, described variously as a beautician, a cosmetologist, a hairdresser, and an unemployed model. *Oh my goodness,* Julie swallowed hard as tears came to her eyes, *it was poor Grace I saw on TV. It's too awful; she was so enthusiastic about going to India and her new life as part of an embracing Indian family.*

According to the articles, Grace had been killed the same afternoon that she and Julie had deplaned together, shortly after they had said their good-byes at the airport exit, Julie shuddered to realize. As Shakuntala reported, only an empty backpack was found, no ID and no reports of missing persons. Hence the original notion that Grace's death might have resulted from an accident. But the police discarded this theory when the autopsy revealed that she had been strangled with a ligature. Some of the articles stated that her throat had been cut, but that was evidently erroneous.

So how did this Sukhdev come into it, Julie wondered. The next article explained it all. A man from Dharavi, a notorious Mumbai slum, had called his local police station to report that he was a neighbor of one Vinay Ratton, who had left a couple of suitcases with him, asking him to hide the stuff for a few days. Curious, he had later looked through the suitcases and found they contained beautiful women's clothing, most of it Indian, but some in Western style; an expensive-looking handbag with a photo of a young European woman and identification documents inside; and an envelope full of American dollars. He knew the goods must have come from some crime and told Ratton to take the stuff away. But Ratton, who had no other place to hide it, kept postponing its removal. When his friend heard the news about the murdered American girl, he knew Ratton's stuff must be connected with that crime. Afraid to be discovered with it and be accused of the murder, he called the local police. After the cops had come and taken away all the stuff, then the Mumbai CID were called in. Vinay Ratton was found and arrested and interrogated in the central police station, where he was jailed pending trial for murder.

Ratton had his own story to tell, which naturally placed the blame on someone else. Ratton was a driver for a big boss in a nearby factory. A few days before, his friend, one Shiv Das, bullied him into borrowing his boss's car for a few hours to do a job that would net them both *lakhs* of rupees. They were to meet an American girl at the airport, take her for a ride, kill her, and hide her body in a place where it would not be easily discovered. The contract was from a rich Indian man, from America, who gave his name as Roop Chand. He gave Shiv Das a picture of the girl so they would recognize her at the airport. This Roop Chand said the girl knew that he could not meet her flight but was sending his "cousin and driver" in his place, so she was expecting them. My friend, Shiv Das says, "It's an easy job, no problem."

"Shiv Das showed me a packet of rupees that this Roop Chand had already paid him in advance and said more was coming when the job was done. I told him, 'I'm doing the driving only, no killing.' He agreed, and so we did what was planned. We met the girl at the airport exit, put her and her bags into the car, and drove to a deserted spot on the airport road. My boss needed his car for the afternoon, so we couldn't drive as far as we had planned. There Shiv Das strangled her, and we hid her body in some bushes off the roadside. This Mr. Roop Chand had told Shiv Das to leave a backpack nearby so if she was found people would think she was a hippie. It looked simple; there was no way anyone could connect this American girl with us. Since Shiv Das couldn't hide the stuff at his house, I managed to leave it with a neighbor of mine.

"Roop Chand told my friend that we could keep all the expensive clothes the girl had brought with her in addition to the money we would be paid after the job was done. Shiv Das was supposed to go to the Maharaj Hotel, where Mr. Roop Chand was staying, to pick up the rest of the money. All I did was drive the car," Vinay Ratton emphasized to the police.

With Vinay Ratton's tale in hand, Mumbai police quickly found and arrested Shiv Das, who was charged as the actual killer. *No rocket science needed there,* Julie reflected. The articles reported that both men had several arrests and convictions for petty crimes and more serious assaults, too, and were probably part of the Indian mafia that operates in the slums of Mumbai.

"If that dimwit Vinay Ratton had been able to drive us further away, into the forest, the police would never have found the body," Shiv Das complained. "We should have planned a better hiding place for the suitcases than Ratton's neighbor; then we would never have been found out."

Julie tracked the case through the pile of articles Shakuntala had arranged chronologically. Once the police interrogated the two thugs, they immediately tracked Sukhdev at the Maharaj under his assumed name of Roop Chand and brought him down to the Central Police Station. There Shiv Das fingered him as the man who had hired and paid them to kill his girlfriend.

With this confession, with Grace's luggage and the cash, and with Shiv Das's possession of the photo, it seemed to Julie that the police had an open-and-shut case against all three men. As one reporter quipped when the police found Mr. Roop Chand, or rather Sukhdev Kohli, at the Maharaj just as his hired killers had stated, "We think that when Mr. Kohli opened the door to his plush suite at Mumbai's most luxurious hotel, he got a big surprise. He will be extending his stay in Mumbai, but no longer in a fancy suite at the Maharaj." *I certainly hope not*, Julie concurred mentally. Yet while Kohli had been quickly located and questioned at the Mumbai Central Police Station, he was not an official suspect, according to the news, but only a person of interest. *How could that be?* Julie thought angrily. The two men who accused him had separately detailed the plot the same way: Grace's clothes and purse, the American dollars stashed with them, and the photograph. How could this Sukhdev possibly exonerate himself? Shakuntala was right—this case twisted and turned like a rattlesnake.

But as the later articles explained, Kohli had denied all the charges leveled against him. "These people who accuse me are only goondas; such low people are liars as well as thugs," he told reporters on departing from his interview at the police station. "They always hide piles of money from their crimes here, there, and everywhere until they can pass it on to their bosses. The police understand this very well. As far as the dead girl, it was very unfortunate, as such attacks give India a bad name with tourists. But

I did not know this girl and had no connection with her or her backpack or whatever the police found. I came to India to see my ailing parents and attend a cousin's wedding. What would I being doing with some European hippie girl going around India by herself? I told the police the same. They certainly have no motive or proof of anything here."

But, then, how could Kohli explain why he was at the Maharaj, exactly where the goondas said he would be? Julie reasoned. The answer was further along in the packet of articles. Kohli had a story for everything, it seemed. Of course, he was at the Maharaj, he asserted. "I attended my cousin's wedding in Mumbai and spent a few days more there on business. There was no secret that I was in Mumbai; the local paper had a big article about successful Indian businessmen in America, and my name was featured. I own a chain of exclusive sari shops in New York; everyone knows me. I'm well-to-do. Where should I stay, at some cheap hotel? Of course I stay at the Maharaj. These thugs know all the comings and goings of rich Indians from America. In their work for the Indian mafia they are always looking for wealthy people who stay at the tip-top hotels and trying to inveigle them into dishonest schemes and rob them of their money. Everyone knows that hotel staff are on their payroll for just such purposes. They come to a man's room and ask if he wants girls, or boys, or entertainment of whatever kind. If a man is fool enough to take them up on it, they extort money from him later. I am never so stupid to get involved with such types. They accuse me now because I refused to deal with them."

What a ruthless manipulator and big fat liar! Julie railed fiercely, recalling Grace's tender, prideful presentation of Sukhdev's photo and then her own encounter with that duplicitous snake at Anjeli's wedding. *Thank goodness I didn't accept his offer of a ride back to Shilpa's house. Maybe that intense stare he gave me was a sign of his suspicion that I had met Grace. And my return stare trying to place him may have confirmed his suspicions. If he'd caught on that Grace had revealed so much to me, he might have murdered me as well!*

As Julie perused the later articles, she was shocked to see that Kohli had not been arrested yet despite the two witnesses and a ridiculously thin story. But according to his attorney—*Good!* Julie underlined the phrase, *Now he's lawyering up; that must mean he's afraid his story won't fly*—his client was an innocent man. "Mr. Kohli is fully cooperating with the police investigation," he trumpeted to the press.

Finally, in the last batch of Indian news clippings, came the most worrisome news: "ACCUSED BUSINESSMAN IN MURDER CASE FREED ON INSUFFICIENT EVIDENCE." Apparently the presiding judge had impeached the goondas' accusations and supposed eyewitness testimony as unreliable and self-serving and had dropped the charges against Kohli for lack of evidence and lack of motive as well. Julie was shocked. It sounded as if the Indian judge had swept persuasive circumstantial evidence under the rug.

Maybe Shakuntala's notions about corruption in law enforcement and the courts were correct. *Bribing a judge, the gift that keeps on giving,* Julie thought sourly. And, indeed, as Shakuntala complained, the whole thing had been very fast-fast.

But not quite so fast, Julie was pleased to note. As Kohli was an American citizen, the American Embassy had pursued his extradition to the States, and now an investigation here was underway both by the FBI—because two state borders and an international border had been crossed in the crime—and the homicide squad in the Queens precinct where Grace had lived. Her mother had filed a missing-persons report that Grace had never returned from India and that she'd had no word of her since she'd left New York. But Kohli had preempted the extradition by voluntarily returning to the city, where he pointed out to the press with his typical unpleasant hauteur that he would be totally free to attend to his affairs. "As they say in America, I have businesses to run, things to do, and people to see."

Free, but still under investigation, you rotten murderer. And it ain't over 'til it's over. This Kohli doesn't know what I know, thought Julie with satisfaction. *I have some information that might just help put him behind bars, where he belongs.* Nobody, not Shakuntala or even the Indian police, knew what Julie knew.

Now the question was: whom should she tell? As Julie sipped her now-cold cappuccino, she considered her options. She would certainly not call the Mumbai Police, with who knew what kind of long-distance phone connection and what kind of English speaker on the other end of the phone and what kind of questions they'd ask her about her trip to Mumbai. Anyway, Kohli was already a dead issue in India.

Julie preferred not to contact the FBI either. Recently they'd run some "counter-terrorism" programs on college campuses, including her own, which, in her view, really trampled on student and faculty civil rights. She'd signed a few petitions against that effort and also added her name to a published letter trying to prevent the deportation of some outspoken but totally innocent professor from Hugo Chavez's Venezuela, so she figured she was probably in the FBI files somewhere.

Okay, that left the homicide squad in the Queens precinct.

✿ Chapter Twenty-One

Let's get this over with, Julie decided, *before I have a week of sleepless nights about it.* She would just call the precinct to find out the name of the detective in charge of the case and make an appointment with him to tell what she knew. She whipped over to her computer and found the telephone number of the precinct. It was one of the old station houses way out in Queens, but she'd take a cab if she needed to. She began pressing the buttons on her phone but then stopped. *Damn, early Sunday morning—maybe the precinct is closed. Oh, stupid thought,* she reversed herself. *Of course someone would be there all the time.* She could at least get the name of the right detective to call during his shift.

Julie dialed through, and after introducing herself to the officer at the desk, she said, "I don't know whom I need to speak to; it has to do with that murder in Mumbai that's been turned over to homicide here."

"Mumbai, where in tarnation is that?" the voice on the other end responded. "I mean Bombay, in India," Julie amended. "In connection with a businessman named Sukhdev Kohli. Let me spell it for you: first name, S-U-K-H-D-E-V, last name, K-O-H-L-I."

"Okay, maybe I can get it that way. Hold on . . . here it is—Detective Michael Cardella. Actually, he's in now, I'll connect you."

A pleasant if inexpressive voice picked up and said, "Cardella."

"Hi, my name is Julie Norman. I teach at NUNY, and wanted to speak with someone about some information I have on the Sukhdev Kohli case. I was told you're the detective in charge."

"That's me. What kind of information do you have?"

"Any chance I could talk to you in person, Detective Cardella?" Julie asked, "It's a complicated story, and I'd rather not go into it on the phone. I could probably be there around noon."

"Noon works for me. Do you know how to get here? It's hell to park nearby."

"Can I get there by subway?" Julie asked.

"Okay, but it's a long trip."

"No problem," said Julie, "just give me the directions." Cardella told her the subway stop and walking directions immediately, surprising Julie, who thought most detectives drove in from Long Island or wherever and wouldn't travel by subway if their lives depended on it. "It's one of those old stations—no elevator and up three flights of stairs," he added. "If that's a problem, I can meet you downstairs."

"No, it's fine," Julie rolled her eyes and responded with what she hoped was a smile in her voice. "I think I can make it if I take the stairs slowly."

Julie typed out everything she could recall about her conversations with Grace on the plane to India. Responding to the voices of the detectives in the true-crime movies she was secretly addicted to, she didn't want to leave out anything out, *"because you never know what might be important."*

Julie followed Cardella's directions from the subway station and easily found the 113th precinct station house, a charming brick relic of old New York, with lovely terra-cotta floral plaques above rows of brown-stone-trimmed, round-arched windows. She admired the antique hexagonal green-glass lantern in front of the door, then mounted the five limestone steps leading up to the entrance. The desk sergeant had been apprised of her appointment and pointed her up the late-Victorian staircase, with its solid, bulbous banisters. The staircase led directly into what Julie imagined was the "squad room," a large space filled with multiple ugly steel desks facing every which way and ill-assorted desk chairs scattered helter-skelter around the room. She was surprised to see that every desk had a flat-screen computer as well as a variety of telephones.

A tall, rangy man looking to be in his mid-thirties rose from a chair he pushed back from a desk covered with folders and papers and walked over to her with his hand outstretched. "Michael Cardella," he said. "Nice of you to come in, Professor Norman." Julie noted his unusually deepset, beautifully shaped light hazel eyes with dark, almost girlish lashes, as she gave his hand a firm shake.

"Please, sit down," he said, pulling over a straight-backed chair to his desk and seating himself. He set out a small tape recorder and set it between them on his desk. "Are you okay with this?"

"Sure," Julie replied. "I realize you need an accurate account of what I'm going to tell you. After all, you don't know me; I could be the witness from hell."

"Why don't you just start telling me what you think you know," Cardella said in a casual tone of voice. "I'll interrupt with questions if there's anything I don't get."

"I'll start with some background," Julie began. "I'm an anthropologist at NUNY, and I do fieldwork in India. I was in India from December 15th to January 15th of this year, mainly to continue my research on changes in marriage and family patterns among Indians who immigrate to America."

As Cardella remained silent, Julie went on. "On the plane trip over in December, my seatmate was a young American woman named Grace, who was wearing an Indian shalwar-kameez. We had a very pleasant conversation during the trip. She told me that she was on her way to meet her fiancé, an Indian man with American citizenship, who was going to marry her in a big, traditional Indian wedding. Naturally, he would be introducing her to his parents and other members of his family. He would also be doing some business in Mumbai—that is, Bombay to most Westerners—while they were there. Then when they came back to America there would be a big wedding reception in New Jersey, where he lives."

Julie noticed that Cardella's expression did not change; she was beginning to understand how the police made people sweat just by keeping their mouths shut. "Grace told me that her fiancé was a big businessman in New York. She was a really sweet person, very sincere, very enthusiastic, maybe naïve, also, in a way. She showed me a photo of her fiancé, but it wasn't that clear. He was wearing sunglasses and was scrunched down in some kind of sports car, but he seemed to be a man in his early forties, handsome in the Bollywood style"—still no change of expression on Cardella's face—*Maybe he's more familiar with Indian culture than I'm giving him credit for,* Julie mused. "From Grace's description, he sounded like a very successful man of the world. Grace told me that he couldn't pick her up at the airport because of some previous appointments but that his cousin would be calling for her in a car and would wait right outside the airport departure door. The cousin would recognize her from Grace's photo, and he would drive her to the Maharaj Hotel where she would meet her fiancé and where they would be staying.

"So when the plane landed, Grace and I walked off together and went to the baggage claim. She had two big suitcases and was wearing a large glitzy shoulder bag with lots of pockets for her various documents, makeup, and so on. Her bags came out before mine, so she said goodbye and wheeled them out on a cart while I waited for my luggage. It came soon after Grace had walked out, and when I finished with customs and exited the airport door, I saw Grace about twenty feet down the sidewalk, wheeling one of her suitcases. An Indian man behind her was wheeling the other bag, and a second man stood by an old car with the trunk lid up and both doors open, motioning them over in what I thought was a rather hurried, coarse manner. I was also very surprised at the appearance of the two men. One, the driver, was wearing washed-out clothes, such as menial workers wear, and cheap rubber thong sandals. The other, the "cousin," was better dressed, but his Western-style pants and shirt were outdated and cheap-looking. It seemed odd that such rough-looking men would be connected to a well-to-do business-man, but I didn't pursue the thought further. I just called her name and gave her a thumbs-up when she turned.

"Then, in my friend's apartment where I stay in Mumbai, I turned on the TV the day after I arrived, and there was a short clip of a person described as a dead European woman whose body was found on the airport highway going north from Bombay. The picture with the news item was kind of fuzzy—maybe what you call a 'morgue shot'"—a brief nod of Cardella's head here—"and the newscaster announced that po-lice were withholding identification. The only details were that she was wearing Indian-type clothes and had a backpack with her. The cause of death was still unknown, possibly a hit-and-run accident.

"I remember thinking 'Gosh, I hope that's not Grace.' I didn't seri-ously think it was; you really couldn't make out the features, and I'd never seen a *real* dead person before . . ." Here Julie paused, looked di-rectly at Cardella, and said, "I mean on TV shows, okay, but never . . ." She faltered for a moment as she thought of finishing with the phrase *in real life* and realized how stupid that would sound. She returned to the facts. "I knew Grace wasn't carrying a backback; she had a big fashion-able purse. And it was my first day in India—I had a lot to do and needed to get going, but I guess I did file the clip away in the back of my mind . . ." Julie's voice trailed off, knowing how lame she sounded. And maybe a little callous, too, like a woman whose career was more important to her than the possible death of someone she knew.

Julie flushed a little, but continued in a more determined voice. "I never did see anything about it again on TV . . ." when Cardella interrupted her for a moment, asking nonjudgmentally, "Did you think about calling the police?"

"I didn't." Julie felt like she was confessing to a crime. "I wasn't sure what I really had to say, and I'd heard about the corruption of the Mumbai police . . ." Here again she trailed off, thinking what a tactless remark *that* was, then continued, ". . . and I was afraid if they dug into where I was staying they might find out I was a paying guest at what is supposed to be a strictly residential building. My friend could get into big trouble for that." Cardella just looked at her with his head cocked, not saying a word, and Julie brought herself back on track. "Anyway, I sort of forgot about it, but here's the punch line. I go to this big fancy wedding, and I'm getting ready to leave, when I see I'm standing next to an Indian man who looks familiar, but I can't exactly place him. An Indian friend comes up and introduces us, me as Professor Norman from NUNY in New York City and he as the bridegroom's cousin, Sukhdev Kohli, from New Jersey. Then the name didn't ring a bell at all, but today I received a packet of articles my friend sent me about this case, and I remembered that Grace had referred to him as Dev at one point, his nickname, I guess. Anyway, he gave me a card, which I just put in my purse without looking at it. Then he offered me a ride home, which I decided not to take, even though I was really tired. He just looked too slick, and he starts with 'I'm staying here a few more days, perhaps we could meet again, *yadda yadda yadda*,' but I'm too bushed to deal with it and more or less just politely brush him off. But it bothered me a bit; this guy really did look familiar. He told me he owns a chain of upscale sari shops, so I'm thinking, maybe I've seen him at some Indian clothing stores; I do buy Indian clothing sometimes, or maybe I saw him on the

Indian TV channel here. But once I got home, I just flopped into bed and crashed and totally forgot about it.

"Okay, I'm finishing now," Julie said, although the detective had not given any sign that he was getting impatient. "So this morning this packet arrived from my Indian friend who took me to the wedding and introduced me to everyone, and it's full of articles about how this guy, Sukhdev Kohli, was accused of murdering his American girlfriend. I know now that it *was* Grace I saw on TV that day, and, unbelievably, he wasn't even brought to trial because he convinced the judge that his accomplices who testified against him are just thugs and that he doesn't even know the dead girl. Then he comes back to America before they can extradite him, and I see in one of the articles that the investigation isn't over and that your precinct is going to be handling it.

"I figure I know things that no one else knows that tie him to Grace in India. She showed me his picture and described him. I saw those two thugs picking her up at the airport, and I was probably the last person to see Grace alive except for her killers. It's outrageous how cold-blooded he is. Imagine—just as cool as can be—he's attending a fancy wedding for his cousin Kumar, where everyone looks up to him as a successful businessman. I wonder if Anjeli—that's the girl whose wedding I attended—knows what kind of relatives her husband has. Anyway, I know I could be of help here. And I'm a reliable person; a judge can't dismiss me as some goonda working for the mafia."

"No question about that," Cardella smiled at Julie's outrage. "But it ain't over 'til the fat lady sings." He turned off the tape recorder and held out his hand. "This is really useful," he said. "I appreciate your making the long trip out here. By the way, has this Kohli tried to contact you?"

"Well, now that you bring it up, I'm not sure. The guy who stays at my apartment when I'm in the field said something about a man calling me who wouldn't give his name. I don't have caller ID, so I don't know who it was. Do you think that could be this Kohli?"

"Hard to tell," said Cardella. "You probably have a lot of guys calling you, I'd guess. Just be careful, though, and I'd stay away from sari shops, if I were you."

As they shook hands and Julie got ready to leave, Cardella said, "May I call you, Julie?"

"Is that with the comma or without," Julie asked with a smile. Cardella looked puzzled for a minute, then got it and joined in her laughter. "And it's yes to both," she said.

"Great. I'll be in touch."

✿ Chapter Twenty-Two

Julie was looking forward to dinner with Anjeli and Kumar. When she rang their doorbell, the door was opened by Kumar's uncle Suresh Kapoor, a man in his sixties whose intelligent, open face radiated a sincere welcome. "Namaste, namaste, come in, come in," he said. "I hope you remember me—I'm Kumar's *taya* Suresh. Ah, I mean uncle, his father's elder brother, as you Americans would say."

"Of course I remember you," said Julie, returning his greeting. She also remembered that he had become a very successful businessman since immigrating to the States in the 1970s and that he lived in New Jersey with his wife and two daughters, whom Julie had also met at Anjeli's wedding. She recalled that one daughter was finishing medical school and would be married sometime this year, while the other was pursuing a law degree. Another inspiring example of the American Dream come true without, it seemed, sacrificing the family values of Indian culture. Kumar's father had mentioned to Julie at the wedding that Kumar had lived with this uncle when he first came to America nine years ago. "That is what we Indian people do for our family," he had said with some superiority. *Ethnocentrism isn't just an American trait,* Julie reflected again as she had then; *it only seems that way because*

we have such an impact on the world, a point she reminded her students
of at every opportunity. Julie felt very comfortable with Kumar's uncle,
whose manner radiated the warmth that made Julie's fieldwork in India
such a pleasure. "How are your lovely wife and daughters? Will I be seeing them tonight?"

"Unfortunately not; they are visiting my wife's sister who is ill and
lives in Ohio. But you will definitely meet them again. My elder daughter is getting married in July, and we insist you will do us the honor to
attend the wedding."

Julie and Uncle Suresh moved into the living room, where the dining
table was set for six and the delightful smells of Indian cooking wafted
in from the kitchen. Anjeli and her mother-in-law, a rather unpleasant
woman, as Julie recalled from the wedding, were lifting lids and stirring
pots on a stove top crammed with jars and bottles of spices and vegetables assembled on plates. "Go, Anjeli, greet your guest. I will make
sure the food doesn't burn," Kumar's mother said, nodding toward the
living room. "I'll just meet your Julie in a minute," she added with a
tight smile. "We don't want her to think I'm the maidservant here."

"Why say such a thing, Mummyji?" Anjeli cried indignantly. "Of
course you must go greet Julie. I'll watch the pots and make sure the
food cooks properly." *And don't think Julie doesn't understand enough
about Indian families to know that I'm the one who would be the maidservant, not you.*

"Well, make sure you don't overcook the food," said the older woman,
making no effort to lower her voice. "It would be a bad impression for
your guest and also a big waste of money." Wiping her hands on a dish
towel, Anjeli's mother-in-law entered the living room to greet Julie.

"Namaste," she said formally, and Julie just as formally returned her
greeting and handed her a box of Italian pastries she had brought from
her own neighborhood. Mrs. Kapoor placed it on a side table without acknowledging it and said, "You have already met my husband's

brother, I think. Mr. Kapoor and Kumar just went out for some last-minute shopping. They will be home very shortly."

"I am so pleased to be here. I have been looking forward to seeing you all again," said Julie, moving toward the kitchen. "I just want to say hello to Anjeli." She gave her young friend a big hug. "Don't interrupt what you're doing, Anjeli; I know how much trouble it is to cook Indian food." *Which is why I don't do it myself.*

"Oh, Julie, I'm so glad you could come," Anjeli said, returning her hug. "I'm cooking all my best dishes tonight—I hope they won't be too spicy for you."

"No way, Anjeli; you know how I love Indian food."

"Please go sit, Julie; I'm just coming out."

"Go, go, Anjeli" said Mrs. Kapoor returning to the kitchen. "I'll take over now." *I bet you will,* Julie thought tartly.

As Julie sat down on the sofa, Kumar's uncle seated himself in an adjoining chair, his face wearing a kindly smile as he complimented her on her Indian outfit, a maroon raw silk shalwar-kameez with an embroidered dupatta. "Ah, you like our Indian dress, Professor Norman, and it suits you also."

"I do, but of course I wouldn't wear all the gold jewelry that should go with it," Julie laughed. "Not riding the subway at night, anyway. And please call me Julie."

"Uncleji, can I get you something to drink?" Anjeli turned toward Kumar's uncle and then toward Julie. "You, too, Julie—what would you like?"

"Thank you, Anjeli, some juice would be fine," Uncle Suresh answered.

"Same for me," Julie said. She knew it was useless to ask Anjeli to join them; she'd be cooking for a while yet under the obviously eagle eye of her mother-in-law, and she would never dare socialize while Kumar's mother worked in the kitchen.

"So," Uncle Suresh said, "my brother tells me you are an anthropologist. A very interesting profession, digging up all those ancient sites and suchlike."

"Well," said Julie, "I'm a cultural anthropologist, so you could say I study people instead of ancient artifacts."

"Ah, even more interesting. And which people are you studying, if I may ask?"

"My current research," Julie explained, "is for a book I'm writing on marriage and family among Indian immigrants in New York."

"Ah, then you'll be studying us," Uncle Suresh replied with a wide smile.

He's no dope, Julie thought to herself, but protested aloud, "No, no, nothing like that. Tonight I'm here only to enjoy the company and the food." *Just a little white lie. A cultural anthropologist in the field is never on vacation from observing and analyzing.* She dismissed the twinge of guilt accompanying her statement.

As Julie finished speaking, the front door opened, and Kumar and his father entered. "Namaste, Uncleji," said Kumar. He bent to touch his uncle's feet but was waved off with a friendly hand. "Hello, Julie. Were you able to find your way here alright?" he asked.

"No problem," said Julie. "Nice to see you again, Kumar." Rising from her chair, she also said namaste to Kumar's father and added, "Can I help you bring some of those bags into the kitchen?"

"No, no, sit, sit," Kumar said. "I'll do it. Sit, Daddyji; just let me drop these bags, and I'll get you something to drink. What would you like?"

His father didn't answer but said instead, "Just see when the dinner will be ready. And tell Anjeli to be quick with these pakoras. We just spent so much time and money to get them; they should be hot or they will lose their flavor." Turning to his brother he said, "Not like the old days, eh *bhai sahib,* when the snacks and pakoras kept coming, coming, coming, no let-up."

Kumar returned from the kitchen with plates of steaming pakoras and offered them around, first to his uncle, then to his father, and then, almost as an afterthought, to Julie. When he again asked his father what he'd like to drink, Mr. Kapoor suggested to his older brother that he join him in a whiskey. "Enough with the juice, bhai sahib. Come, come join me; I don't want to drink alone.

"Well, alright, just a small one," Suresh agreed. "I have to drive home tonight."

Well, Kumar, Julie thought, *then you could ask me if I'd like a scotch too.* She knew that drinking expensive liquor was not uncommon among upper-middle-class Indian men, except, of course, for the orthodox, and the custom had definitely carried over into the immigrant community as well. But even if Kumar did drink whiskey, which was likely after so many years in America, he would never take a glass in front of his father and his father's elder brother, however Americanized the latter seemed to be.

Kumar poured both his father and uncle drinks from the little cupboard and joined Julie on the couch.

"You know, Julie . . ." Uncle Suresh began, then interrupted himself, "I really like this American informality . . ."

As he hesitated, Julie said again, "Yes, please, do call me Julie; even my students sometimes call me that."

"Bad idea," interrupted Kumar's father. "All this cozy-cozy relations between professors and students, parents and children, this calling by the first name, has bad consequences. No one knows who is who, and it results in a breakdown of the family and all the social institutions of law and order. Our Indian way keeps things clear and lets everyone know where they stand."

"That's true," said Julie agreeably. "I try very hard to remember all the different kinship relations when I'm in India so I don't insult someone by accident. But it's pretty complicated for an American—we have a much simpler system. Just a few terms—*mother, father, uncle, aunt, cousin, in-laws,* that sort of covers it—and no one feels insulted if you get it wrong."

"True, true," said Uncle Suresh. "Our system must be confusing to you . . . older brother, younger brother, older sister-in-law, younger sister-in-law, mother's side, father's side . . . but all part of Indian culture. We never want to lose that. It's hard to explain to someone in America."

"Especially the part about mother's side and father's side, and the importance of elder and younger," Julie said. "And it *is* significant. It explains why people behave in different ways toward each other. I think—hope—after half a dozen field trips to India I have it down now."

"Well," said Kumar, a little sourly, "the difficulties are not just on the Indian side. When I first came to America I was introduced to people called someone's uncle, or aunt, or brother-in-law or cousin, and I thought, Who is this, his father's brother, mother's brother, or his brother's wife's brother, or his sister's husband, or which cousin on which side? Very confusing. Just new from India where such things matter, I was very tense about getting it wrong and insulting someone, as you say about India. Of course, now I know you can't insult Americans over confusing relationships or how much respect you need to show them."

"I'm not sure that's entirely true," said Julie, trying not to be argumentative. "Americans do want respect, but perhaps for us respect is based more on what people have accomplished or on their wealth, rather than something due them because of their age alone or where they fit into a family. Sort of goes along with American individualism."

"That's very clever, Julie," said Uncle Suresh. "Yes, in America it is the individual and his own achievements that are the center of everything, whereas among Indians, it is the family. I think you must have learned these things from your profession as an anthropologist."

Julie ducked her head in modest acknowledgement. "Yes, Mr. Kapoor, that *is* the kind of thing we study. That's what makes anthropology so interesting." She decided this was a good opportunity to discover more about Sukhdev Kohli, so she continued, in what she hoped was a casual tone. "Speaking of relatives, I met so many at the wedding, I couldn't remember them all. But I do remember one man; he looked a little like that Bollywood heartthrob, Roshan, and he very kindly offered me a ride home. He looked familiar to me, but I couldn't quite recall from where. My friend Shakuntala Jatani—her people are friends of Anjeli's parents—introduced him as Kumar's cousin, but I don't know exactly what she meant by that. His name is Sukhdev Kohli; perhaps you know who I mean?"

Julie did not miss the long look that passed between Kumar's father and his uncle. *What does she know?* Kumar's father was wondering. *Is this all an innocent act she's putting on for us? Just because we speak English with an accent, these Americans always underestimate our intelligence.* "Ah, so you met Mr. Kohli," said Kumar's father. "Yes, he is Kumar's cousin, as you would say here, on my wife's side. When he first came to America many years ago, he also stayed with my brother Suresh." Here he nodded in the direction of his elder brother, who dismissed the importance of that help with a wave of his hand.

"It was nothing at all; it was my pleasure to be able to help out the family," he said with becoming humility.

Kumar's father continued with some pride, "Mr. Kohli has become a very rich and famous businessman; his shops attract even Western celebrities, and he lives in the most posh suburb in New Jersey."

Uncle Suresh kept his gaze fixed on Julie's face as his younger brother imparted this information. She kept her expression just as impassive as his. "Do you keep in touch with him, here in America?" she asked with a straight face.

"Oh, yes," said Kumar's father. "He is very helpful to the family. You know Kumar is thinking of going into his own business, and Mr. Kohli has been most generous with his advice. He has many, many contacts in the Indian community. Once we decide to make the move, his assistance will be invaluable."

"Oh, I didn't know you were planning to leave the bank," Julie said, turning to Kumar. "What kind of business are you thinking of going into?"

"I'm not sure," Kumar said abruptly, obviously wanting to redirect the conversation and clearly implying that it was none of Julie's business.

At that moment Anjeli and her mother-in-law entered the room, placing steaming bowls of food on the dining table and asking everyone to sit down. Before Kumar's father did so, he replenished his own whiskey glass to the top and managed to add a little to his brother's glass as well before Suresh could put his hand over the top.

Julie's mouth watered at the array of dishes in front of her. She knew, of course, that the invitation to sit down would not immediately include Anjeli, who, as soon as everyone else was seated, darted back to the kitchen. "Just let me fry the *pappads*, and I'll be right back," she said to no one in particular.

Julie noticed that Kumar and Anjeli had hardly spoken to each other. Not a surprise. One of the drawbacks of joint-family living was that husband and wife had little privacy, a situation not entirely due to a lack of space. Cultural restraints limiting the affection that could be expressed in public between husband and wife were a basic difference between the Indian family and its American counterpart. The importance of the parent-son ties in the former contrasted to the primacy of the marriage ties in the latter.

A brilliant Indian psychoanalyst, Sudhir Kakar, had recently written about the subject of intimacy in Indian families, and Julie heavily relied on his interpretations in her fieldwork and writing. Kakar forthrightly noted how, in the relationship of young Indian couples, much of whatever strength the bride enjoyed derived from the power of sex. It gave her an important edge, for in most cases—even today among all but the most cosmopolitan, upper-crust urban families—the husband as well as the wife was probably chaste and had little or no experience of sexual intimacy. Through her sexual allure, the wife might be able to subvert the traditional, religiously sanctioned norms of Indian family life, which emphasized the loyalty between the husband and his parents rather than between the husband and wife. If the son's traditional obligations to his parents should decrease, with his loyalty and affection transferred to his wife, that could cause a great deal of worry to his parents and, indeed, to all his elders.

As the person closest to the new bride on a daily basis, the mother-in-law's special burden was to make sure this alienation did not occur. And this was an even heavier burden nowadays, when the son and his new bride often lived on a different continent and were exposed to a value system completely opposite to those of the Indian family. Julie could see this tension in every action of Kumar's mother, both toward her son and toward Anjeli. With mothers-in-law like Anjeli's, Julie could not quite work up the sympathy to accompany her intellectual understanding.

"Do you mind my asking when you came to America, Mr. Kapoor?" Julie ventured, turning to Kumar's uncle. "I know there have been many changes in the lives of immigrants here over the last twenty or thirty years."

"Indeed, there have, Julie. I have lived through the good old and bad old days. I came in the late 1960s before there were a lot of Indians here who, like me, had come as students. Many of us intended to return to India after graduation, but as economic opportunities opened up, we changed our plans. We were able to do well in the American economy. Of course you know how we Indians save our money and help each other out. In that way I was able to open a business and have some modest success. Things have altered somewhat, I'm afraid."

"Yes, I can tell you that from personal experience, Uncle," Kumar said glumly. "At my bank they are already laying off people. And it's not just my bank—the whole financial industry is going down the tubes."

"I see the good-old-days part; what was the bad-old-days part?" Julie inquired with interest, when Kumar had finished speaking.

"Well," answered Uncle Suresh thoughtfully, "back then Americans didn't know much about India, and more than once when I said I was

Indian, someone would ask me 'which tribe?' Even one educated man once asked me if Hindus were reincarnated as cows after they died." He laughed, though not unkindly, at these memories. "Yet in those days people were very interested in us Indians, and in our culture, too. We were no threat to them, so perhaps that's why they were so hospitable. And of course, we also didn't know a lot about America and made mistakes we'd laugh about among ourselves. But then as more Indians came, American hostility toward us grew. More economic competition, more neighbors and shopkeepers who looked different, darker skinned, the environment became less friendly."

"Not so friendly these days either," said Kumar with some asperity.

"Well, yes and no. Not as bad as the 1980s, with those dotbuster types."

"What a funny name, Uncle; who are these dotbusters?" Anjeli asked. By this time, since everyone had eaten at least one helping, she was able to take a respite from ferrying the food back and forth and had joined them at the table.

"Oh, Anjeli, just a bunch of stupid people who harassed us Indians. In the 1970s, when many Indians were opening businesses in New Jersey, the local people didn't like the competition. Just as happened in your Jackson Heights. But in New Jersey, it got rougher. Vandals pitched stones through the windows of Indian businesses, and some people got badly beaten up even. By the 1980s the increase of the Indians generated a lot of resentment, even though our communities had little crime and our children were winning top awards at schools.

"They called these hoodlums *dotbusters*, Anjeli, because one day, in the late eighties, a Jersey City newspaper received a letter warning the Indians that if they didn't leave the city, serious things could happen. The signature was a dot with a slash through it, the dot representing the bindi that Indian women wear on their foreheads."

"Oh, yes," Julie confirmed, "I do remember reading about that when I started my research on the Indian diaspora."

"Yes, well, anyway, the day after that letter appeared in the papers, two thugs broke into some Indian man's home and beat him almost to death. They were mostly Gujerati there; apparently these thugs just picked a Patel at random out of the phone book—such a common Gujerati name, hundreds of them, like Smith for Americans. But then an Indian doctor leaving his hospital was also severely beaten by three men who attacked him for being a 'dothead.'"

Anjeli put her hand over her mouth in fear. "A dothead! But men don't wear bindi," she cried out, obviously very much disturbed.

"Of course they don't," continued Uncle Suresh, "but these"—he started to say one word but out of respect for the women present, continued with another—"these ignorant people didn't know that. They don't know anything; that's the problem. Anyway, the doctor never recovered, and the three attackers were acquitted at the trial, even though later the judge criticized the police for their sloppy investigation."

"America is a very racist country, Anjeli; don't be so shocked," Kumar said, rather unkindly, Julie thought.

"Well, all countries have their flaws, Kumar," said Uncle Suresh, "and racism is always made worse in a bad economy, isn't it? In general now I think Indians are treated quite well here. What do you say, Kumar?"

"I don't think I agree, Uncle; maybe the racism is just more subtle. And since 9/11, there's even more suspicion. Brown skin is not trusted. These Americans don't know the difference between people from India or the Middle East, wherever. Because Sikhs wear turbans, people think they are Muslims, so a Sikh was killed because of that. After 9/11, Sikhs were cutting their hair and other Indians were shaving their beards—not a good time to look like this Osama bin Laden fellow. And just recently, some stupid politician called an Indian journalist a *macaca*, meaning a monkey, I think."

"Well, it cost him the election," Julie contended as Kumar paused, "That's some progress."

"While your examples are true, Kumar, considering the horror of September 11, I think the backlash against Indians was relatively small,"

Uncle Suresh continued in his reasonable voice. "Muslims, of course, were a different thing, targeted by the American government and many of them deported. And immigration applications dropped down a lot for all foreigners. But Indian people here are very patriotic, getting very active in American politics also. That's a good sign, I think. Why, an Indian was recently elected governor of the state of Louisiana!"

Here Kumar almost interrupted but held back until his uncle had finished speaking. "This governor of Louisiana," he said somewhat angrily, though he didn't look at his uncle as he spoke, but rather at Julie, as if it were her fault, "is a convert to Christianity, so does he really count as an Indian?"

"But, Kumarji," Anjeli said hesitantly when Kumar had finished, "I read that Sonny Caberwal—you know that Sikh model for Kenneth Cole—has refused to shave his hair and take off his turban or even cut his beard. That is very good, don't you think?"

Uncle Suresh and Julie could both see that Kumar was in a mood to argue, and his uncle jumped in before Kumar could speak. "Come, come, let us drop all this politics. We were strangers here, and America was very good to us." Turning to Mrs. Kapoor he said, "Bhabhiji, this was a fabulous meal you and Anjeli put together for us. I think the food here is even better than in India."

"It's not finished yet, Uncle; let us try some of these European pastries Julie brought us."

Julie surreptitiously looked at her watch. "Come, Anjeli," she said, "let me help you put the dishes in the kitchen, and then we can bring out the pastries."

Over dessert Anjeli mentioned to Kumar's uncle that she was now working at NUNY for a professor who specialized in Indian religion. "Maybe I can even start taking some courses without paying tuition," she said enthusiastically. Julie beamed.

Kumar's uncle nodded approvingly, a complete contrast to Kumar and his parents, who sat in silence. "Come now, Satish," he said, turning to Kumar's father but including Mrs. Kapoor in his conversation, "this is good news for Anjeli and the family. In America everybody works, and work is rewarded. Yes, that's the American way. My daughters also plan to work after marriage; it is a good thing for women to have outside interests."

As the conversation became desultory, Julie prepared to leave. Kumar's uncle again reminded her of his hope to see her at his daughter's wedding. Looking happily at Kumar's parents he added, "And soon there may be another wedding of a daughter, isn't it, Satish?"

Kumar's father made a sour face. "Yes, perhaps we will find a boy here for Lakshmi, but even so, where will we get the money for the wedding?"

His wife added, looking snidely at Anjeli, "Yes, the money will be a problem; some commitments that we had counted on did not come through."

Anjeli's eyes began to fill with tears, and Julie made an effort to divert her attention by making exaggerated preparations to leave. She thanked Mrs. Kapoor profusely for the excellent dinner and said her good-byes to Kumar, his father, and his uncle.

"Will you be alright getting back, Julie? It's quite late now," Kumar's uncle asked. "I would be happy to drive you home."

"No, no, please stay," Julie replied. "I'm used to the subway, and the stop is right by my house." Anjeli walked Julie to the elevator, where Julie gave her a big hug meant to convey her understanding of the difficult situation. "Do keep in touch, Anjeli," she admonished.

Julie had downplayed any fears regarding her late departure, but she had recently become more mindful of her late-night activities after Detective Cardella's concern about those mysterious telephone calls whose source she still hadn't discovered. And in fact, Sukhdev Kohli, who was still enjoying his freedom, certainly knew where to find her. She'd impulsively bought a pepper spray cannister, which she kept in her bag these days, though she had no real confidence that she could wield it effectively. *I'll just watch my own back more vigilantly!*

Chapter Twenty-Three

Dev—as he thought of himself (Americans had such a hard time with the whole moniker, Sukhdev)—leaned back in his office chair and dialed information. Julie Norman at a Chelsea address, no problem. She didn't even have the sense to use a first initial. She might be school-educated, but Dev was beginning to think she wasn't too smart about life in the real world. America was a cutthroat place, and if you didn't look after yourself, no one else would. Survive the messes, like this stupid Grace business, and move ahead. You didn't need three college degrees for that. Let Grace's parents threaten him with a civil suit. Wait until they found out what lawyers cost!

This damn Julie person at the wedding, though. What bad luck! Hundreds of people there, and that buttinsky Shakuntala had to show up with all the details of his family tree, his sari stores, blah blah. Would this professor put two and two together? According to a recent conversation with Mrs. Kapoor about the visit Julie had made to their house, she had poked her nose into the Kapoor's continuing relationship with him. Was it just curiosity, or had she befriended Grace and heard every detail of their romantic drama? *Let's face it, I've dug myself into a hole with that idiot. Well, I've taken care of that little mess, and if it becomes necessary, I'll take care of this Julie mess too.*

Had she looked at him suspiciously at the wedding? As if she knew him? Hard to decide. She seemed the typically outspoken American woman; every idea in her head popped out of her mouth the minute she thought it. If she'd made the connection between him and Grace, she probably would have given herself away. But it couldn't hurt to make sure.

"Hello, is this Professor Norman? This is Sukhdev Kohli. I met you at Anjeli and Kumar's wedding in Mumbai in January. How are you?"

"Oh," Julie almost stuttered. "Fine, busy. How are you? How did you get my number?"

Dev smirked, even though no one could see him. *Excuse me, Miss Ph.D, did you ever hear of a phone book? You're right in it under N. As dumb as Grace. I can hardly believe it. She should demand her tuition money back.* "It's in the book. Look, I was recalling your appreciation for our Indian culture, and I thought you might enjoy a fine Indian dinner some night. I know a special South Indian restaurant that prepares some delicacies you may not have tasted as yet."

"Um, this is a busy couple of weeks for me; it's midterms," Julie explained, trying to keep her voice friendly. Dev tried to gauge whether she was blowing him off because she really was busy or she had a boyfriend or she suspected him in connection with Grace. "Could I take a rain check?"

"Certainly," Dev responded politely. "I'll try you again soon and will look forward to seeing you." He hung up the phone in some disappointment but would just bide his time. He needed to know exactly what Julie remembered of her conversations with Grace and if there was anything in them that would lead to her pointing a finger at him. If Julie *did* think she had information, he needed to know what she would do with it. He hoped none of this had to go further but also knew that, as the Americans say, "ya gotta do what ya gotta do."

A few days after Sukhdev Kohli's call, Julie was home grading her midterm papers when the phone rang. She picked it up on the first ring, and a familiar voice said, "Professor Norman?"

"That's me," Julie answered, recognizing the speaker. "Is this Detective Cardella? I was hoping you'd call. Is there anything new on the case?"

"Maybe we could talk over dinner, Julie. There's a lot to tell. And drop the Detective Cardella, okay?"

"Dinner's great. And I think I remember your first name is Michael."

"Only my mother calls me Michael. Mike is fine."

Sitting over their menus at East of Eighth, a local bistro with excellent food, large portions, and reasonable prices, Mike Cardella responded carefully to Julie's eager question about where the Kohli case was going.

"So, okay, the case has widened; it's much more complicated than we thought at first. This Kohli character is a real piece of work. Apparently he took out a couple of life insurance policies on this Grace, and now the case involves insurance fraud. We're handling that part at the precinct because it took place in Queens. The FBI is handling the murder investigation because, and I quote, 'the suspect used foreign commercial travel and facilities to pay money to someone to cause Grace's death.' There *is* evidence from here that Kohli was connected to Grace because her family had met him, and other people saw them together; also Grace told them about going to India to meet his family. But your sworn testimony that you knew Grace and recognized Kohli from his photo will be very useful in showing he lied about not having any connection with her *in India*. I copied your tape for the FBI people, and you'll probably be hearing from them down the line. And the insurance fraud gives this creep a really big motive, something that was lacking before."

"But I don't understand. How did you tie Grace's murder to insurance fraud?"

"Most nonprofessional criminals do dumb things," said Cardella. "When the Feebs were investigating the murder, they took control of Kohli's cell phone and traced a number of calls to various insurance companies. I won't bore you with all the charges, the whereas, and wherefores, but the long and short of it is that Kohli had called several insurance companies trying to get a one-million-dollar life insurance policy on Grace, with himself as primary beneficiary. That's pretty high stakes for an unemployed model or cosmetologist or whatever she was.

"He calls one life insurance company saying that his fiancée— Grace—wants to buy this policy for herself; of course *he's* really buying it with the idea of collecting the death benefit later on down the road. So this company informs him that for a one-million-dollar policy, the applicant has to come in person for a medical interview with urine and blood samples. But for a $500,000 policy, the medical results can be mailed in with the application and the premium. So not only does this SOB trick Grace some way into taking the blood and urine samples and get a five-hundred-grand policy, but then he doubles up, calls another insurance company, and gets the same story and has the blood and urine samples from the lab sent to this company, too! So you do the math—how much does he have riding on Grace's life?"

"Umm, one million dollars?" Julie queried doubtfully.

"Duh, yeah, that's right." Mike laughed. "For a minute there I thought you were going to take out a pencil and add it up on a napkin."

Julie laughed too. "I did pass statistics for my doctorate," she said, "but just barely. Go on, this is really fascinating. The arrogance of the man."

"Yeah, this is where these types always trip up," Mike asserted. "I've seen it a hundred times. Kohli's big mistake was not only filling out Grace's application with some false info on her job status and salary, but both the insurance companies and the medical lab handling the mailing of Grace's tests were out of state. So now we add postal fraud to the charges. This guy'll be selling samosas in prison to make his cigarette money for a long time to come. The postal fraud division is death on violators. Plus we've found some serious downturns in Kohli's sari shops. Income on the slide and big expenses—Grace's new Mercedes, tuitions for his kids in private nursery school and kindergarten—you know what those run these days?—and a new, upscale condo for himself on the side, something, by the way, he didn't bother to tell his wife about. It all adds up."

"Samosas?" Julie asked, "You seem to know a lot more about Indian culture than I would have thought. No offense meant, but I did notice you didn't have any questions about some of the terms I used."

"None taken, Julie," Mike responded. "I sort of got into it sideways. I started working on some homicide cases with a really good Indian detective at the precinct here, Rajiv Sharma. He was a beat cop before, mostly dealing with store burglaries, street robberies, that kind of thing. He gained a lot of trust in the community, moved up to detective, and we've partnered in a lot of cases in the Indian community. He knows about the Kohli case, and I've told him about you. We thought maybe if you could get out to Queens some afternoon, we could all meet and exchange ideas on some of these cases involving violence against women. It'd be an education for me, for sure. You think we could arrange it?"

"Absolutely, Mike. I'll give you a few available dates, and you can get back to me with what's convenient for you and Rajiv."

"Will do. You know, Julie, there's not that much crime, and especially not violent crime, in the Indian community. But what there is often involves domestic violence. Domestic assaults and even spousal murder is nothing new to me, not only in the Indian community but all over the precinct, but one difference I've noticed is that quite a few of these Indian wife-abuse cases wind up in murder by fire. How would you explain that?"

Julie marshaled her thoughts. "Well, fire does have a special *sacred* meaning in India associated with purification; it's used symbolically in weddings, and cremation of course, and you may have heard about the old Indian custom of sati, where a widow would immolate herself on her husband's funeral pyre. Perhaps that's been retained, unconsciously, in the immigrant community's psyche, even when it's a death by murder. But it might also just be that most Indian immigrants don't have access to guns or the money to hire a hit man, and a woman's sari catching on fire while she's cooking is an inexpensive, plausible way of making a murder look like an accident. That's certainly a problem that has attracted a lot of attention in India."

"Hmm, could be that simple. What's amazing is that these husbands don't usually cover their tracks very well. They break down and confess pretty quickly and wind up doing heavy time in places where take-out Indian food isn't very available. I mean who else are we going to suspect? It's kind of sad, actually. You'd think divorce would be a lot easier in the long run."

"Yes, an American might think so," Julie agreed. "But the Indian situation is much more complicated. Divorce, even for men, still has a stigma attached. Marriage is taken very, very seriously in Indian culture, even among Indian immigrants."

"So . . . speaking of marriage," Mike glanced at Julie's empty ring finger, "why isn't a smart, beautiful girl like you married?"

Julie laughed inwardly, thinking of all guys who had asked the same question. She recalled one guy in a bar, wearing the Armani suit and black-tasseled loafers that screamed greedhead Wall Streeter at her, who had hit on her with just that phrase, followed by the lame-o nugget, "Hi, I'm Chet; I'm an attorney." He had gotten her stock reply, "Hi, I'm Julie, and, thanks, but I already have a lawyer." What Julie said aloud was "Do you want the short form or the long form, Mike?"

"In your case, I've got time for the long form."

"Okay, you asked for it. Guys today . . ." She shrugged. "Like a colleague in film studies—not a complete jerk but full of himself. We're having coffee, he leans over into my face and asks me the same question, twisting off his wedding ring beneath the table so I can't see him slip it into his pants pocket. 'Julie,' he says sonorously, 'you're what the Italian directors in the fifties called *la maggiorate fisiche*—physically advantaged we'd say.' I replied that when I thought of all the married men cheating on their wives with the *physically advantaged* if they could get them and the less advantaged if they couldn't, it seemed like the Indian custom of arranged marriage had much to recommend it. I told him my mom was going to make a *shiddach,* an arranged marriage, for me pretty soon, so if he were really interested, he could start on his divorce, buff up his resumé, and get in line."

Cardella laughed in spite of himself, and Julie continued more seriously. "I thought one relationship a couple of years with ago with a visiting professor from Texas might go someplace, but his job was in Texas, so were his kids from the first time around, and I'd never leave New York, so that was one hurdle. And it wasn't a perfect fit in other ways too. Now I suppose my work's kind of taken over my life. I guard my free time pretty carefully. At least until I finish this book I'm working on and get my promotion." Julie smiled and added, "So a guy would have to be pretty foolish to take me on." Mike's face slipped into a quirky smile but then, Julie noted, reverted to his impassive detective face, a neutral but thoughtful expression as if he were filing away Julie's comments in his head.

"So how did you get into such an all-consuming field as anthropology, Julie," he continued in an interested voice.

Julie answered by stealing a quote from her favorite Israeli novelist, Amos Oz: "'When I was little, I wanted to grow up to be a book.'" Mike grinned at the image, and Julie continued, "But eventually I learned that I'd grow up to be a *person,* and that's when I decided to be a teacher, eventually a scholar and professor and a writer. It was a great choice.

I enjoy teaching tremendously, and the travel I do for my research introduces me to terrific people of every description. And cultural anthropology is fascinating, maybe a little like your detective work, careful observation and analysis of what makes people tick—and applying it in a small way to make the world a better place . . . that last is my parents' legacy. How about you, Mike? How did you become a detective?"

"I enlisted in the service after high school and thought I might even make some kind of career in it, but it wasn't for me. Should have gone to college when I got out, but I got married instead—yeah, instead"—he answered the implied question in Julie's raised eyebrows—"and joined the police force. I always wanted to do something with the law, my marriage didn't last long, so I went to John Jay College on that split-shift program they have for cops. With a day job as a cop, I really wanted to explore subjects that I'd always enjoyed, so I took a liberal arts degree with a major in American history, the Revolution, the Constitution, the whole works. My dad was thrilled; can you believe it?

"It's late in the day, I know, but both my parents are actually immigrants, my mom from Ireland, my dad from Sicily. He especially bought the whole ball of wax, the founding fathers, the Bill of Rights . . . Every time my aunt would say, 'history, shmistory—what kinda degree is that? Ya gonna open up a history store?' he'd shush her. 'Annamarie, this is America; everybody should study these things. People died for them.' She'd curse him in Sicilian dialect under her breath, but I'll never forget how he stood up for me when a lot of my colleagues thought I was wasting my time. Maybe someday I'll get a graduate degree or even go to law school." He ducked his head toward Julie. "Hey, maybe I should turn off my microphone?"

"No, no," Julie protested sincerely, "please go on."

"So, okay, I made detective, starting out in robbery-homicide. But it was so depressing. Mostly these stupid young guys from the urban ghetto, they make a gigantic mistake—waving a gun at someone—and wind up with hard time on felony or felony-murder raps. And if they

ever get out, there's nothing going for them anyway. So I stayed in homicide but specialized in fraud-related murders where the arrogant bad
guys, like this Kohli, do it for the money, thinking they can outsmart the
dumb cops. Most of them don't even need the money, at least not the
way an ordinary working stiff does, for the basics, to support a family."

"Mike?" Julie asked tentatively. "Do you think I could be of any help
here in getting more information from Kohli? He called me last week,
and I brushed him off, but politely, so I could keep the door open if you
thought it would do some good."

"Don't even think about it," Mike said emphatically. "We don't need
you playing Nancy Drew. Your testimony will certainly be useful, but
what you've got isn't the kind of incontrovertible evidence that would
convict in court. Kohli's defense lawyer would make mincemeat of it.
Like, 'how do you know *Grace* was the girl he was meeting. Did she tell
you his name? You only have *her* word for it that they were going to get
married, right? She could have lied to you.' Leave it alone, Julie. This
guy isn't just a creep, he's a dangerous creep."

Abashed and disappointed, Julie assured Mike she took his words
seriously.

"And speaking of danger," Mike paused, "I can see you're an adventurous lady, you go all over the city . . . maybe wearing Indian clothes
sometimes, right? Rajiv's heard about a couple of rape cases that we
aren't sure are connected but seem to involve Asian women or women
wearing Indian dress, like that. One was that Halloween rape case. Did
you read about? It actually happened near where you live—in that renovation site on Chelsea Piers?"

"Oh, gosh," Julie gulped. "I did read about that. I was right around
there then. My sister had brought my little nephew in for the Chelsea
Halloween block party. We had such a good time—of course we left
before dark—and I recall thinking, 'Oh dear, that poor woman being
assaulted that same night just a few blocks away?'"

"I don't mean to scare you, Julie, and Rajiv isn't sure yet where the Indian angle fits in, if at all, but if you're going to be out late wearing Indian clothes, just keep your third eye open, okay."

"Thanks, Mike. That's good advice, and I intend to follow it."

"Hey, Jeannie," Julie waved to her friend sitting on the lobby bench as she entered the building after her dinner with Mike. "Kind of late for you to still be here, isn't it?"

"It's only 10, Julie. When I was a girl we thought nothing of being out 'til all hours of the night at dances and whatnot. But you missed your friend. He was looking . . ."

"Wait a minute, Jeannie," Julie interrupted. "What friend? I didn't expect anyone to come by tonight."

"Yes, exactly. When I came in from the park he was searching the bell list, so I asked if I could help. He asked did I know Professor Norman—he was just passing by and took a chance you might be home. A distinguished-looking Indian man. I thought he must be connected with your work. Very well dressed for a professor, I must say. Forty years with the garment union, I know my onions about men's suiting. I explained that I couldn't let him into the lobby; I hoped he understood but the building is very strict about security. But he could leave a note with me and I would give it to you. But he said it wasn't important." Jeannie gave Julie a sly look. "A new admirer, Julie? I hope I didn't scare him away."

❀ Chapter Twenty-Four

On his lips he says Ram, Ram, *but in his belt he carries a dagger.*

—*Indian saying*

The apartment was very quiet; Kumar was still at work, and his mother was out with her friends, so it was only Anjeli and Kumar's father at home. Angeli was in the kitchen thinking about the current state of affairs. The hostility between her and her mother-in-law was ongoing. She was outraged that her mother-in-law had not brought with her any of her wedding saris or the gold jewelry she had taken from Anjeli's purse when she had left for New York. Outraged, but not really surprised, knowing as she did now the difficulty they would have providing a dowry and wedding for Kumar's sister.

She didn't like being around Kumar's father, either. Of course, she treated him with the respect and distance required by custom, as far as that was possible within the confines of the small apartment. But she felt he looked at her in ways inappropriate to their relationship, and it seemed to her he often brushed too close to her body as he was passing by. She acquiesced to his seemingly innocent requests to massage his feet or prepare his bath with no outward hesitation, but still felt distinctly uncomfortable, and she tried to avoid being alone with him in the apartment.

Now, as she checked the pots on the stove, she heard some footsteps behind her and knew it must be Kumar's father. She turned around and asked in a low voice, "What do you want? Is there something I can do for you?"

"There *is* something, Anjeli. We are alone now and . . . you are so beautiful; you are a temptation to any man that sees you." He took a few steps forward, grabbed her shoulders, and pulled her toward him, pushing his face close to hers and holding her so tightly their bodies were pressed together all along their length.

"Let me go immediately," Anjeli said through gritted teeth. "If you don't, I will scream for help. And then the police will come, and you will go to jail. Don't think I'm afraid of you!" Anjeli *was* afraid, in truth. She had never realized what a big and powerful man he was. He was trying to lift her off her feet and carry her from the kitchen when she exploded with a rage that came from deep inside herself, a rage she never knew she was capable of. He put her down and let go of her immediately, stumbling backward with his hands held high as if to ward off an attack from her.

Anjeli shook her head in a dismissive gesture as much to herself as to the seemingly crazed person before her. She would never have believed she could feel such anger and, yes, hatred for another human being. That he was obviously under the influence of alcohol was no excuse. Her upbringing did not desert her. She stared at her father-in-law, her face composed into a mask of hauteur though she felt only disgust. Why should she, a model of decorum and honor, be forced to listen to such vulgar talk and be victimized by this horrible man? How awful for her own father-in-law to comment on her beauty. Had she designed her beauty for herself, had she purchased it for gain, or could she do anything to disguise it? Enough! She did not deserve and she would not tolerate such behavior from anyone. "Leave the house," she said almost airily, flicking her dupatta back over her shoulder as she turned away to the stove, ostentatiously stirring the pot that rested on the flame. "You will not treat me like a servant girl who must do your bidding."

Although cowed, her father-in-law continued to move toward her. She took the pot off the stove and threw it at him with all her force, the rice pullao she was cooking falling to the floor. "Enough! You have taken advantage because Kumar is at work and your wife is out of the house. You are betraying your family. This time I will keep quiet, but if you ever approach me again I will tell Kumar."

Gathering his strength, her father-in-law sneered at her. "Kumar will never believe you. Is this any different than what happens with your professor? Don't try to fool me with your innocence. Meeting your professor at night, and who knows how many other men you meet. Why not me?"

"Do not be misled by my obedience. I am a good wife and have done nothing to deserve this treatment. Go now, and don't come back into the house until Kumar and your wife are here, or I will call Kumar at the office and maybe call the police as well. You are contemptible," she laughed at him outright.

"Shut up! How dare you laugh at me? I could kill you for that!" her father-in-law shouted at her.

"Just go, go now." Anjeli demanded. *If he ever tried anything like this again, she would show him no mercy. She would tell Kumar and force him to recognize that a reckoning had to come and that they could not go on as they were.*

As Mr. Kapoor stormed out of the apartment, he almost fell over his wife who was kneeling on the floor in the hall. She looked up, startled, as if she were interrupted in doing something, and he briefly wondered if she had heard anything of what had just transpired. "Oh, I was just looking for my keys. I dropped them as I tried to open the door."

Ignoring her response, he pushed the elevator bell and said over his shoulder, "I'm going to the corner for a newspaper. I'll be back shortly."

Since her father-in-law's attempted assault on her a week ago, Anjeli was careful about being in the apartment unless her mother-in-law or Kumar were also there. Today as she arrived home from work, she quietly entered the apartment and heard Kumar's parents talking in their bedroom. She then slipped into her own bedroom, hoping for a short rest before they demanded their tea. Even when her bedroom door was closed, they would sometimes open it without knocking. Their carping never stopped: she came home too late, the tea was cold, her clothes were unsuitable, she did not take adequate care of Kumar, she spent too much money, her friends—*And who were they?* Anjeli wondered. *I have no friends except for Gita and Julie*—were unsuitable. Although Kumar's mother constantly referred to the help she gave Anjeli in cooking and food shopping—indeed she insisted she be in charge of it—her help was more trouble than it was worth. Anjeli would escape by rushing to the bathroom with some excuse so as not to scream back at them.

Now, as she lay down on the bed, she couldn't help but hear Kumar's parents, quite clearly, through the thin walls that separated them. It sounded as if they were having an argument. "What do you want me to do?" Mr. Kapoor was asking in a plaintive but hostile voice. "I have spoken to Kumar about his wife's behavior, but he doesn't listen to me." "You have to be more forceful, Mr. Kapoor. You must speak to the girl herself." his wife retorted. "She is the wrong girl for our family. Disobedient and a spendthrift. Kumar himself took her to buy a coat while my coat is still from last year. And Kumar hardly buys anything for himself. We should never have allowed him to marry this girl."

"What could we do? He would have no other."

"We should have stood more firm. The girl's parents have no money, no status, her father is only a civil servant. So many girls from the business class we could have found. Our Kumar is a catch; he deserved better, and so do we. You went along with his choice only because the girl is so good-looking. You men, all you think about is sexual allure. What good is that without money? Her parents only put on a show with the big wedding. There was no dowry to speak of, and you need to remember that we also have a daughter to marry off. Where will we get the dowry for her? This was a big mistake. But mistakes can be fixed, and I have some ideas on that, you can be sure. Divorce is not out of the question. If it comes to it, we can order Kumar to do it."

Anjeli lay silent as a ghost on her bed. She started to weep, restraining her sobs so she could not be heard. She would have to tell Kumar about this conversation. It was more than her life was worth to continue living with these horrible people. Was it possible that Kumar would listen to his parents and divorce her? She could not bear to think about it. Her life would be ruined. Anjeli only hoped that she and Kumar would not have a child until these awful people left her alone. She honestly felt she could kill them for ruining her married life.

I will not stay another moment in this apartment until Kumar comes home, Anjeli decided. She rose from her bed and went into the living room to get her coat. Even if she had to walk the streets in the cold and mist that was turning into a hard rain, she would go. But before she could put on her coat, the Kapoor's bedroom door opened, and Mrs. Kapoor came storming out. "Here you are, Anjeli. Home so late? What excuse now? And going out again! Please make us some tea. And some snacks—not that sweet stuff you gave Mr. Kapoor last time. You know he has this diabetes and cannot take all that sugar."

Anjeli removed her coat and did as she was told. After putting the tea things on the table, she sat down opposite her mother-in-law. "Why do you treat me like this, Mummyji? What have I done wrong that you try to make my life so miserable?"

"You miserable? And what about my son?" Mrs. Kapoor shot back. "You are ruining his life. How hard he works for you, and you give nothing in return. What Indian husband helps so much in the kitchen as my son, Kumar? Your parents never gave the proper gifts suitable to this marriage . . ."

Anjeli would not let her mother-in-law continue. "My parents," she defended them, "gave beautiful wedding saris, all gold embroidered, and many items of jewelry. And where are these things? You took them away, 'to keep them safe,' you said. But you have kept them back in India . . ."

Mrs. Kapoor cut Anjeli off in turn. "Safe, safe, whatever small amount of things they gave. Much they promised but gave only little. My friend in India whose son just got married received a car and a house full of furniture from the bride's family. And the girl was beautiful also. It was our foolishness to let Kumar be swayed by your beauty from the obligations to his family. You have no respect for us, his parents. You disobey me on the simplest things. Always running off to work or some other excuse to leave the house. Spending time with that loose girl Gita from next door. What a bad influence, corrupt, boys coming in at all hours, smoking even on the street when she thinks no one is watching. Don't think we don't see it.

"Kumar works like a dog just to keep you in saris and shalwar-kameez. You eat up all the money he makes. He wants to go into his own business—where will he find the money for that if you do not save on his behalf?"

"That is not fair! I also work hard. I took this job so I could help Kumar save."

"You took this job so you could meet men, have a life for yourself outside marriage," Mr. Kapoor, joining them, cut in aggressively. "I know America. I know how women here treat their husbands, running all over the place, bossing them around, being so independent." In spite of his bluster, Mr. Kapoor was, however, a little bit frightened. He did not really think that Anjeli would tell Kumar about what he now thought of as "the incident"; still less did he think she would go to the police. But . . . he couldn't be sure. It would be such a disgrace to the family if he were ever jailed, even if only for a night and even on such baseless charges. *What to do?*

Here Mrs. Kapoor interrupted his thoughts, saying to Anjeli in a scornful voice, "Because of your beauty, you think you can do anything. You cannot do anything. I will speak with Kumar and have him take you in hand and show you your place. And if he will not, then I will. You will find out, Anjeli, that I am someone to be reckoned with."

Soon after this encounter, Mrs. Kapoor was at home alone, deep in thought about the best plan of action to get Anjeli out of the way so that Kumar could marry again. *What fools we were to accept her*, she berated herself. *Who is the best person to see about taking steps?* Mr. Kapoor's older brother Suresh would not be suitable. At dinner he had shown himself too friendly to that Julie person and to Anjeli herself. And while he might understand their need for money, she didn't think he would be sympathetic to their plight. No, the best person would be Sukhdev Kohli. As a junior relative from her mother's side, he must defer to her and accept whatever obligation she placed on him, no matter how burdensome. He also owed them heavily for all the help Mr. Kapoor's brother Suresh had given him when he first came to America.

Now he is successful, Mrs. Kapoor mused, and innocent though he may be of the charges in this recent police case, he obviously had connections that could be useful to her in some way. At the very least he might have some good advice about what she might do about Anjeli, advice requested and given in the most indirect way, of course. He would know about divorce laws in America, how much they could expect to get if that were an option—or even about other things . . . things she would not even admit clearly to herself.

She would tread carefully with Kohli, get a feeling for his capabilities— She would call him right now and make an appointment to see him. She could always tell Mr. Kapoor she was attending her Sat Sang.

Sukhdev Kohli ushered Mrs. Kapoor into his office in the back of one of his exclusive sari shops, telling the manager not to disturb him under any circumstances. After bowing to touch Mrs. Kapoor's feet in defer-ence, he sat down in one corner of a little sofa facing an Indian inlaid coffee table and beckoned Mrs. Kapoor to the chair opposite. He started to offer some chai and snacks, but she waved the offer away, saying, "No, no, I have come on some important business, to ask your advice, and I don't have so much time."

"Whatever you need, Auntiji. Please ask away. I am your humble servant."

"I will not beat around the bush, as they say in America, Mr. Kohli. I have come to you to help solve a family problem. We made a big mistake permitting our Kumar to marry Anjeli. He was entranced by her looks— everyone is, even my husband! Her parent's finances were already going downhill, and whatever they spent on the wedding—you were there, you know how expensive those things are—must have come close to leaving them almost penniless, with hardly anything left for the dowry. At the time Kumar persuaded us to go along with his choice. He had to return soon to his job in the States, so there was no time to back out of the ar-rangements and find someone else. Now we are here, and things have gone from bad to worse. Kumar's job is at stake with this big downturn in the American banking system, and Mr. Kapoor received very little from his

business, which was almost bankrupt when he retired. We were depending on Kumar's income to invest in some business. Our plan is to look for
a husband for Lakshmi here. But even these American-settled boys make
demands. So, what to do? I ask your advice. Is divorce a solution?"

"Well, I wouldn't count on that. True, what they call *no-fault divorce*
is easy to get here, but American divorce laws usually favor the woman.
In this state, perhaps even division of the property. But if there isn't
much property, even without a child, the man would probably have to
provide some kind of support to his wife, if only for a couple of years,
maybe pay her tuition at some school so she could train for a job. And
Anjeli could argue that—theoretically, you understand—any gifts given
to her by her parents at marriage were for *her*, and a judge might easily
agree that your family would have no right to them. This dowry thing
is complicated; even the experts are not sure to whom it belongs. But
if Anjeli got a lawyer—these women's groups like Badi Bahen provide
them free—they would probably hire some Indian culture expert to say
the dowry belongs to the girl. I understand there are not many of the
dowry items here, but still . . . And paying a divorce lawyer itself costs
money, lots of money. Is there any life insurance. That is something you
might want to find out about. And of course there are no children yet,
I hope. That makes it easier. Do you think Anjeli would want to stay
here if she were divorced? You know in India she would have much less
chance to remarry and have a life there."

"How is that our concern? And what means would Anjeli have to stay
here if Kumar divorces her? She only has some small part-time employment that could hardly maintain her in such an expensive city as New
York. So let her go back to her parents and see if they will take her in.
Or that sister of hers—they are supposed to be so close—but she has her
own brats and husband to take care of."

"Yes, but these women's groups often provide support for the wife
to remain here because they know of different agencies that can help.
I am only trying to tell you a divorce could be quite costly for Kumar.

And also, I am talking of no-fault divorce here, which means both parties accept equal responsibility and agree mutually. Would Anjeli agree to that? Or even would Kumar agree?" Now Kohli paused to give Mrs. Kapoor some time to think over what he had said.

When she kept silent, he continued. "If, however, you could catch Anjeli in some wrongdoing, like an infidelity, then she might be more willing to accept a divorce on your terms regarding financial arrangements."

"That's an interesting idea, Mr. Kohli. Anjeli works for some professor at a university in Manhattan. He sometimes calls and asks her to stay late in the evening and that he will drive her home. I can't say we have proof of anything—yet!—but that could be the case we are looking for."

"Then let me start with this for now: You ring me the next time this professor offers to take Anjeli home late at night. Just leave me the date, time, and place. I will take care of the rest . . . But you must bring me a photo first, to make sure we have the correct girl.

"Don't wait too long on this thing, Auntiji. Such problems are best resolved quickly. And if a divorce will not work . . . there are other ways, unfortunately more costly, but very certain of the desired result. I have experienced men whom I can employ for such work . . . There would be not need for you to worry, just a phone message of a date and time when your daughter-in-law will be alone in your apartment . . ."

"I understand perfectly. First I will accept your effort to get evidence that Anjeli is having an affair."

ꕥ Chapter Twenty-Five

"I hope Anjeli will restock this Darjeeling while she's out shopping; here's the last of it," Mrs. Kapoor told her husband as they sat down for tea and snacks at the kitchen table. Suddenly the phone rang, but neither one picked it up. Soon a message came on: "Hello, Anjeli, It's Phil. We're on for the wine and cheese after the conference Friday night. We'll leave afterward promptly at 8:30 so you won't be home too late. I'll drive you, not to worry. Thanks."

His tea finished, Mr. Kapoor went to rest in their bedroom. Mrs. Kapoor immediately went to the phone. "Kapoor here. Friday night, 8:30. The professor and our daughter-in-law will exit the NUNY main entrance. The driver must compare the photo. We don't want time wasted on wrong information."

"See, Anjeli, I'm as good as my word—8:30 on the button. Come on, my car is just down the hill." Professor Fleagle ushered Anjeli into the car with a mock bow. "Beauty before age," he said. At her puzzled look, he explained "A little joke. It is the reverse of our English proverb 'age before beauty.'"

"Oh, I can understand that," Anjeli said, settling down in the seat. "We think the same in my culture."

Before buckling up, Anjeli gave Professor Fleagle one more chance to avoid the long drive to her home in Queens. "You are very kind to drive me, but it is not really necessary. The grant pays for late night transportation. I could take a taxi; see there is one right there at the end of the street . . ."

"No, my dear, I wouldn't hear of it. There's no traffic now. We will make good time. We can dissect the conference on the way. I value your opinion." Fleagle stretched his arm along the seat back, his fingertips brushing Anjeli's shoulder. "You did a fine job tonight. Everything ran like clockwork. And the buffet table looked beautiful. Your exquisite taste, I'm sure. I suspect you have a lot of untapped skills." Unaccountably to Anjeli, he turned his head toward her and winked. "You know," he continued, "you should be thinking of taking some courses while you're working here. We could set you up for a master's degree in a year, year and a half tops. That's if you don't decide to have a baby and ruin that lovely figure of yours. You could start this summer with my Eastern philosophy course. You'd have an edge on the other students, and I'm sure you'd get a top grade." He turned to smile at her.

"Thank you, professor. I will think about it," Anjeli replied politely.

As Fleagle removed his arm from the seat back to make a sharp turn into a street that would lead to a short cut to Queens, he glanced into his rearview mirror and frowned at a cab on his tail making the same turn. Although the roof light was off, signaling a passenger inside, the cab's back seat appeared empty. The driver—he looked like a Pakistani or Indian—*So what else is new?* Fleagle thought—seemed to be peering intently at Fleagle's vehicle rather than looking at the road ahead. The professor slowed down to let the taxi pass him, but the driver remained behind, close on his rear. *What the hell is all this about?* Fleagle wondered. *Is this bastard following me or what? Uh oh, or is it Anjeli that he's following?* Fleagle stepped on the gas and didn't speak to Anjeli again until he reached her neighborhood and needed specific directions to her house. When he stopped the car in front of her building, he got out and went around to the passenger side. Thanking her again for her contribution to the conference, he returned to his car and drove off.

Anjeli consulted her watch and was glad to see it wasn't even 9:30 yet. *Imagine,* she thought, smiling to herself, *on a Friday night at this time back home I'd just be leaving some film with my friends, and we'd be on our way for ice cream and a long conversation about the film.* She looked up at her lit window and saw Kumar waving down to her, his mother standing beside him. She waved back, hoping they had seen Professor Fleagle on the sidewalk. They would see he was just some ordinary middle-aged man, nobody for her handsome husband to worry about. Maybe that would stop their nagging about her job. Altogether, Anjeli felt pleased about the evening as she walked into the lobby.

Suddenly a figure jumped out of the darkened hallway at her, startling her into bumping back against the lobby door she had just closed. "Hey, pretty lady," whispered Tommy Moran, stretching out his arms to pin her to the door. "Don't you know you shouldn't be coming home after dark by yourself? You could get in trouble that way. Me and Bubba can protect you. Just say the word." *Bubba?* Anjeli bit her lip nervously. *Was that his dog? That horrible animal with all the teeth? Is this man drunk?* Anjeli wondered, though she could not smell any alcohol on his breath. *Maybe on drugs?* His words seemed slurred. But how could she judge such a thing? And what should she do?

"I know hubby and the old folks are home, so we can't have any fun right now," Tommy went on, leering at her frightened face. "But some day we'll have the place to ourselves, and then I can show you a real good time. Um, you don't need to give me your key . . . I have my own little tricks. Later, baby." Abruptly he removed his arms from the door, turned, and walked up the staircase.

Anjeli pressed one hand over her thumping heart and pushed the elevator call button hard several times, trying to catch her breath. When the door opened, Kumar was there, frowning. "What the hell took you so long to come upstairs, Anjeli?" he asked, pulling her in by the arm.

"Nothing, Kumar," she replied. "Some people must have been holding the elevator door open, and it took a long time to reach the lobby."

The next day, in the empty apartment, Kumar's mother sat heavily on her bed. She dredged up all her resentments against Anjeli that had been gathering like dark clouds since Kumar had deprived her of all she deserved by insisting on marrying this wretched girl so quickly. *No wealth, no business, such a simple place they lived in—no proper furnishing. All this we suspected at the bridal viewing. What was the need to rush? And such a disobedient girl. No respect at all. These goings-on with this professor. And now this disgraceful enticement of Mr. Kapoor. The temptress! And threatening to call the police on him. What shame on our family reputation! This nightmare must be ended. Divorce might not be sufficient.*

Chapter Twenty-Six

Anjeli dragged herself out of bed, relieved that Kumar had risen early, taken breakfast by himself, and left by the time she came into the kitchen to set up morning tea for her in-laws. She had dressed quietly in her room, carelessly throwing on the same creased shalwar-kameez she'd worn to the office the day before. She clipped her hair severely back and coiled it into a dowdy bun at the back of her neck.

"You're looking very pulled down, Anjeli," Kumar's mother greeted her, adding sarcastically, "Not dressing up for your professor any more?" Anjeli would not dignify Mrs. Kapoor's remark with a reply, but in her heart she felt perhaps there might be a grain of truth to it. Kumar seemed more heavily burdened with money worries each day, and she knew that her additional income was in fact no longer just useful for extras but almost a necessity. In some indefinable way she could not articulate, she felt that she *was* using her comeliness—and her willingness to take on extra tasks for Professor Fleagle with which she was not

216

wholly comfortable—to retain her job. She wished she could be breezy about declining to work late hours the way Kimmy was. When the professor had asked her officemate to stay late for the conference, Kimmy had winked at him brazenly and said "All work and no play makes Kimmy a dull girl, professor," and he had merely smirked, almost in complicity, Anjeli thought.

Anjeli's wariness must have been evident to Professor Fleagle, too. As he was setting out their schedule, he interrupted himself to solicitously wrap an arm around her shoulder and "command" her to sit down and partake of his breakfast danish and coffee before beginning work. "Is something wrong at home, Anjeli?" he asked with concern. "I know an extended family household is not easy to handle. Very little of the private time a new bride needs with her husband, eh? I have a little knowledge of how young Asian women have to juggle family and intimacy issues, the kitchen and the bedroom as it were, eh?"

Baap re, Anjeli thought. *This is not the road I want to go down.* Professor Fleagle's arm felt heavy on her shoulder, and the horrible thought struck her: *What if Kumar's mother has some magical TV set that could see me here, as my kindergarten teacher had told us she could if we didn't do our homework? Only five years old then, and I can still recall my fear!*

"Is it some legal matter, Anjeli, a visa problem? Perhaps I can help. I'm well connected with the immigration people. I've helped a lot of my Asian assistants with their immigration status, divorce proceedings, that sort of thing."

"No, no Professor Fleagle. Thank you anyway, but it's nothing like that. Professor Norman is my friend, and she would be happy to help if anything like that came up. I would never impose on you for such a thing."

"Now, Anjeli, I know how much you admire Professor Norman, but I wouldn't depend on her help. American women are so busy, busy, especially when they're climbing the career ladder . . ."

"It's kind of you to be concerned, professor, "Anjeli replied, "but I don't want to take up your time with such things. We should get to that PowerPoint presentation you need for next week."

"Just remember you can come to me any time, my dear." He gave her shoulder a squeeze. "Alright, let's get started as you say. I have a set of those slides of God and Jiva standing in mutual exposure to illustrate the tripartite Tantric philosophy of sexuality serving three purposes: procreation, pleasure, and spiritual liberation. Please choose two slides for each heading; each will be on for thirty seconds as I discuss them, and when we've made the selection we'll work on integrating my text with the images."

An hour into her task, Anjeli's stomach was churning with a mixture of emotions. Professor Fleagle had assigned the slide review in such an ordinary way that she'd never expected to see such an array of explicitly sexual visuals. One of them she recognized as similar to a stylized icon on one of the professor's cards—he had a variety of them apparently designed for different audiences—and the thought prompted her to steal over to his desk and filch one from his top drawer. *I need Julie to guide me,* Anjeli realized. Despite her college degree and her excellent English grades, Anjeli lamented to herself that she was so unacquainted with American codes of conduct that she had no means of determining what was right behavior for anyone, including herself. Involuntarily almost laughing, she thought of how Kimmy or Gita would love to be a consultant about her dilemma—*"What exactly did Fleagle say, Anjeli? Describe the pictures in the slides. Ooh, hot, hot, hot."* No, no, Anjeli sobered up, *only with Julie would she feel comfortable enough to even mention her problem.*

Julie picked up her office phone on the first ring and tucked it into her neck while she continued making notes. When she heard Anjeli's voice, sounding hesitant yet distressed, she put down her pen and held the receiver more closely to her ear. "Is everything alright, Anjeli?" Julie asked.

"Julie, I know how busy you are, but would you be able to see me for just a little bit today?"

"Of course! As long as you'd like. Come over at your lunch hour; we can meet in the faculty cafeteria or here if you prefer."

"No, no, not the cafeteria, Julie. Your office . . . I will come at noon."

Julie's office door was open when Anjeli arrived, but she closed it quickly behind her.

"I am not used to American ways. I know that," Anjeli began even before she took the chair Julie offered her. "I want to show you something." She fished Professor Fleagle's card out of her purse and pushed it across the desk to her. "What do you see, Julie?" she asked, not sure what she hoped Julie would say—that she was overreacting and should get on with her job or that she was correct to be disturbed and must take some action.

"Hmm," Julie began, picking her way across what she could see was a minefield. Not only did she recognize the icon as an artful drawing of a couple entwined in each others' bodies, but the Web site listed—tantra*phil*iac.com—was not only a nod to the site's author, Phil Fleagle, but also to the content of his Web page. As Julie gathered her thoughts, Anjeli sped forward in an uncharacteristic way. "You see, this Tantric philosophy—that is part of his field. I know that it is ancient Hindu literature about sex . . . I'm not sure exactly, but I *do* know that never, even in college, would we students look upon such images as he assigned me today. Others like this, but more, how do you say, so you can see everything that men and women are doing with each other. Maybe he thinks because I am a married woman that there's nothing bad about my seeing such things. Other professors, even some students, will come to his lectures where he shows such pictures, but imagine mummy or daddy knowing of this work I do . . ."

Julie noted Anjeli's lapse into Indian phrasing as a measure of her unconscious retreat to a more culturally familiar world. She could see tears forming in Anjeli's eyes and came around the desk to hug her.

"I don't want to make too much of something, Julie," Anjeli continued tearfully. "Professor Fleagle is the same with everyone. No one seems to take offense. Once when Kimmy came in late, I thought he would be angry with her, but he only said, 'Big night out—I mean in—with the boyfriend?' And Kimmy just made a little cute face and shrugged her shoulders. And I heard her tell another new assistant that Professor Fleagle is 'a really good guy. Not uptight like some of the profs.' Julie, I can interpret that word *uptight*, that's probably what I am considered. If the professor sometimes puts his hand or arm on me when he talks, even though I know it is the American way, to make better communication with someone, yet I do not like it. Or maybe it is seeing American culture through the eyes of Kumar and his parents. They are very uptight! No, Julie?" Anjeli and Julie both smiled at her brave quip.

"And he is very nice to me, always having coffee breaks and asking if I need help with legal problems or personal things at home. He gives me extra hours to work and drives me home if it is late." Here Julie raised her eyebrows a little, and Anjeli noted the implication of doubt. "Maybe, Julie, I should overlook some things. Or should I try to make my own feelings known to him? But I do need this job. Kumar is having more difficulties, and his parents being there costs us so much more money."

"Anjeli," Julie said firmly, "you are not overreacting, at least not from your cultural perspective, which I think Professor Fleagle should understand with his expertise in Eastern cultures. Scholars at his lectures viewing the graphic pictures you describe may not blink at them, but you are not a Western scholar of philosophy. If he is as kind as you say, I think you should inform him of your discomfort and ask him to assign such tasks to other persons who would not feel as you do. But let's not rock the boat just yet; wait until we've located the life jackets, okay? First I want to talk to a colleague who knows Professor Fleagle better than I do. I'll check out some things and get back to you soon. Here at the office, not at home," Julie added seeing a look of near panic fleetingly cross Anjeli's face. "Try to hang in 'til then without acting any differently . . ."

"I will do that, Julie. I will do nothing until I hear from you. And thank you so much. You are like my mother and aunty and big sister all in one here. I have no one else."

"This is a good time," Julie's close friend Jill Lockwood told her. "I'll be right over." Jill was as good as her word. She was Julie's best friend at work, and they had become personally close as well. Jill had been at NUNY longer than Julie, and her involvement in college governance gave her an ear to the ground and a knowledge of where the bodies were buried—something Julie had deliberately avoided. Julie briefly described Anjeli's dilemma about Professor Fleagle and continued, "I don't know this Fleagle at all. I only got the job notice from the bulletin board; now I'm beginning to think I should have checked him out more carefully. Some of the things Anjeli told me may be only a matter of culturally different styles, but other things do seem inappropriate. What do you know about this guy?"

"I haven't had that much to do with him myself," Jill began cautiously, "but I can tell you about something that happened between him and a student of mine—no names obviously—that may be relevant. Fleagle might argue this is just undocumented gossip, but you know that's not my style, and you can make up your own mind. I will say that if I'd known you were sending a lovely young Indian woman over there, I might have given you some warning.

"A couple of years ago I had an excellent student of Indian-Fijian descent. Her great-grandparents were sugar-cane workers brought to Fiji by the British, and her family included several generations of labor-union activists with both her mother and grandmother as feminists ahead of their time. She was a little older than our traditional students, and with our common political interests we became quite friendly. She needed money and applied for a part-time job on Fleagle's grant—funny how all his grants have room for part-time assistants—perfect openings for a female foreign student. Since I did know Fleagle from a curriculum committee, I put in a good word for her, and she got the job.

"When I went to his office I was really impressed by the diversity of his college work-study assistants. Really, Julie, it was like one of those Benetton ads—every size and shape and color of young women: Asian, Hispanic, black, white—it was such a gorgeous mosaic, some of the students in native garb. It seemed like an ideal setting. Only, later, did it strike me that I never saw any young men working for him . . .

"Well, after a couple of months I asked her how things were going. She expressed her gratitude to me, but I noticed she seemed hesitant in speaking about Fleagle himself. Finally, I winkled out of her that she thought her boss was somewhat inappropriate in his behavior with her and some of the other, younger, assistants too. 'Too much hands-on,' she said, too many coffee breaks in the office where he sat too close to her, placed his hand on her knee, or spoke of personal subjects she thought were out of bounds. Now, Julie, you're won't believe this, and it wouldn't work for Anjeli, given what you've told me about her, but my student said to him, 'Professor Fleagle, there's an interesting study I just read on sexual harassment that stated that most women students find their professors old, ugly, and weird. My grandmothers struggled against bosses like you in the cane fields a hundred years ago. I want a formal written evaluation of my work from you, and I want to finish out this semester without any more such sexual innuendo, or I know where to go for help.' She told me that Fleagle huffed and puffed—my words, Julie, but you get the picture—and apparently that was the end of it. She's going to law school now. I did give Bobbie Baxter in counseling a heads-up in case any students came to her with a similar complaint, so you might want to check with her."

Good idea, Julie thought. Bobbie could evaluate Anjeli's complaints better than she, and if Anjeli could save her job by getting Fleagle to discontinue the most disturbing aspects of his behavior, that would be best. If not, Bobbie could help them devise a fall-back alternative.

Anjeli was determined to put in as much time as she could on her job until she heard from Julie, so when Professor Fleagle suggested closing up early one afternoon because of a torrential downpour, she couldn't prevent an involuntary frown from crossing her face. "Why, you greedy little child," Fleagle stood close to her and wagged his finger in her face as if talking to a five year old with her hand in the cookie jar. "You don't want to lose a couple of hours pay. Well don't worry, baby, daddy's the one who fills out the time sheets." He took an umbrella from his elephant foot stand—an office decoration Anjeli particularly detested— and as they left the building entrance, he drew Anjeli close to him for the fast walk to his car. "Mm, cozy to be inside in a storm, isn't it?" he shivered suggestively as he tossed the umbrella in the back seat. Anjeli sat close to the passenger side window, well aware that her thin cotton kameez was soaked despite the umbrella and that her bra was showing through. She draped the ends of her dupatta down over her chest as she saw Fleagle glance towards her.

"Anjeli, Anjeli," he intoned, "you seem unhappy lately. Is something wrong at the office? Are the other girls unkind to you for some reason? They could be jealous. You know, even as an 'older married woman'" he used air quotes around the phrase with his nondriving hand—"you have a better figure than most of them." Anjeli kept her face blank and averted. *Gita was right; all men are the same,* she thought more with irritation than anger. *They do not even see how they are the cause of a woman's problems. Always other women are the first they blame—even Kumar. Don't see Gita, don't call Julie, they are teaching you bad ways.* Anjeli nearly sputtered the words aloud, it seemed such a valuable insight.

"You can talk to me, Anjeli, even if it's a marital problem. I told you, I was married once, a long time ago, also to a foreign woman, which, as you know, means being married to a family. In America there are solutions that are not possible in India. You don't have to run home every day to be browbeaten by your husband or his parents."

"Beaten?" Anjeli, only half-listening, turned to Fleagle. "My husband would never beat me. He is very handsome, and he knows I love him, and he loves me. Just that he is young and trying to handle so many problems at once. And with his parents living in our small apartment we have no space to talk things out."

"No, no, *browbeaten.* It means suffering verbal abuse, like when they criticize you all the time. There are legal remedies, like separation. Or divorce. Or you can find other sources of companionship and affection. Do you understand what I'm saying, Anjeli?" Anjeli avoided answering his question by looking out the window, but the heavy rain obscured any landmarks that would indicate how close they were to her house. As a great clap of thunder sounded and wild streaks of lightning zigzagged down from the sky, Professor Fleagle turned onto a short paved pathway that dead-ended at the entrance to a small park.

"I have to stop for a little until the rain lets up. We can talk for a few minutes."

For some reason, maybe because her talk with Julie had given her confidence that she could negotiate the difficulties with Professor Fleagle and keep both her job and her self-respect, Anjeli turned on the seat to face him. She addressed him in what she hoped was a steady, mature voice. "Yes, I am glad we have an opportunity to talk, as there is something I would like to explain to you. I would like to be *candid*, which is a good word and one of your favorites. I was upset the other day because I had to review all those slides of sex . . . sexual . . . sexual positions. I think you are so used to such images that you don't realize some of us are terribly embarrassed by them—more than embarrassed. I don't know the right words. But I am sure you understand me, and perhaps now that you know, I hope you can modify your assignments to me. I want to keep my job with you . . ." Her voice quavered.

"Of course, I understand," Professor Fleagle agreed, moving out from under the steering wheel as he spoke. "In the future I *will* take care with your tasks as you suggest. But just think about it differently for a moment. You and your husband together could watch such images to improve your intimate relations. I have helped many young couples with such advice. They are arousing, yes, but also artistic and religious and spiritual all at once. You see, Anjeli, youth alone is sometimes not such an advantage. Experienced older men such as myself, with special knowledge of how to give women pleasure . . ." Completely missing the appalled look on Anjeli's face, Fleagle leaned toward her, threw her dangling scarf ends backward over her shoulder, and embraced her waist with both hands. "You Indian women have the genes of the goddesses. Let me teach you how to enjoy your body."

Anjeli shook herself as if out of a trance and pushed Fleagle back, pummeling him with her small fists. "How dare you treat me so?!" Anjeli shouted at him. "I will report you, yes, to the college authorities, and you will lose your job."

Fleagle smirked, holding Anjeli off. "You are a very stupid, naïve girl," he chuckled. "Here's an English phrase you don't comprehend: *he said, she said.* You can't *prove* anything to the *authorities*, as you so quaintly call them, but you have proved to me that you are entirely ungrateful. Unlike many of our office team, believe me. Hmm, maybe I should call that handsome husband of yours and tell him how you invited my advances. Bad things can happen to stupid girls who cross me. Think about that."

"My friend Professor Julie will help me," Anjeli shouted at him, breaking one hand free and smacking Fleagle's face. "She already knows about you. Just drive me to the subway station immediately."

"Faster than you can say Jack Robinson," Fleagle yelled back at her, starting up the car and driving a few blocks to a subway station Anjeli didn't even recognize. "And you've just quit your job in case you don't know it." He reached across her and shoved open the door, practically dumping her out onto the rain-soaked street. "You're not to come to my office again. Your back pay will be in the mail." He paused and barked at her disappearing back, "Maybe."

Anjeli did not know where she was, but luckily there was an attendant at the subway station who was able to give her directions to her usual subway stop. When she finally reached home, she was drenched. As she entered the apartment, her clothes dripped water on the floor, and Kumar's mother immediately started berating her. "Why are you so wet? See, you are dripping water all over the floor. If you catch cold, who will do the work around here? You expect me to do it while you rest in bed?"

Anjeli was too upset to reply. As she moved toward her bedroom to change her clothes and dry her hair, Kumar walked in the door. "What the hell is going on here?" he asked.

"One moment, Kumar. Let me get into some dry clothes, and then we can talk over dinner," Anjeli replied dispiritedly.

After changing her clothes, Anjeli tried to calm herself as she prepared dinner. When she had served Kumar and her in-laws, she sat down herself. Turning to Kumar, she said, "I won't be working any more; the grant money that paid my salary ran out."

Kumar's father preempted his son's response, grumbling, "Useless girl. She can't even hold a job."

As the rain didn't seem to be lessening, Julie decided to pack it in and and take her papers home to grade over a take-out dinner. After braving the wet commute home, she dropped her folders on the dining table and listened to her messages, only paying half-attention while she flipped through her take-out menus. At Anjeli's tremulous voice, she put down the stack of restaurant brochures to listen more carefully. "Julie, it's Anjeli. I must be quick. I won't be coming in to the college any more. I will call you . . ."

Sukey—as Soo Kee had Westernized her name—knew she'd stayed out a little later than she should have, but her parents wouldn't be calling her; the timing was wrong And Friday nights up by Columbia there were always some people around, even on the side street where she had her off-campus apartment. After several months of anxiety settling into her new life, she felt safe—and confident about her internship at Columbia's journalism school. Tonight's party, an opening for a new multiculti women's zine, had been really cool. The heavy rain had finally ceased, and the skies had actually cleared later in the evening. She thought she had struck just the right note with her appearance—her long black hair clipped on top but loose to her waist, her new lycra layers covering her down past her butt but not hiding her shape, her long legs encased in stretch jeans—displaying both her femininity and her contemporary chic. She looked carefully behind her before keying open her lobby door—it was an old tenement but actually pretty well-maintained—but as she unlocked her apartment door, she felt someone behind her push her into her foyer, shut the door, and knock her hand from the light switch. "Don't turn around, don't yell, I'm not here to hurt you. I only want us to experience bliss and divine union together. I love you tiny dolls. I know just how to make you like it. Pretend that I'm your boyfriend; I bet you have one mummy doesn't know about, right?" The man thrust her ahead into the darkened studio room and pushed her face down on the futon that served as her bed. "Just pretend it's all a dream," he spoke softly, pulling off her shoes, jeans, and underwear. "It will be a sublime experience of infinite awareness." When he was finished, he warned her not to turn on the lights or call the police. "And, truthfully, wasn't that a remarkable fusion?" he asked rhetorically as he exited the apartment. Shaking with fierce anger, Sukey quietly crept over to her phone, dialed 911, and then crept back to her window, where she cautiously raised her head to peer outside. She saw her rapist clearly as he stood in the streetlight, gazing up at her apartment, an expression of satisfaction washing over his face. He was gone before the police arrived. They gathered her bed covering and clothing as evidence and gently led her to the squad car for the trip to the hospital for the necessary examination.

Chapter Twenty-Seven

As Julie walked into the station house, Mike and a middle-aged Indian man were waiting for her at the entrance. "Good to see you, Julie," Mike greeted her. "This is Rajiv Sharma, the detective I told you about who works the Indian-related crime in our area. Rajiv, this is Julie Norman."

"How nice to meet you," said Julie, shaking Rajiv's outstretched hand. "I really appreciate your giving me this time."

"My pleasure; I'm always interested to talk about my work."

As a couple of detectives exited the station house, one called out to Mike and Rajiv as they passed. "So, is this your anthropologist consultant? She doesn't look anything like the pictures I've seen of Margaret Mead."

"Yup, this is Professor Julie Norman, and she *is* an anthropologist, and she *is* gonna do some consulting right now." He turned to Rajiv and Julie. "Mei Jun is a good Chinese restaurant near here. Sound okay?"

As Julie and Rajiv sat down at a corner table at the restaurant, Mike spoke personally to the owner and ordered for them. "We'll be here for a while, okay, Mr. Chong?"

"As long as you wish, Officer Cardella. It is our pleasure to serve you and your colleagues."

When Mike returned to the table, Julie and Rajiv were already in animated conversation. "Mike probably told you about my interest in immigrant Indian families and particularly in domestic violence. I'm hoping you can give me some background on the issue from a police perspective," Julie was saying.

"Domestic violence within the South Asian immigrant community is a very neglected problem," Rajiv responded. "Our own information about it is mostly anecdotal. The abuse that leads up to it comes in bits and pieces through complaints that later don't go anywhere. The wife's family and friends usually persuade her that sending her husband to jail overnight will only make things worse. The abuse reports from the hospitals generally have the same results. Of course, with a death, we investigate and make our own report. But it's hard to get in-depth information about domestic violence; I'm sure you know that the Indian community doesn't want this problem aired in public. It is hard to investigate these incidents properly when people are so secretive about their family life. It's even hard to know exactly how widespread the problem of domestic violence is. The South Asian women's groups say maybe 20 to 25 percent of families; that's a lot lower than the American rate, but it still adds up to a lot of suffering. If more people would report it, we could get a better handle on the statistics and maybe what to do about it."

"Yes," Julie agreed, "I do know the difficulties. I always explain to my students that the sense of shame that attaches to family problems in Indian culture is largely absent in America. When caught in some sexual indiscretion, our politicians say 'sorry' and apologize, their wives always 'stand by their man,' and it's on to the next scandal."

"Yup," Mike interjected, his eyes dancing with mischief. "Remember last year the police in some western state caught a married senator soliciting in a men's restroom at the airport. Even with all the publicity, he didn't give up his wife; he didn't even give up his seat—not the toilet seat—the one in the Senate."

Julie and Rajiv smiled broadly, then Julie continued more seriously. "I see the Indian extended-family system as one of the most crucial cultural factors impacting the incidence and response to domestic violence. Two or even three generations living together, that's almost nonexistent in America, so it doesn't crop up in our domestic assaults very often. But in the Indian diaspora, I think it's an important factor. Do you remember, Rajiv, that recent case in Canada where a doctor killed her husband? She was so angry that he didn't stand up for her when she challenged his parents' attempts to control her life that she knifed him in the neck during one of their arguments. She pleaded self-defense, claiming she was struggling to wrest the weapon away from him and killed him accidentally."

"I do remember that case," Rajiv responded. "The prosecution decided to go for manslaughter, but even then couldn't do better than a hung jury, and the judge freed her. Looked to me like death by extended family. And this wife was educated; she had options; she could have just left him. Not like a lot of the immigrant women we deal with, who don't have many skills and sometimes don't speak very good English. What are they going do if they don't like the family situation?

"And so often in the immigrant community it's more likely that the husband rather than the wife will have family and friends here," Rajiv continued. "So if the husband wants a divorce to marry another woman, or his parents want to free him for a better match the second time around, what can the wife do? His side is Johnny-on-the-spot, and *her* family and friends are an ocean away. She's cut off here, isolated, no viable options in sight. And, as you must know, Julie, even if she asked her family in India for help, what could they do? They'd probably just advise her to stay in the marriage and make the best of it, especially if there's kids." Rajiv grimaced, shaking his head. "And the violence can easily lead to a killing. Divorce by itself might not be enough for the husband and his parents. An American court might award the dowry back to the wife, or some women's group might help the wife stay on her own and get custody of the kids—absolutely unacceptable to the husband's side. So some of these guys—or their parents—look for the better mousetrap called murder. Those are the cases we get. Unfortunately, sometimes, before the husband or his parents can do her themselves, the wives, who are truly suffering emotional anguish, beat them to the punch by killing their husbands themselves, and maybe even their kids.

"It's very tough on the women," the Indian detective concluded, "but, you know, the men don't always have it easy either. The conflict between a man's obligations to his wife and his obligations to his family is a very intense situation; it can tear even the best husbands in two. And then you can add to that the genuine stress some of these guys are under—money problems, some of them are heavy into gambling or drinking, or maybe there's some secret sex life that they don't want to give up."

Mike shook his head sadly. "This stuff is so hard for me—speaking as a typical American I guess—to understand, the idea that a woman's folks wouldn't stand up for her, that she wouldn't have support from them. Americans say 'home is the place where when you go there, they have to take you in.' That means your parents' home. Only the worst families in America would lock out a divorced son or daughter if they needed some space to get their life together, especially if there's grand-children involved."

"That *is* a significant cultural difference," Julie assented, nodding, "compounded by the geographical distance between a woman and her family. It's what leaves immigrant women particularly vulnerable. Even if a woman's family in India might be supportive, being so far away really complicates things. Unfortunately I'm familiar with this situation firsthand." Here Julie paraphrased her conversation with Anjeli's mother about how Julie would be the only person on her daughter's side in the States. She also summarized her observations from the family dinner—how scornfully Anjeli's in-laws treated her.

"Unfortunately," Julie added, "although Anjeli's parents *had* investigated her husband's family in India as well as their resources in the time allowed, they had no resources in New York to check out the husband's employment situation. They had to put their trust in what his parents told them. It turned out that they exaggerated the level and security of his position, and his salary was not what they had indicated. A professional investigator might have dug more deeply. Today, with Indian families so dispersed across India and even on other continents, it's hard for parents to learn all about each other as they did in the past. So a lot of parents, especially of the girls, are hiring a private investigator before they settle the marriage. I think it's an excellent idea, especially if the boy has lived in America for a while—check out whether maybe he's already got a wife or a girlfriend here and also, if his parents are going to live with the couple, what the backstairs gossip is on them." *Like I wish Anjeli's parents had done,* Julie thought.

"Hey, that's a great idea for our retirement, Rajiv," Mike teased his partner. "Maybe we could set up as private investigators together, 'arranged marriages our speciality.'"

Julie, thinking in dismay of Anjeli, scolded him with a look.

"These contrasts between Indian and American culture are very useful to think about," Rajiv said, shaking his head side to side in agreement in the Indian manner. "More of our colleagues should learn these things. It is not just academic; this knowledge can help us in our work."

"Absolutely," Mike concurred. "I've made enough wrongheaded judgments in cases because I was ignorant of the cultural factors at play. It's like walking into a minefield . . . like our invasion of Iraq."

"That's a great image," said Julie, "and some folks in the Pentagon finally got the same idea. They've hired a few anthropologists to introduce our officers and troops to Iraqi culture."

"There's another dimension of the in-law thing that I'm thinking about as we talk." Rajiv spoke hesitantly, as if he were organizing his thoughts. "In our Indian culture it is the husbands' parents who in some ways have the largest stake in their sons' marriages. As you know, Julie, traditional Hindus take an almost *religious* view about the *bloodlines* descending to the next generations. Very unlike America, eh, where couples are adopting children from here, there, and everywhere. It would be very hard to imagine an American homicide where a father killed his daughter because he thought she polluted his family bloodlines. But I recall several such tragedies in our Indian immigrant communities. One, in Chicago, I think, an Indian girl married a lower-caste Indian man she had met at work. Her father, who lived nearby, felt completely disrespected by this 'pollution.' So one day he carried a full gasoline can in plain sight to his daughter's house, showered the house with it, and set the whole place on fire, killing his daughter and his grandchild. He confessed to the police as if he thought they would sympathize with him. He didn't understand that things that might carry weight in India, like caste, have no bearing here at all. Even with an anthropologist's expert testimony, this 'cultural defense' failed."

"There was another similar case, in Texas, I think," Julie noted disconsolately, "but it was a black man the Indian girl had married. So the father, on a visit from India, also sets the couple's home on fire, killing the whole family, including a grandchild, with whom he obviously felt no ties at all."

"And it's not only the male parents involved in these lethal cases," Rajiv offered. "Recently in England, a mother-in-law, an elderly woman with many grandchildren, wanted her son to get out of his present marriage so she could arrange a 'better' one for him. But she also wanted to make sure the children stayed with him. So she concocted a story that her daughter-in-law was having an affair with some guy at work and hired a gunman to kill the poor girl. It goes on and on. I hope, Julie," Rajiv's face expressed concern, "that these stories will not make you think badly of our community; I am recalling them only to find their patterns, as you say. In police work, also, we always seek the patterns. Isn't it so, Mike? Sadly, while my files are endless, they are not usefully organized or indexed."

Only Mike's chopsticks were still actively dredging up the remains from his rice bowl, but no one was ready to leave. Julie grabbed the check when it came, asserting, "This one's on me, guys. My grant pays for informants' time. In fact, it's an ethical commandment of the Anthropology Association.

"Many thanks," Mike and Rajiv assented together.

"Grandmothers, grandfathers, this is incredible," Mike contended in response to Rajiv's stories. "Here, a woman is murdered, the first person the cops look at is the husband, or boyfriend, or significant other, whatever they call them these days. But the grandparent generation . . ." he paused, shaking his head. "that sounds so weird to me—and my father's Sicilian. It's hard to imagine any of my dad's relatives killing their own children or grandchildren . . . I mean unless they had a really bad case of Sicilian Alzheimer's . . ."

Julie looked inquiringly at Mike. "Sicilian Alzheimers, I'm not familiar with that . . ."

Mike practically choked on the food he was shoveling into his mouth with suppressed laughter. "Sicilian Alzheimer's is when you forget everything but the grudges," he said, breaking into uncontrollable guffaws that splattered some of his rice around.

Julie joined in his laughter but then added seriously, "But the joke isn't entirely off base here. Domestic violence, like mental illness—*real* mental illness," she cocked her head toward Mike, who snickered back, "not only occurs in every society, but it does seem to follow cultural patterns in the methods and the motives, perhaps. Ultimately, though, I've come to believe its primary dynamic is male dominance and power. Of course, certain male profiles feed off this power more than others: the outsized ego who thinks the law doesn't apply to him because he was the high school football hero or mother's little darling, or, conversely, because he's making up for early feelings of inadequacy by dominating and abusing women later on. And alcohol and poverty play a role, too, in many cases."

"I'd agree, Julie," said Mike. "In most of the domestic violence I've seen, not the immigrant cases, I mean, where it's usually the husband or boyfriend killing the wife or girlfriend—though the reverse happens sometimes too—the motive is frequently the guy's new flame and maybe a pile of life insurance that fuels the fire, so to speak." He paused thoughtfully and added, "Actually fire seems to play less of a role in American cases than in Indian ones."

"What do you think, Rajiv?" Julie asked. "Does American domestic violence have a different pattern of methods and motives from Indian

ones, which often involve issues of caste or dowry, and often collabora-
tion with the in-laws? It seems to me that cultural differences *do* play a
role here."

"Interesting question, Julie. I'd have to think about it. You know,
maybe you should look through my files some time; you might see
something in them. But I'm with the women's groups all the way on
this. The more we educate people about domestic violence, even if they
don't like to hear about it, the more we have a shot at preventing it. Or
at least, helping the victims. And things *have* changed. Once, some years
ago, a representative from one of the women's groups tried to talk to
our precinct captain about it, and I think he gave her all of seven minutes. That wouldn't happen today."

"I should hope not," Julie said indignantly. "And I do see some kind
of a joint effort here, Rajiv. Your police expertise and files, and your
being Indian, would give a lot of weight to my anthropology research.
Maybe you could even speak to one of my classes sometime. Here's my
number; give me a call, and we'll arrange a convenient date."

"Okay, professors," said Mike, "time to see our futures in our fortune
cookies. Rajiv, you first."

Opening his cookie, Rajiv announced with surprise, "Hmm, there
might be something to these things. I quote: 'A man with two friends
always has a teacher. One friend teaches him right conduct to follow, the
other, wrong conduct to avoid.' What's yours, Mike?"

"Domestic felicity is in your future." Mike blushed as Rajiv winked
at him. "Domestic felicity? After our conversation I'm not sure there is
such a thing. Okay, Julie, your turn."

Julie flourished her slip as she announced theatrically, "I just took
over that PI firm for arranged marriages, guys. It says 'Man is the head,
but woman is the neck that moves the head as it wants.'" And in a sudden, fluid motion, she steepled her hands together in the air and moved
her head side to side in the measured rhythm of an Eastern dancer.

"A perfect *apsara*," Rajiv murmured appreciatively. Mike just stared
in admiration.

Chapter Twenty-Eight

With a frown of annoyance at the doorbell, Anjeli turned the burner to low and walked to the door, keeping the chain on as she opened it. Before her a neatly dressed man held out a plastic photo ID card draped over his checked shirt and tie. "I am from TRN Cable Company, madam. There is some trouble with the cable lines in these apartments. I must check the connections. It will be a few minutes only. Otherwise you may have interruption in your television reception."

Kumar would be furious at that. Anjeli pictured him and his father on the couch with their drinks, angrily working the remote to recapture a disappeared screen of half-naked girls and the loud fake laughter that screeched all the way back to the kitchen. Anjeli undid the chain and let the cable man enter. "Do what you must; I will be in the kitchen. I have something on the stove."

No excuse for burning the Kapoor's food now, she thought miserably, *with no job to go to. But that did not mean they can make me their maid. I will compel Kumar to stand up for her in the bitter battles his parents started and will confront him over the control of my dowry pieces once and for all. I will call Julie from a pay phone as soon as I can, and Julie will guide me to outside help, women's organizations, even lawyers. I knew my worth now; I will find another job.*

As Anjeli bent over the stove, the man moved swiftly behind her. Before she could even utter a cry, he seized her neck in his two hands, squeezing the life out of her. He disdainfully let her body fall to the floor. *Too bad fire was not an option; it was so useful in putting an end to difficulties.* Quickly he drew on a pair of latex gloves and moved from one bedroom to the other, pulling out dresser drawers and scattering their contents, and yanking clothes from the closets. Not a scrap of jewelry worth taking for himself, just cheap plastic bangles and ordinary saris. "Pah!" Returning to the kitchen he bent down and yanked the chain from Anjeli's neck and ripped off her gold earrings from her ears. *A little something for my trouble,* he thought. He looked through the peephole in the door to scan the hallway and left as invisibly as he'd arrived.

When Gita came back from running a few small errands, she saw Anjeli's witchy in-laws walking to the subway. Mr. Kapoor was dragging the wheelie he used for their Jackson Heights shopping, and Mrs. Kapoor was dressed a little better than usual, probably going to her Sat Sang. Now that Anjeli wasn't working anymore, she'd probably be home cooking and cleaning, and Gita decided she'd drag her over for a tea break, just for an hour anyway. As she exited the elevator, she smelled something burning in the hallway. At first she thought it was probably old Mr. Delaney dropping his lit cigarettes in his garbage bag again. She'd told him off about it a million times, but he never paid attention. *He's one his son ought to put in an old folks home already.* Gita looked in the incinerator room. No smoke there. *Hmm.* She bit her lip anxiously; the burnt smell seemed to be coming from Anjeli's apartment. Maybe she was getting a head start cooking dinner for the Kapoors. *And maybe burning it . . . accidentally . . . on purpose. Who could blame her?*

Gita rang the bell and knocked loudly on Anjeli's door several times, calling her name. No answer, which worried her—you could hear the doorbell from anywhere in these matchbox apartments. She waited a bit and rang and knocked again, then took Anjeli's key from her key ring and gingerly tried the lock. "Anjeli, you there?" Gita called. She didn't see anyone in the living room, so she raced back to the kitchen where a pan of food was smoking on the stove. She gasped at the figure of Anjeli lying on the kitchen floor in a twisted position. With shaking fingers she pushed the buttons on her cell to 911 and then turned off the flame under the smoldering pan.

When the cops arrived, they first checked Anjeli's life signs, which were negative. The young male cop pasted a crime-scene notice on the closed door of apartment 6A and shooed away the few neighbors who had gathered in the hallway. "Awright, awright folks, nothing to see. Please go back to your apartments." The older, female cop shepherded Gita back to her own apartment next door.

Some minutes later, Rajiv and Mike, their ID cards looped down their shirtfronts, pushed their way through the knot of punked-up teenagers at the front door of the building and took the elevator to the sixth floor. "What's with the louts and loutessas playing house in the lobby?" Mike asked Rajiv. "The leftovers of the old neighborhood before the tide deposited the 'dotheads' in the building," Rajiv sneered. As the elevator door closed, they missed seeing one of the louts, his red ridge of hair bristling like a cockscomb, who flew up the stairs at the back of the hallway.

They knocked at the Kapoor's door, and the uniformed cop inside cracked it open to admit them. " Back here to the kitchen." He led them through the ransackled apartment. "There's the vic on the floor." He pointed down to a beautiful young female clothed in a shalwar-kameez. Mike uttered a Sicilian expletive as the two detectives looked down with sorrow at the murdered woman, her neck twisted at an angle impossible in life, her eyes open wide more in surprise than fear. On the stove was a frying pan full of vegetables. Rajiv and Mike looked at each other with the same thought: *A burglary gone wrong? Or made to look like a burglary gone wrong?*

"Everything's just as we found it," the young cop asserted. "The medical examiner's on her way." He took a little notepad and began to drone his report to the detectives. "Neighbor in 6B, Gita Khosla, rang the bell and knocked at the victim's door to check out the smoke. When she didn't get any answer, she opened the vic's locked door with a key she'd been given previously. The vic was on the kitchen floor, just like this; she didn't touch or move anything, just called 911 and turned off the burner under the pan. She's a smart, plucky college kid," the cop editorialized, "and, quote, 'Anjeli's friend, insofar as that bastard husband and his witchy parents let her have friends.' Her English is perfect," the cop added. "She said she had a 'lot of stuff' to tell us." The cop took the two detectives on a tour of the seemingly vandalized bedrooms. "Maybe a botched burglary?" he offered. "My partner's with the neighbor now, and the ME should be here as quick as traffic allows."

The cop left the kitchen for a minute and returned with a decoratively covered address book in his gloved hand. From the front cover's list headed 'Important Numbers' he read, "Vic's name is Anjeli Kapoor. She lives here with husband, Kumar; he works at a bank in lower Manhattan—here's his number—and his parents live with them . . . Um, the first name on the page isn't her husband's, though. It's a 'Professor Julie' with a NUNY address and telephone number . . ."

Before he could drone on, Mike grabbed the book in his own gloved hand and stared at Julie's number.

"What's up, man?" Rajiv looked at him, startled.

"It's Julie's Indian friend," Mike grimaced, "the one whose wedding she attended in January. She told us about her at lunch, remember? Anjeli's wedding was where she met Kohli, the guy indicted for killing his girlfriend. Julie was supposed to act like Anjeli's 'big sister' here. How am I gonna tell her?"

"Not by phone for sure. Call her. If she's home, get right down there; take care of it in person, and I'll wait for you here."

"I owe you one, Rajiv," Mike said, peeling off his gloves, punching his cell buttons, and speaking urgently into the phone as he left.

In under an hour, Mike rang Julie's downstairs bell. "You'd better sit down," he said, entering her apartment. "I've got bad news—real bad news. It's about Anjeli Kapoor . . . She was killed today. In her apartment. Rajiv is still out on the crime scene, and I'll have to go back, but I wanted to tell you in person. The ME's not there yet, so we don't really know the details."

"Oh, this is terrible, Mike," Julie said, tears welling up in her eyes. "I should have kept in better touch, insisted we see each other more. She was all alone here."

"Don't go that route, Julie," Mike admonished. "It's not your fault. She had a husband and his parents here"—Mike sardonically preempted Julie's response—"Yeah, I get it that they were part of the problem, not part of the solution . . ."

Making an effort to compose herself, Julie told Mike she had to phone some people in India, "right now" she asserted. "I don't want her miserable in-laws to be the ones to tell Anjeli's family. Just stay until I'm finished, okay? Oh, god, her parents will be devastated. And her sister, they were so close. I'd better call Shakuntala, my friend who introduced us. She and her husband can contact Anjeli's family."

"You don't know any details," Mike reminded her. "Just offer your condolences." With a shaking hand, Julie dialed Shakuntala's telephone number. Her friend answered sleepily, but the moment she heard Julie's voice, she cried, "What's wrong, Julie? Something bad must have happened or you wouldn't be calling at this hour."

"Put Ajit on the extension," Julie said, and when she heard him on the line, she cried the awful news into the phone.

"Oh, Julie, that's horrible, horrible," Shakuntala sobbed. "You were right to call us first. We shall call her sister and Prem, and then they can tell her parents."

"Thank you," Julie wept, "I'll call you again as soon as I know more."

As the bored crime-scene cop scanned the street from the apartment window, Rajiv dialed Kumar's work number. His face turned thoughtful as the receptionist told him that Mr. Kapoor had called early this morning to indicate he would not be in today, but could she take a message? *So where is this absent husband, and how long before he turns up to learn of his wife's violent death? Assuming he didn't know of it already, possibly?* Rajiv asked himself.

"The ME's wagon's just pulling up, detective," the cop broke into Rajiv's thoughts, and Rajiv stepped out into the hallway to await them.

As the medical examiner and her staff began their work, she answered Rajiv's questions succinctly. "The autopsy will determine exact cause of death, but it looks like manual strangulation with these neck bruises. Forensics could get lucky here. A couple of new techniques in retaining fingerprints from a body could get you a print match from AFIS. It'll take a while, but maybe we can give you some joy on that score."

"Ah, that would be very good, doctor," Rajiv replied. "And you'll let us know about any signs of past violence? We are suspecting the possibility of domestic violence here."

"You got it," the ME replied. "Is there anyone to identify the body?"

"The neighbor who found her," Rajiv said, "but we'll get a family member down for the official ID as soon as one of them shows up."

Rajiv followed the crime scene techs around the apartment as they dusted for prints. In both bedrooms the dresser drawers had been dumped open, and their contents were scattered all over the floor. Clothes had been dragged from the closet and flung on the bed. "Your garden variety burglary . . . ?" the tech offered. "You'll need the family members to ascertain if anything's been taken."

Nah, Rajiv thought *No signs the lock was tampered with, so the killer probably used some ruse to get in, a break-in in broad daylight, plenty of neighbors going in and out, and why this particular apartment?* It didn't compute as a burglary to him.

Rajiv stepped back into the living room to let the crime scene techs do their work. Anjeli's body had been removed, and the female cop who had been babysitting Gita had returned to the apartment. It looked like the crime-scene people would be there a while.

At a loud knock on the front door, Rajiv let in a disconsolate Mike. "Thanks again, Rajiv I just stayed while Julie called some people in India who'll contact Anjeli's parents. She was on a guilt trip about not keeping up with Anjeli like she should have, but she seemed okay when I left. We'll be talking." Mike then opened the front door again and pulled Rajiv after him into the hall. "Who's this punked-up kid hanging around down the end of the hallway? Looks like one of those louts from the lobby. What's his story?"

"Let's find out, Mike. This Gita neighbor told the female cop that one of those 'effin' creeps'—her words—was obsessed with Anjeli, always leering at her, even following her in the street, calling her his 'beautiful lady,' saying how he'd protect her." Gita thought he was a little off, drugs maybe or just not playing with a full deck. I was planning to get to him; let's do it now."

As the two detectives started casually down the hallway, the young man called out to them. "Hey, detectives, it was the beautiful lady that got hurt, right? I told her and I told her Bubba and me would protect her, but she just never listened."

"She did get hurt, fellow," Rajiv said in a measured voice. "Do you know anything about that? I'm Detective Sharma. What's your name?"

"Moran. Tommy Moran. Sometimes the gang calls me Tommy Mo-ron, but they're just jealous 'cause the beautiful lady never pays atten-tion to them. She was frightened of my dog, Bubba, but I told her she had nothin' to worry about with me around."

"Can we talk out of the hallway, pal?" Mike asked, after introducing himself.

"Sure, I live in 2B. Follow me down." Tommy started skipping down the stairs, Mike right behind him, while Rajiv said he'd take the elevator and meet them there. Rajiv spoke through the open doorway of 6B to the cop inside. "Here's my cell number. We'll be in 2B. Anyone from the family comes up, they don't go to the toilet alone before we get there."

Tommy and Mike waited outside Tommy's apartment for Rajiv to arrive. As he stepped off the elevator, Tommy turned to the detectives and spoke earnestly as he opened his door gently. He seemed oblivious to the miasma of cannabis floating above their heads inside the stuffy apartment, whose windows were closed despite the heat of the day. "Now, when we first go in, Bubba'll jump up and growl, but that don't mean nothing. He's just afraid of strangers. As soon as I tell him you're my friends, he'll smile at you. You'll see."

What Mike saw as he followed Tommy was a huge brindled pit bull jumping upright to embrace the kid with his front paws. *Crap*—Mike stepped back a couple of inches—*this freakin' dog's as big as a horse.*

As the dog looked over Tommy's shoulder and saw the two detec-tives, a low, throaty growl erupted. Tommy patted the animal down to the floor and spoke to him loudly enough for the detectives to hear. "Don't worry, Bubba; these are my friends. They're gonna find the guy who murdered our beautiful lady. See?" Tommy waved Mike and Rajiv in, "Bubba knows you're my friends now. Lookit how he's smiling at you." As if in obedience to Tommy's remark the dog bared more big, white, sharp teeth than his mouth seemed to have room for.

This is Bubba's smile? Mike thought sourly. *He looks like he's getting ready to chew my leg off. Somebody should recommend a new dog dentist to Tommy.*

Mike and Rajiv hesitantly took seats on the lumpy, dog-haired-covered couch. "So," Rajiv began as Tommy pulled up a kitchen chair to face them and Bubba stretched himself contentedly on the floor nearby, "the beautiful lady upstairs. Was she your friend?"

"Nah, not my friend. Not like those sluts I hang with. I know the difference. Me and Bubba, we just woulda protected her, that useless husband of hers, never home, letting her go out on the street by herself, how could he keep her safe? Yelling at her all the time. He didn't deserve a beautiful lady like that. And see, somebody got to her, didn't they?"

"Well, maybe, did you want to scare her a little, show her how much she needed your protection, Tommy? You got inside her apartment somehow, she told you to get lost. You didn't mean to hurt her, right?" Rajiv asked. "But if you couldn't have her, no one could?"

"No, man you got it all wrong. I'd never hurt the beautiful lady. I told her once I could get into her apartment, see, to kind of scare her, but I didn't really have no key."

"We were told that sometimes you'd follow her in the street, call after her, threaten to sic the dog on her. Is that true?" Mike interjected.

"Sure, Bubba and me, we'd follow her sometimes, to protect her, but we'd never hurt her," Tommy replied indignantly. "See, he was mistreated before. I got him from Mr. Delaney upstairs; his son thought he would be good company for the old guy. But one time I visited him, I saw he forgot to put out water for Bubba. And he smoked so much, the apartment was full of secondhand smoke that Bubba was breathin' in. So I asked if I could take care of him, and he gave him to me, and now Bubba would only hurt someone if I told him to. Right Bubba?"—here Tommy patted the animal's head, and the rictus that he called a smile appeared on Bubba's face again.

Oh, god, dumb as a sack of hair, him and his grinning dog both, Mike thought, rolling his eyes at his partner.

"Okay, Tommy," Rajiv continued patiently. "So you were down there with your gang most of the morning. Did you see the beautiful lady's husband?"

"Nah, we didn't see anyone come in and out but a few old ladies with their shopping. And the beautiful lady's mean old folks, they went out but didn't come back. And that ugly bitch who lived next door, she sped in and out, probably for cigarettes; she's always got one hangin' out of her mouth. A real bad example for the beautiful lady." Tommy was thoughtful for a moment. "'Course, there's the back door down the alley by where they put the garbage. It's always open. Somebody coulda got in that way." Mike made a note, and Rajiv rose.

"We'll need the names and addresses of your friends downstairs," Mike said. "Someone'll be taking their statements later. Don't plan to take any Caribbean cruises for a while, okay?"

"Huh?" Tommy asked. "Oh, you mean on a boat? No, I can't do that. They don't allow dogs on those big boats, I can't even take Bubba on the subway."

"It's okay, Tommy, we appreciate your help," Rajiv said.

Mike rolled his eyes and added as they exited the apartment, "And, Tommy, open some windows,. Smoking dope even in your own apartment is still against the law."

"So what do you think, Mike?" Rajiv asked as they returned upstairs. "I think we're just spinning our wheels with him, but he did give us that point about the open alleyway door. That could be why no one saw the killer enter or leave."

"Yeah, that fits. You'd have to scout the block to discover it, but Kumar could certainly know it was there," Mike sighed. "So where's the absent hubby? Out with another woman while someone offs wifey, or what? According to Julie they were like the sun and the moon at their wedding, but it was an arranged marriage; they hardly knew each other. How fast could that turn sour, especially with the buttinsky in-laws?"

Chapter Twenty-Nine

At the sound of a key turning in the lock, Rajiv and Mike walked to the door to confront a handsome young Indian man who stared at them aggressively. "What is all this?" he sputtered as Rajiv interrupted him authoritatively.

"You are Kumar Kapoor, Anjeli Kapoor's husband?"

"Of course I am, who else would have our key?"

"I am Detective Sharma; this is my partner, Detective Cardella. Please come in and sit down. We have some bad news for you." When Kumar seated himself on the couch, Rajiv told him that his wife had been killed, cause of death not determined yet, it may have been a botched burglary . . .

Yadda, yadda, yadda, Mike thought to himself, his arms folded across his chest, his face impassive, gauging Kumar's reactions.

Kumar's face dropped into his hands, his features creasing into an expression of anguish. Tears stood in his eyes when he lifted his face. "How could such a thing happen? Was it a robbery? We have no valuable things here. Did someone come to kill my wife? Who would want to kill my beautiful Anjeli? She was such a devoted wife. It is my fault—I did not protect her enough. Now I've lost her! Tell me, who killed my beautiful Anjeli?"

"Those are all questions we plan to find the answers to," Rajiv continued. "After we finish talking here, you'll have to come with us to identify the body at the morgue. Your neighbor Gita found her, but of course we need an official identification."

"That Gita," Kumar exclaimed angrily. "How is she involved? One of her criminal boyfriends murdered my Anjeli? They all take drugs, you know. She has parties day and night . . . I had forbidden Anjeli to spend time with her."

Yeah, and you should hear what she says about you, Mike thought grimly.

"Well, see, we would have told you as soon as we got here," Rajiv interrupted, "but your receptionist said you weren't coming in. And there was no cell phone number for you listed in your wife's address book. So, um, can you tell us about that?" Rajiv pursed his lips and cocked his head as if he were ready to believe whatever Kumar told him.

"I had some private business. I left early and tried to call Anjeli later in the morning, but there was no answer, so I just left a short message."

"That's alright," said Rajiv. "Your cell phone records will show that. Could you give us your cell number, please? Is there a reason why your wife didn't have it listed?"

Mike had to stifle a smirk at Kumar's discomfort; you could just see the guy's thoughts whirling madly. "Oh, these cheap cells I buy, they never work properly," Kumar stammered. "I change them all the time. Anjeli didn't bother writing down all the numbers. Umm, I used a pay phone today."

Rajiv eyed Mike; they didn't have to tell Kumar right this minute that the Kapoor landline phone would show LUDs if there had been a call and the number of minutes it lasted. "Oh, so could you tell us something about this private business that took you out of touch while your wife was getting killed?" Rajiv asked, with a straight face.

"Now listen, you," Kumar fumed. "You can't just accuse me. I know my rights I'm a citizen with a responsible job and influential relatives here, not some illegal Bangladeshi dishwasher. I loved Anjeli. I would never hurt her. Okay, I was up in the Bronx all day; I can prove it," Kumar continued, "so don't think you can pin this on me."

Rajiv and Mike eyed each other again; odd turn of phrase for a bereaved husband.

"Hey," Rajiv replied equably. "We want to get to the bottom of this, just like you do. You have an alibi; let's hear it, and we can move on."

"One minute," Mike said. "Let's get the tech's tape recorder . . ."

"Go ahead, detective, I have nothing to hide," Kumar said in resignation. "Look, I dated this American girl I met at work before I was married. I was a young immigrant, alone. You understand, Detective Sharma?" Kumar turned toward Rajiv. "She thought the relationship was more than it was. I didn't think my marriage would be arranged so soon. After, I never actually told this girl I was married, just sort of avoided her, and I never told Anjeli about her, either. Then one day, her brother calls here, threatens Anjeli that I have to give him money for his sister or he'll do us damage.

Where was I supposed to get such money?" Kumar asked Rajiv plaintively. "My job is not so secure now, my parents are here—more expenses, money is short." Kumar stopped abruptly, working himself up to righteous anger. "Anjeli got a job but earned so little. And her boss was always calling here, 'Anjeli, stay late; Anjeli I'll drive you home,' and that Gita next door encouraging her to act like an American girl . . ." His voice trailed off.

"Yes, yes," Rajiv picked up the thread smoothly. "These Indian women learn American ways quickly when it suits them."

Kumar calmed down a bit. "Well, Anjeli and I quarreled about this girl, and I told her I would borrow some money to pay off the brother, and we could put it in the past. But she says, 'Who will lend you money? We could never pay it back,' and takes out her little purse of gold jewelry hidden for ourselves and says I can sell some pieces so this man won't 'burn' us as he threatened. She is very angry, though, and says if we do this I must stand up for her to my parents and get more of her dowry back from them. They say they have left it in India, but who's to know the truth? Some they left in India, but some they may have taken here and put in a bank without telling us. Who knows? They needed money for my sister Lakshmi's college tuition, and they had to start on a dowry for her marriage. Also my father had retired earlier than he had intended, and his income was not what he had counted on. It was my duty to help them, but there wasn't much I could do. I have no money.

"So for this man Al, we chose some pieces we had hidden ourselves here; I got a few thousand dollars for them this morning—see I have this receipt . . ." Kumar pulled a wrinkled slip out of his jacket pocket. "I brought the money to this man's house as we arranged he lives somewhere in the Bronx that I never heard of, near some Arthur Avenue. It was two trains and a bus. I got lost; it took hours to get there and back. You can check with him; here is his telephone number."

Mike took out his cell and put it on speakerphone. "We'll just do that right now," he said, dialing the number and laying the cell next to the tape recorder.

"Al here," came a rough voice.

"Al, it's Kumar. Uh . . ."

"You forgot something . . ." Mike prompted in a whisper.

"I forgot something," Kumar began haltingly.

"What's this crap, Kumar?" came the earsplitting response. "You take two hours to get here, I'm late getting back to work, you're seriously short of what I asked for, and now you get home and you forgot something? Maybe you forgot another grand that stuck to your pocket? I don't think so. And don't you come sniffing around my sister again. I saw her giving you the sad eye today; she's dumb enough to let you back in her life. The line went dead. Fahgeddaboutit. It's over."

"You see," Kumar said, with a touch of arrogance, "that proves where I was when Anjeli was killed."

But it doesn't prove you weren't involved, now does it? Mike reasoned.

As the key was heard in the lock again, Mike almost laughed aloud. *It's turning into the stateroom scene from the Marx Brothers' Night* at the

Opera. *Enter the "witchy" old folks. Just in time for tea, but no Anjeli to wait on them hand and foot.*

Mrs. Kapoor walked inside imperiously, staring down Rajiv and Mike. Mr. Kapoor followed her unsteadily, pulling a plaid canvas wheelie bag behind him. "What is this crime scene poster on the door? Who are these people in our apartment, Kumar?" Mrs. Kapoor asked. "Your father and I have had a long day, and we would like our tea. Where is Anjeli?"

Rajiv advised the Kapoors to sit down. "We have bad news for you," he said. "Your daughter-in-law was killed this afternoon." Mike read Mrs. Kapoor's face like a book. It said, "So what's the bad news?"

Mr. Kapoor merely looked befuddled, though he looked fearful, too. "How killed?" Mrs. Kapoor asked. "Was this a burglary? Has anything been taken from our house?" she turned toward Kumar, signaling her concern with a narrowing of her eyes.

"We haven't determined that yet," Mike interposed. "You can help us. You folks can survey your bedrooms, see if anything's been taken there." He turned to Rajiv. "I'll finish up here; you can take Kumar to the morgue to identify the body. Tomorrow, first thing at the station, we'll get the LUDs on this landline and Kumar's cell. We'll take it from there."

Mike's cell rang; it was Julie, still sounding shaken and sad. "Mike," she said, "I was so upset, I forgot to tell you something about Anjeli. It might be important. Anjeli was being sexually harassed by her boss at NUNY. She talked to me about it at length, and last week she left me a disturbing message that she wouldn't be coming to work any more. I have the professor's card she showed me to indicate her concerns; I forgot to give it to you. Give me your fax number, and I'll send it over."

"That'll be great, Julie; we'll give this guy a look first thing tomorrow."

🏵 Chapter Thirty

Julie's fax of Professor Fleagle's tantra*philiac* card was in Mike's machine when he sat down at his desk the next morning. "Hey, buddy," he phoned Rajiv's extension. "I'm coming down. Julie clued me into something worth checking out. This Professor Fleagle at NUNY was sexually harassing Anjeli . . . So maybe did she threaten to blow the whistle? He visits her to tamp things down, and the situation gets out of hand. It might be worth turning over a few rocks . . .

The two detectives threaded their way through the hallways to the NUNY philosophy office, drawing a few sideways looks at the badges decorating their jacket pockets. At the department reception desk they announced themselves to Kimmy, as the receptionist introduced herself. She picked up the phone to alert Professor Fleagle. "Two NYPD detectives for you, professor . . . ," she paused. "Cardella's the hottie, and the chubby Indian is Sharma . . ." another pause and Kimmy smiled saucily at Mike and directed the detectives to Fleagle's office.

"Hottie, hottie," Rajiv winked at Mike, as they entered Fleagle's office. The professor rose from his desk chair at their entrance, stroking his goatee, then came around his desk to firmly shake their hands. "Can

I get you gentlemen anything? Kimmy can bring in coffee, or tea if you prefer . . ." this to Rajiv.

"If you're having something, we'll have coffee, black," Mike said abruptly, cutting Rajiv off before he could answer.

"Excellent," said Fleagle, returning to his seat behind his desk to phone Kimmy to bring in the beverages. The professor leaned back in his chair, his mind furiously racing, though his genial smile remained pasted on his face. *I can't believe that stupid girl actually reported me to the police,* he thought. His instinct told him Anjeli wouldn't have reported his "attack," as she'd call it, to her husband, with his parents undoubtedly listening in; *that would open up a can of worms that would only make her situation worse . . . but it's possible she might have told that damn "Professor Julie," as she'd called her, and that buttinsky had stiffened her spine, coercing her to bring in the cops. Well, I've been there, done that, walked through worse minefields, and nothing had stuck . . .*

"So, detectives, to what do I owe the honor of this visit?" Fleagle began. "Not about one of my students, I hope." He thanked Kimmy for the coffees, and Mike noted his eyes following her rear end as she sauntered out the door.

"No, it's about Anjeli Kapoor. We know she doesn't work here any more. Can you tell us something about that?" Mike asked forthrightly.

"Hmm, well, the . . . uh . . . grant ran out . . ."

Rajiv made a note in his pad to check those records later if necessary.

Mike kept silent, and after an awkward pause, Fleagle started up again. "Oh, and yes, it seemed that her husband was not happy with her working here; her in-laws were here from India . . ." he turned to Rajiv and said in a conspiratorial tone, "You know what that's like, I'm sure."

Rajiv refused the opening, and Mike asked casually, "Professor Fleagle, where were you yesterday between the hours of 10 A.M. and 2 P.M.?"

Okay, Fleagle sighed inwardly, *it wasn't his attack on Anjeli. These cops might not technically be hicks like those dummies out in Ohio, but they're just fishing all the same.* "I was here in my office most of those hours, though I did take lunch with a colleague in the faculty cafeteria for about an hour," he responded, half a smirk twisting his lips. "May I ask why you want . . ."

Before he could complete his sentence, Mike broke in to drop the bombshell. "Do you know that Anjeli is dead, Professor Fleagle, murdered yesterday?" To Fleagle's credit, Mike's usually reliable bull puckey detector judged that the professor was genuinely surprised, even shocked. But, hey, he could just be watching an Oscar-sized acting job here. "So is that a no? you weren't aware of this?"

"Indeed I was not, and I'm very sorry to hear it. Anjeli was doing very well here, and I was encouraging her to start some courses this summer to fit in with her office hours." Then, realizing the contradiction between that remark and the grant money running out, Fleagle backed up a bit. "Uh, I was hoping I could shift some grant money to save her job," he added lamely.

"You were pretty friendly with her, we understand," Mike said ambiguously. "Do you know anything about someone crowding her, maybe conflicts at home, something that might point us in the direction of finding her killer?"

"Well," Fleagle said expansively now, "Indian women, Asian women in general, I know quite a bit about this—Asian philosophy is my specialty. When they come to America, they are often caught in cultural conflicts. They want independence, but don't always know how to distinguish between Americans who genuinely want to help them and those who might do them harm."

And, um, which category do you belong to, professor? Mike asked himself.

"They may dress or talk a certain way," Fleagle continued, "not understanding the signals they send, which might get them in trouble. Where an American girl might know how to handle herself in today's sexually explosive environment—*like Kimmy; I bet she knows how to chat you up or smack you down to her advantage,* Mike thought—". . . an innocent like Anjeli might have her decisions clouded by cultural ignorance. She did speak to me about some such things on occasion. Maybe she became involved with someone, didn't know how to stop a friendship she had started. I'm afraid I have nothing specific to offer though."

"Okay, thank you, Professor Fleagle. That looks like it for now. Rajiv, drink up." Mike downed his own dregs and abruptly grabbed his partner's cup, then blandly reached over to take Fleagle's cup as well. "We'll just we'll drop these outside. You've been very helpful, and we appreciate it. Rajiv, give the good professor our card." Rajiv handed one over. "Call us if you think of anything else. And it's possible we'll need to talk to you again, so please inform us if you plan to be taking any research trips to the Far East, okay?"

"Mike," Rajiv complained on the way out, "you practically spilled my coffee all over my lap. And don't think I didn't see you tucking the prof's cup into a plastic bag just now. You know involuntarily acquired DNA is still a very gray area."

"Yup," said Mike. "We'll cross that bridge when we come to it."

Mike dropped Fleagle's coffee cup into the precinct's evidence room, and the two detectives planned to separate for the tasks ahead. "We need to check Kumar's claim that he called Anjeli the day she was murdered," Mike said. "That'll be enough to get the Kapoor LUDs. The phone records will indicate whether Kumar actually showed such tender consideration for his wife's anxiety about Brother Al as he said he did. If he lied, we'll bring him in to the station for a more formal interview and dig a little deeper into his relationship with his wife. I also want to dig a little on Fleagle . . . That stuff may be too hot for your tender ears, Rajiv," he grinned.

Mike took the stairs two at a time, got the process started on the landline phone LUDs and Kumar's cell records, and sat down at his computer to check out the good professor. It wouldn't be the first time a professional man offed a woman to shut her mouth and keep his job. Kimmy had given them a copy of Fleagle's class schedule and office hours, which indicated he'd been at the college, either in class or his office, during the hours when Anjeli was killed. That didn't necessarily mean anything, though; with his vaunted connections to the Asian community, he might have a whole roster of mutts who could blend into Anjeli's neighborhood and have done the actual killing.

Meanwhile he'd start with the card Julie had faxed him. The listed Web site was loaded with mystical-sounding text accompanied by explicit art photos extolling the Tantric philosophy of sexual intercourse. "Interested parties" were sent on to a Yahoo text-messaging site for the "sexually adventurous multicultural woman who appreciates a mature man and a sublime intimate experience." There, under the heading "40s–50s Love, Asian Preferences," Mike found phil's snarky sexual quips and explicit sexual invitations as well as some bragging rights about his sexual equipment. *Gross, but not criminal, unfortunately.* He printed out the page; maybe Rajiv'd pick up on something beyond the obvious.

There's gotta be more on this guy, Mike speculated. *They don't start this crap in their fifties.* He googled the name *Phillip Fleagle,* not really expecting much—*I mean how famous a philosopher is he?*—and shouted "Bingo" as a newspaper story from Massillon, Ohio, from about ten years ago appeared on the screen. Mike scanned it quickly. It seemed that Fleagle's wife, a young Filipina, had disappeared without a trace, and the police were never able to move the case forward. *Oh, yeah.* Mike started dialing the Massillon PD; with luck, someone might still be around who would remember the case. It was easier than he thought: a desk sergeant referred him to a Lieutenant Clark, who'd actually been there at the time.

"Mainly we still keep the case open because the family—good people, the wife's brother and sister-in-law—call us once a year at least, to see if anything's been discovered. They told us Ismelda, that was the wife's name, had said the marriage was going way bad and if any-thing ever happened to her to look at her husband. This Fleagle was an arrogant S.O.B., practically taunted us to find the evidence that he killed her, but we just couldn't get anywhere. Then right away he starts dating some student of his from India or Indonesia, some country like that, but that's not against the law either. Anyway, he left his job that summer and disappeared. We'd collected his DNA, so if anything ever turned up we could possibly still nail him. Probably not too likely, but it could happen . . ."

Mike filled Clark in on Fleagle's current incarnation, "same old, same old, a person of interest in a sexual harassment thing, also with an Asian woman, maybe a murder. I'll get back to you if anything pans out."

Mike felt like he was on a roll the next day when the police tech dropped the Kapoor landline phone records and Kumar's cell phone LUD printouts on his desk. *Not a lot of traffic to or from the Kapoor landline. No call to Anjeli the day she was killed, but no surprise there. Kumar's pay phone message, my butt.* He noticed the call from the past week to Julie's number, probably the message about Anjeli losing her job that Julie had mentioned; he'd check the date with her. Then he was startled to recognize Sukhdev Kohli's office number showing up in a few very brief calls, all but one under a minute. One was from the day just before Anjeli's death. Of course they were all freakin' relatives, but these were no kissing cousins chewing the fat; it looked to him just like information being passed along or people setting up meets. With Kohli still under indictment for Grace's murder, his office phone should be good for a court order for a tap; he'd get on it right away. There was practically nothing on Kumar's cell LUDs either. The couple of Bronx exchanges—Brother Al's number—were consistent with Kumar's claim about contacting him to calm him down and set up their meeting. And there was the one early-morning call to his Manhattan bank job on the day of Anjeli's murder, which tallied with what Kumar had already told them.

A phone call from Rajiv downstairs broke into Mike's review of the phone records. "Get down here, Mike; useful results from the ME. She just faxed the report from Anjeli's strangulation bruises. Fingerprints on her neck match up the kazoo through AFIS with one local thugeroo named Harish Desai. Visa and citizenship applications from twenty years ago, and since then a rap sheet as long as your arm, everything from turnstile jumping when he was an itty-bitty baby skell through burglaries, robberies, time here, time there, escalating violence, on parole now, with guess who providing him intermittent employment when he's out of the joint? The big uncle and do gooder, Sukhdev Kohli, whose sari shop in Queens is providing him with the necessaries of human life as we speak."

"That's it, my man," Mike rose from his desk. "That's the connection. Let's get that arrest warrant and take this Harish down right now. On our way with a couple of uniforms, and if his boss is there, we'll pull him in alongside as a person of interest. This Kohli is all over the street like dog doo; you gotta carry a popsicle stick at all times."

Harish Desai sat in an interrogation room at the precinct house facing Rajiv and Mike across a standard-issue formica table. "He doesn't look as much of a skell as I thought he would," Mike offered across to Rajiv. "Nice clothes, shined shoes, very slick for a guy who goes around brutally murdering lovely, innocent young women who never did him a bit of harm."

"That's what makes you so useful to Kohli, isn't it?" Rajiv asked Desai, who was slouching back in his chair, a been-there-done-that attitude painting his face.

"I know my rights, detective; I want to call my lawyer. I have nothing to say to you until then."

"Be our guest, Harish," Rajiv continued, "but your fingerprints are literally all over the victim's neck. If you want to talk to us, we know you didn't just pick this apartment out of a hat; someone set it up. Maybe we can talk to the DA, they can do something for you down the line. Maybe you didn't mean to kill her? Just to scare her, make her unconscious to buy yourself some time while you raked through the apartment for some goodies? We know Kohli has a lot of control over your life—he can do you damage, you couldn't say no. We're gonna get the wizard behind the curtain in this thing for sure. You think Kohli'll take the fall with you? We don't think so. We think he'll toss you to the sharks. You want to chew on that?"

"Hmm, yes, detectives, I can do that," Harish said thoughtfully as he was led back to his cell.

Mike joined Rajiv back at his first-floor desk with the pages from Fleagle's Web site, eager to get some action going. He made sure that the tap on Kohli's office phone had been set up, and he looked for some results there down the road. But Rajiv had one more piece of business to spring on his partner. He waved a faxed Compu-Sketch portrait of a man's face, which utilized the newest police technology, under Mike's nose. "Do you recognize this guy?"

Mike looked closely at the drawing. "I wouldn't have before yesterday, but after our visit to NUNY I would say it looks just like our good professor. Where the hell did that come from?"

Rajiv picked up the note that had accompanied the sketch ID. "A Detective Danielle Ortega from the one-three in Chelsea sent these over to me. It's part of some rapes she's trying to connect. Remember that Halloween assault on the Chelsea Piers, a woman in a sari? Well, that vic turned out to be a mature woman, a social worker who had not only brought in the perp's used condom dripping his DNA all over the floor but had also spent an hour or so chatting with him over coffee, so his identity was burned into her brain. Ortega distributed her sketch around West Side Manhattan precincts first and dug up two more rape cases of Asian women, one of them a journalism student at Columbia, also an acute observer, who confirmed her rapist's identity through a photo array that included this sketch. A third victim, an orthodox Muslim who doesn't speak English and was reluctant to come to the Greenwich Village precinct that handled the case, was reached at her home and made the ID there through a photo array as well, so all bases are covered. Both these rapes yielded DNA evidence too, from the student's bedspread—she was raped in her apartment—and the other women's clothing. So this Ortega broadened her distribution because here she's got the face and the DNA, but who's the perp? She was going to try the West Side colleges next, but that could have taken forever if Julie hadn't dropped that dime on Fleagle."

"Rajiv, this is great news. Even if he's not involved in Anjeli's murder—and he's not home free yet by any means—he'll definitely be looking at very hard time on the rapes. Maybe that'll be some consolation for Julie, too. Let's confirm this scum's ID right now so this Ortega can get her warrants for Fleagle's office, computers, the whole ball of wax. And don't forget his personnel records from their human services office or whatever its politically correct name is these days. In fact, I'm going to call Julie and see if she can dig up anyone at the college who remembers when this guy was hired, what his application looked like, and what he claimed was the trigger for leaving his last job. This crap from his Web site"—here he slapped his sheaf of Fleagle's printouts on Rajiv's desk—"has to be just the tip of the iceberg. His hard drive will be hot as a pistol—diaries, trophy writings, fantasies, guaranteed. These lowlifes are all the same. Let me tell you what I learned from a Lieutenant Clark of the Massillon, Ohio, PD."

As Mike told his tale, Rajiv listened intently, wagging his head briskly in his characteristic side-to-side motion to acknowledge the plausibility of Mike's information.

Julie was indeed somewhat consoled by Mike's news that at least her lead on Fleagle had helped bring in a really bad guy. Anjeli's death was too great a sacrifice, but at least it yielded up someone dangerous to women. She was even able to smile at his remark that "If there's any justice, he'll do so much time he'll need Viagra to start up again when he gets out."

When he summarized his information about Fleagle's first wife in Ohio, Julie wasn't totally surprised to hear it. "Did I ever tell you," she said with a small embarrassed laugh, "that I'm a women's-channel docudrama freak? And you'd be surprised how many of these cases are solved even after fifteen or twenty years."

Mike responded silently with a crooked smile. "Which leads me to an idea I had. Could you dig up someone who was in on Fleagle's hiring or knew him pretty well back then? The Chelsea precinct is grabbing all his personnel and computer files, but his backstory first hand might give me a better handle on him."

"I'll sure try, Mike," Julie replied, making a note.

Chapter Thirty-One

Julie caught Mike at his desk early in the morning a few days later. "Check your e-mail, Mike. I was able to dig up a retired faculty member who was actually on the department P and B that hired Fleagle, and I sent you the gist of our conversation."

"Thanks, Julie. That'll move us forward on him. Let me catch you up. The autopsy gave us Anjeli's actual killer, made to look like part of a burglary gone bad, but that was as phony as a two-dollar bill. No motive; we know he was just a hired gun. And guess who he works for? Sukhdev Kohli. Can you believe it? We think Kohli paid him for the murder, and we're working on the doer's giving him up. We're looking for more evidence. We haven't got Kohli's motive yet, and we're tracking other possible players. That'll take some time. But, say, are you going to have any holes in your schedule this week? This Detective Ortega from the Chelsea precinct on the Fleagle thing, she said Rajiv and I could be flies on the wall for his lineup and interrogation in the next couple of days. We're going to be right in your neighborhood. So if you're free, maybe we could all meet afterward, grab a bite, whatever, and we could catch you up on both cases."

"I wouldn't miss it for anything," Julie replied. "I want to hear every detail."

Mike forwarded a copy of Julie's e-mail about Fleagle to Ortega in Chelsea and to Rajiv downstairs. Like she'd said, it wasn't evidence, but it was all of a piece with what they were learning about this creep. Without any preamble, Julie had written:

So this professor said, "Fleagle wasn't my kind of guy, sort of full of himself, and condescending to our committee." She didn't think his research specialty, Eastern Philosophy, was a great fit with our students or the NUNY mission, which is teaching oriented, but actually a phone call to one of his references indicated he was a very engaging teacher who filled his classes. Fleagle told our committee he was happy to teach the Phil 101 courses, the entry level nobody ever volunteers for . . . That was a real plus. His resumé showed a lot of grants—mostly small stuff for creative teaching, conference organization, that kind of thing, so that was in his favor too. (FYI, Mike, colleges love grants because they bring in overhead cash with no effort on the college's part.) While she recalled that his scholarly articles were from "pretty arcane journals," philosophy wasn't her field and, as she told me, "we're not Harvard," and his apparently strong teaching skills sold a lot of the committee. Here's the really germane, part, though.

Julie had bolded what followed. *This professor did recall feeling—and apparently this was a committee consensus—that Fleagle's former colleagues* **"were unusual in their reticence about him personally."** *And when they asked him about why he had left his previous college rather precipitously, he explained that he had recently become a widower and wanted to leave a place that had "bad memories, you understand," a line she remembered verbatim as she had found his expression of grief somehow inauthentic, a little over the top, almost like he was speaking lines from some old British film. She'd figured that most couples who build a life someplace, if one dies,* *even in an untimely manner, the other would want to stay where they'd presumably made friends, had a social network . . . But, bottom line, they needed someone urgently, Fleagle was certainly a reasonable candidate, and she "wasn't going to go to the mat against him." (The idea is, Mike, if a new pick doesn't work out, you can always reject his appointment the following year without cause or his tenure on down the road.)*

Scrolling through the rest of his e-mails, Mike was surprised to find an instant one-line reply from Ortega:

Thanks for the info; it's uncanny that our Halloween rape victim used the exact same words "full of himself" in describing her rapist.
    "Ten years and this blowhard hasn't changed one iota," Mike muttered to himself.

Mike sat at his desk, reviewing what they had so far on Anjeli's murder. Realistically, the suspect list was already cut in half. Mike ticked off that doped out Tommy Moran as a no-starter, and questioning his little army of hooligans had led nowhere. Brother Al was really off the short list, too. He had nothing to gain from Angeli's death. And checking him out, they'd found, surprisingly, that he was a pretty upstanding citizen. A Seabee with an honorable military discharge, steady construction employment, no record, a wife and son, and a decent place in a solid working-class nabe—he didn't compute. The worst that neighborhood people could say was that when he was too deep into the bookies, he'd drive his van with his head ducked below the window to avoid them. But ultimately he'd pay up, and there was nothing there. Fleagle, Mike figured sourly, was only a weak possible. He was alibi'd by Kimmy—all right, they wouldn't have accepted her word alone—and classes full of students; in fact a student had actually come to see him during his office hours. That he drew on a network of punks for hire to produce Harish Desai—who worked for Kohli—was a million-to-one chance. Fleagle might drop something, though; he was a lip-flapper, and those guys sometimes dug their own graves with their big mouths. That'd have to wait 'til they got to his interrogation at the one-three, a couple of days off. He'd keep in touch with Ortega on it. But it wasn't likely.

Mike drummed his fingers on his desk, impatient to get the past few days' tapes of Kohli's phone taps. Getting Harish cold and his concrete connection to Kohli was a big step forward, but they'd need a lot more to tie Kohli to Anjeli's death. What Kohli's motive could be? Could he have had some kind of relationship with her like he did with Grace, and she became inconvenient? Mike didn't know how likely that would be, given her character and the family relationships Julie had drawn for him. He'd certainly want to check with Julie and with Rajiv to see if there was some kind of cultural context they could supply that would make Kohli a halfway decent suspect. The phone tapes were a better bet, like if Harish would call him from the jail, let something drop. He had an undeniably tight link to his boss going back years; it probably wasn't the first time Kohli had gone to bat for him. But this was murder and airtight; Harish wouldn't be taking just short time on assault, not even if he owed his boss. If the DA could exploit that, maybe arrange something with Harish down the line, he'd give up Kohli in a New York minute. But Harish was just doing it for the money and wouldn't be privy to Kohli's motive.

That was the missing link. That's what they had to hope the Kohli phone tap would supply. Just the Kapoor LUDs showing some one-minute phone calls to Kohli, even the one on the day before Anjeli's murder, wouldn't be enough to hold Kohli, though it would be enough to bring him in. He'd definitely lawyer up—and any mouthpiece worth his salt would wave away the records of any phone calls between the Kapoors and Kohli as just a natural occurrence between close family members. *So,* Mike thought, *the call records might not trap Kohli, but maybe they'll catch him off guard before his lawyer gets there. Worth a try, anyway.*

"So, Sukhdev, you're not even out of the woods on Grace's murder, and you're already in another trick bag just like it," Mike taunted at the elegantly dressed businessman opposite him in the interrogation room.

"My attorneys will have something to say about that, I think," Kohli countered.

"Get them in here it'll be our pleasure," was Rajiv's mild rejoinder. "We have enough to hold you, anyway. And I don't think your buddy Harish wants to go down for this alone."

"Harish, Harish, who is this man? Another desperate thug like those two in India. You have a short memory, detective," he said, staring insolently at Mike.

"This interview's being videotaped, my man," Mike responded. "We're getting the popcorn ready for the doer as we speak. So let me hear it right now; Are you going to post his bail as well as your own? How will that go down with a judge? I don't think the 'respectable businessman, ties to the community' thing is going to work here once the judge sees these phone transcripts. And if you cut Harish adrift like you did with those two hoodlums in India, what, Harish is going to take the max on this by himself?"

Kohli pointedly ignored Mike's remarks. "So I'm free to go now, isn't it?" he smirked. "You can talk to my lawyers from now on; I'm a very busy man."

Mike sat on the edge of Rajiv's desk, his face expressing his disappointment. "Okay," he mused aloud, "this thing with Kohli isn't going to go anywhere fast. Eventually we'll get him, one way or the other. But I think we have to look at who brought him into the picture to hire Harish. We haven't looked deep enough into Kumar here. After all, he regarded Kohli as the family big shot who was going to advise him on improving his financial situation, start a new business, maybe get a fresh start with a better marriage, someone whose family had bucks, get his mitts on more dowry to help out that sister of his and his retired father. We don't want to overlook the possibility that Kumar was exploring all these angles with this cousin or whatever he was.

"And we've got the LUDs on Kumar showing that he lied about his phone call to Anjeli the morning she was killed. So much for the loving husband, eager to assure his anxious wife that they were now safe from Brother Al, the big bad wolf. Let's start with that to bring him down here."

"Yeah, that'll work," Rajiv agreed, "though when we told him about Anjeli's death and later at the morgue—you didn't see him like I did—his shock and grief seemed real to me."

Mike was a little more skeptical. "Grief, guilt—in my experience one doesn't necessarily exclude the other," he argued. "The guy gets jealous or desperate for whatever reason—real or imagined—and he has someone handy he can hire to solve his problem. Then he's shaken by what he set in motion—I'm not talking about a stone-cold killer like Kohli here, just a regular guy—but it's too late. Something like that Ram character in that Indian story you were telling me about—he felt love and even believed in his wife Sita's innocence, but then the pressure of his people got to him, and the end result is the same—pow! She's out of there. His grief and guilt are real, too, but the deed's done and can't be undone."

"So, Kumar," Rajiv probed, "we know from your phone records that you never called Anjeli to leave her a message like you claimed. Can you explain that?"

"Look, I was ashamed and embarrassed at having gotten us into all that trouble with Al, him threatening her and all that. I want you to know I truly loved Anjeli. She was a good wife, trying hard to please me, working for extra money. She tried to please my parents, but they had so much of their own worries about money. Anjeli didn't deserve my getting her into such a mess. And I couldn't properly protect her from those hooligans in the building—have you checked them out thoroughly? And that Gita person with her dangerous friends? I tried to keep her safe. Anjeli could be naïve about Americans . . .

"My folks kept harping on me all the time: 'You must divorce her; we must find someone with more wealth; her family is nothing; she is not a good wife; look how she behaved with that Professor Phil; we let you marry her too quick-quick; you would look no further.' That is correct, detectives; I was stubborn about that. 'We did everything for your life here,' they said. 'Now it has not worked out, and you must separate from her and look for a new, better marriage.' What was I to do? But to kill Anjeli? Never, never would I do such a thing. Are you thinking that I hired someone to do that? How would I even know such a low person? The only thug I know is my own boss at the bank," Kumar smiled weakly. "And how could I pay such a person? You know my financial situation."

"Any more questions, Mike?" Rajiv turned to his partner, who shook his head.

"Not at this time. But we may want to talk to you some more, Kumar. Stick around the city."

Back at Rajiv's desk, the two detectives agreed that they were probably at square one again. Though mindful of the cops mantra—take nothing for granted, be wary of everyone—neither one credited Kumar with involvement in the murder. Mike sighed, reminding Rajiv of their lunch conversation with Julie and the only other possibility for the one-minute phone calls listed on the Kapoor landline. "Déjà vu all

over again. Time to bring in the creaky old folks, pal. Let's hear what
they have to say."

"Do we need our attorney here?" Mrs. Kapoor asked Rajiv haughtily
when the detectives came to the apartment to "invite" her and her husband down to the station house.

"You are entitled to one, of course, if you can afford one. And you
have the right to remain silent. If you are arrested and can't afford an
attorney, the court will appoint you one for free."

Mrs. Kapoor's sniff at that remark indicated her assessment of public
defenders.

"For now, we'd just like to talk to you, get a few explanations . . ."

No money for a big lawyer, Mrs. Kapoor knew. She reluctantly shepherded her husband out the door with her, warning him out of Rajiv's
hearing to keep quiet. "We must not volunteer anything," she jabbed
him in the side for emphasis. "I have read that even the most innocent
people are put into jail because they talk and try to explain themselves."

Mr. Kapoor looked at her in puzzlement. What did he have to explain? Again he wondered if it were possible that Anjeli had told someone about "the incident." Maybe this Julie person? Could they suspect
him because of that?

At the precinct, the detectives separated the husband and wife into
different interview rooms and had a cup of tea brought to each. Mike
took the husband, Rajiv the wife, making sure the cameras were running
on both. Mike indicated to Mr. Kapoor that there were a number of calls
between the Kapoor household and Sukhdev Kohli's office. "Do you
know anything about that?" he asked. "Were you just keeping up with
your relative here? Maybe some discussions about how he could help
your son in opening a business? We know you were retired and your
son's job was possibly insecure."

With Mike's question, Mr. Kapoor realized "the incident" was not known to the police, and he became more confident. "You don't understand our Indian relationships at all, detective," Mr. Kapoor sneered at Mike. "You see, Mr. Kohli is my *wife's* relation. I have more caste than he, even if he is richer than I. Not everyone is like you Americans where money counts above all. Perhaps my wife had these lengthy conversations you mention. I also have my own very respectable relatives here; my elder brother has been here even longer than Mr. Kohli and has done quite as well. He is planning a big wedding for one of his daughters, who is a doctor, and of course we are invited; we could certainly call on him if we needed to make a loan."

"Okay, so how were your relationships with your daughter-in-law? Did you get along?"

"She was a very selfish girl. I was very angry at her sometimes. She couldn't even keep her job, little that it earned her. And her boss calling her at all hours—was that a proper thing for my son to hear? She was a beauty, I admit, but that brought us down. Our son would have no other; her family had no wealth, no status, but what to do? All this is Mrs. Kapoor's department. What has this to do with our burglary and Anjeli's death?"

Without answering, Mike made an excuse to leave the room for a moment and knocked at Rajiv's interview-room door. After a few moments Rajiv joined him. "Rajiv, unless this is another Oscar-sized acting job, I don't see this guy as the organizer for Anjeli's murder. I'll put in the time, but the connection with Kohli doesn't fit. He doesn't seem to have any idea about the Kohli phone calls—some kinship thing. You can check it out when you see the video. He certainly disliked his daughter-in-law and would have liked a match with more wealth for him and the missus. And maybe he also came on to Anjeli and she threatened to tell Kumar. But I don't see him with the focus to be the decider. He can just stew a bit. I want to check on those Kohli phone taps."

Mike returned to his desk to hunt up the phone techs—*they needed something concrete on tape to nail Kohli's motive or his conspirator, or they'd be stuck here forever*—and saw a manila envelope topped with a scribbled post-it on top: "Tape inside, hope it brings you joy, this is one closed-mouth guy." Mike actually crossed his fingers as he sat down. He swept his desk clear, whipped out his tape recorder, put on his headset for maximum clarity, inserted the tape, and pressed play. Twenty minutes into it, he found what he'd been hoping for.

Carrying the manila envelope, Mike sought out Rajiv in the interview room where he was still questioning Mrs. Kapoor. He knocked on the window, signaling his partner outside. "We're paddling forward now," Mike told Rajiv ebulliently as he handed him the tape and recorder. "Listen to this."

Rajiv smiled broadly as he heard the brief phone conversation. Like Mike, he understood the caginess of both caller and recipient in not identifying themselves. Of course you didn't have to be a rocket scientist to figure that no one but Kohli used his private office phone. The caller was clearly a woman; both voices could later be IDed by voiceprint technology. "Your man did well," the caller spoke first. "But we cannot get your money as quick as we had thought. Do not worry, the dowry remains safe in India; we are good for it. Just a little patience, please . . ." A man's voice interrupted the caller, "Do not call me again." The phone banged down.

Rajiv reentered the interrogation room and reseated himself opposite Mrs. Kapoor, picking up the thread of their interview, Mrs. Kapoor's take on her daughter-in-law. Some of it was old hat to him already from Gita's and Julie's observations. "So, you were saying, you didn't think the marriage was a suitable one?"

"Exactly right, detective, though what could we do about it? Kumar would not think of divorcing her—'What would her life be either here or in India?' he asked us, as if that was our worry. She made me very angry, she did not even see how she had ruined my son, so handsome and hardworking, a catch for many girls with better backgrounds than Anjeli. Hanky panky with her boss 'Phil.' She even thought she would cut her hours of work and go back to school instead of getting a job that paid more. And then she quit altogether. Yes, she angered me. My husband, unfortunately, is too kind a person to push Kumar; he is not worldly and doesn't fully understand the demands of America, though we have visited here before."

"Well, according to your phone records, you spoke with Mr. Kohli several times recently. Did you feel that he could give you better advice than your husband? Were you banking on your kinship with him to help you out?"

"Banking? What does this mean here?" Mrs. Kapoor asked indignantly. "Is bank theft involved now?"

"No, no—by *banking* I mean *depending* on him," Rajiv replied.

"Oh, I see," Mrs. Kapoor nodded complacently. "Well, yes, we spoke several times. He is an excellent businessman with contacts in the community that might be useful to Kumar if he left the bank. His legal, financial, and such knowledge could possibly assist us in different ways. He was aware of a wide range of possibilities."

"Such phone conversations would take quite a while, wouldn't they, Mrs. Kapoor?" Rajiv pounced. "But your phone records show your calls with Kohli to be way under a minute. Even one the day before Anjeli was killed. You know, the kind of call that just transmits information . . . a date, a time, a place. Can you explain that?"

"Oh . . ." Mrs. Kapoor stammered, "just the day before? Well, I must think. Perhaps, yes, I recall I was making an arrangement for us to meet for a more lengthy discussion about Kumar . . ."

"No information about when Anjeli would be alone in your apartment, Mrs. Kapoor? When it would be convenient to have a burglary occur that would eliminate your daughter-in-law from the scene? Then how do you explain the phone conversation between you and Mr. Kohli *after* Anjeli's murder, which clearly shows you planned to pay him for something he'd done for you? Money that would come from your obtaining Anjeli's dowry items that you had hidden in India? This is not just from a list of phone calls; we have a tape of this conversation," Rajiv told her forcefully.

Mrs. Kapoor looked thoughtfully at Rajiv. "I believe it is time for that public defender you mentioned. I have nothing further to say."

Chapter Thirty-Two

Detective Danielle Ortega met Mike and Rajiv outside the old one-three stationhouse on 26th Street and shook their hands as they introduced themselves. "Early vintage, like our place," Mike admired the old brick-and-limestone building. "No elevator I bet."

"Yes, it's 1918. These paneled wooden doors with the metal medallions are original, but the inside's been sort of renovated for modern interviewing techniques, computers, and so on. I'm on the top floor—"

"Up the stairs, just like me," Mike smiled.

"—But we'll be doing this in the new, first floor area."

Rajiv said "Thank goodness," and Ortega waved them past the police receptionist at the grungy, paper-laden steel-case desk that was jammed up almost to the front door. As they walked to the squad room's video-viewing area, they saw three Asian women sitting inside. One, wearing a shalwar-kameez with a scarf covering her hair and most of her face, sat in a chair a little apart with a young man by her side. As the cameras started to roll, Ortega signaled for the young Muslim woman and her brother and translator to accompany her to the lineup-viewing room where Fleagle's lawyer was already waiting. The girl's face was a mask of fear, but also determination. Her brother's hand on her arm gave her the courage to put this terrible man in jail forever, she hoped. She had been advised to take her time; she would, to show how certain she was, but in her heart there was no delay. "Number four," she said in halting English after some minutes of looking the line up and down.

"Are you sure?" Ortega asked.

The young woman emphasized her answer to her brother, who repeated in English "Number four."

"Thank you." Danielle gently led them from the room, expressing the hope that the girl might eventually be able to testify at the future trial. When her brother translated Danielle's remark, his sister looked aghast and spoke rapidly to him in her native language. When she finished, her brother explained to Danielle that this could never be; her appearance at a public trial would forever ruin her chances of a decent marriage. "Not to worry," Danielle replied, looking at the girl, with great empathy. "We can always take a deposition."

She then returned with the mature social worker who had been the Halloween rape victim. Wearing a smart sari and choli combination, the woman walked gracefully alongside Danielle to the lineup room, passing Fleagle's lawyer who was whining some complaint to Ortega, which both women ignored. The victim looked at the line of men up and down carefully, returning to the middle of the line twice. "It's number four, definitely," she stated. She told Danielle that if they wanted, they could have each man, in different order, speak the sentence "I've seen many such festivals in India," and she would close her eyes and identify her rapist again, that's how sure she was. Fleagle's lawyer should have loved the idea, Danielle thought; great for him if she made a mistake. But the woman's unflappability gave him pause, and he passed on the offer.

The third woman, looking more Chinese than South Asian and dressed in the most current college fashions, was also very forthright in her identification of number four. Like the Halloween victim, she also volunteered to hear the men speak a sentence about how she would enjoy the rape, and she would reidentify him by voice. Again Fleagle's lawyer waved away her offer. Ortega thanked her as well; she knew that the last two women at least would be sterling witnessess when the time came.

When returning to the squad room, she asked Rajiv and Mike what they thought. "I don't want to jinx anything, "Mike said, "but bring me a fork. This turkey's done. I wonder, though, in another case Fleagle might be good for, in Ohio, if on down the road you could give me copies of his intimate computer writings, Asian-women fantasies, like that, that might suggest he disappeared his first wife, a young Filipina, about ten years ago."

"You got it. You're welcome to watch the interview now. How long can it take with these identifications and DNA matches on all the rapes?"

Danielle left them at the video area while she went over to the interview room where Fleagle was sitting by himself, a cocky smirk on his face despite his jail greens and what he must know they had on him.

"So, Detective Ortega," Fleagle greeted her leaning over the table in a flirtatious manner.

"Can you believe that scum?" Mike erupted, his growling quickly shushed by Rajiv.

"Have you met my attorney yet?" Fleagle continued in a relaxed manner. "His Armani suit is a clue to how good he is and how fast he's going to get me out of here, don't you think?"

"I don't think anything of the kind, Mr. Fleagle," Ortega smirked back at him while leaning back in her chair.

"That's _Dr._ Fleagle, if you don't mind using my proper title," the professor emphasized.

This time Mike got out half a mocking Sicilian epithet before Rajiv again shushed him. "Is this how you interact with your TV, my friend? Remind me never to watch the tube with you." Mike acknowledged his partner's remark by raising his hand to his mouth and zipping his lips.

Ortega spit her evidence back at Fleagle. "Do you know that we have three positive IDs and DNA from a suitcase full of clothing and your condom? I bet even your lawyer is going to suggest a plea offer in your own interest. And don't think for a minute he's going to let you mouth off on the stand with all that sexual crap that you have in your computer."

Fleagle readjusted his body defensively on his chair, though his face still seemed ignorant of what was actually awaiting him. "You know, detective, a lot of these so-called victims ask for it. Look at these students—their bodies exposed, belly, hips, and butts on display, what is a virile man to think?"

Mike exploded too fast for Rajiv. "A virile man has to rape innocent or drugged women? Gimme a break."

"All this sexual-harassment business," Fleagle continued, "acquaintance rape, allegations of date-rape drugs, these are merely new laws to deprive a highly respected professor such as myself of the voluntary, consensual sexuality of his students or adult partners. I enrich them, and they enrich me . . . I don't deny it," Fleagle crossed his arms on his chest as if he'd just solved his problems.

"You know, *Dr.* Fleagle," Danielle sarcastically drew out the title, "the Chinese have a saying: 'If you have a big problem, make it small. If you have a small problem, make it disappear.' Do you realize your problem is so humongous you couldn't bury it with a bulldozer? But let your fancy lawyer figure it out; that's what you're paying him for." She gathered her papers and left the room as the guard took Fleagle through the other door.

"So okay, guys, we're done here," Danielle approached Rajiv and Mike. "I won't forget those printouts you asked for, Mike."

"Danielle," Mike and Rajiv started together, and Mike continued, "We're meeting a friend at a nearby restaurant for lunch or whatever it is by now. She's an anthropologist who's actually been of great help in both this and our murder case out in Queens, an Indian wife who was her friend. Do you have the time to join us?"

"I would like that," she agreed as Mike dialed Julie's number on his cell.

The three detectives walked down to East of Eighth, where Julie and Mike had met before, and found Julie already sitting at a small outside table when they arrived. After introductions were made, Julie led the group into the garden, explaining, "Happy Hour starts soon, and when it gets mobbed, you can't even hear yourself talk. Frederico'll give us a corner table, and we can stay as long as we want. He knows my mom and I close the place when we meet for our marathon catch-ups."

As soon as they were seated, Mike and Rajiv brought Julie up to date with the forensics and phone LUDs that led them to book the thug Harish, establish the Kohli connection, and then finally implicate Mrs. Kapoor as a conspirator or accessory or whatever the charge would ultimately read. "With the possibility of multiple charges, though," Mike added, "I'm afraid we can all safely take a couple of 'round-the-world cruises and still be back in time for the convictions. Justice will be done as far as it ever can be in a murder, but not as soon as it should be."

"Yeah, but with Fleagle, it'll be sooner than that," Danielle observed to Julie, "and we could even say Anjeli started us off. Who knows how long it would have taken if she hadn't given you his card and then you hadn't faxed it on to Mike and Rajiv?"

"And you too, Danielle. If you hadn't put the rapes together and sent out that sketch, Fleagle would still be out there," Rajiv congratulated her. "Now thanks to both of you, at least Fleagle's a wrap!"

Rajiv lightened the atmosphere a little with a recapitulation of his and Mike's first interview with Fleagle—"hottie, hottie"—and Mike's coffee-cup caper, and then, at Mike's urging, Danielle acted out her Fleagle interrogation for Julie, who joined in the laughter. Mike noted that Fleagle had come on to Danielle exactly as Julie had described the married prof who had once come on to her, "leaning into her face, speaking sonorously." His observation led to a spirited discussion of how similar all these lowlifes were, and then the four of them bounced from theme to theme: cultural defense, the legitimacy of surreptitiously collecting a suspect's DNA, evildoing in-laws—with Julie recapping the ways in which Mrs. Kapoor had felt herself wronged by her son's marriage and how all her resentments had come together, driving her to her ultimate lethal action.

"Well," said Danielle, "I still think it's weird, but I guess in some ways Indian families are like Cubans. My brother's wife is Cuban, her family's a bunch of *blancos* who left Castro's Cuba eons ago, and they spend every Sunday at his house lined up like the Inquisition, dumping on their dark-skinned son-in-law: Why he doesn't do better by their daughter? Why do they have such a crappy apartment? Why can't they afford Catholic school for their kids? I'll say one thing though, his wife stands up for him one hundred percent . . ."

"If only Kumar had stood up for his wife against her parents early on, he might have saved her life," Mike grimaced, as Julie nodded in agreement, again close to tears.

"Lieutenant Clark?" Mike tucked the phone into his shoulder as he pored over a sheaf of papers on his desk. "Mike Cardella here. How're you doing? Look, on these rapes, we got this Fleagle dead to rights. He won't see daylight 'til forever. But trawling through the pornographic crap on his hard drive, I found something for you that might reopen your cold case on his wife, Ismelda, is that her name? There's a bunch of this Tantric B.S. with complaints about how her sexual allure was a false front, she wouldn't go along with his skeevy sexual fantasies, but the kicker is some soupy poems or whatever you'd call them about him returning her to the water that 'is our womb'—I'm quoting here, I couldn't make this stuff up—'near, yet like Sita, below the earth.' I know a little about that part; it's from some Asian story . . . Anyway, if he owned any property with water on it, a pond, river, whatever, you might want to check it out."

"Thanks, buddy, you'll be hearing from us."

❀ Epilogue

A woman leaves her home twice in her life, and she is carried both times:

the first time when she marries and is carried to her husband's house in a palanquin,

the second time when she dies and she is carried to the cremation ground.

—*Indian folk saying*

❀ Points for Discussion

Drawing on the story *The Gift of a Bride*, discuss the following questions.

1. How has ethnography changed with urbanization and globalization?

2. How does the view of other cultures from the inside help us view our own culture from the outside?

3. How do anthropologists use participant-observation in studying other cultures?

4. Culture is in the details; how do details give us insight into a culture?

5. What is cultural relativity? Does cultural relativity mean we cannot make personal judgments about the values and practices of other societies?

6. What range of techniques and sources of information do anthropologists use to understand another culture?

7. What is engaged anthropology? How is it different from earlier anthropological methodology?

8. What is ethnocentrism? Are all cultures ethnocentric? Does ethnocentrism have any positive functions? Negative ones?

9. What are some of the elements of American culture regarding gender? How do these differ from some of the core elements in Indian culture?

10. Discuss some ethical issues in cultural anthropology. What ethical issues appear in this story, and how would you respond to them?

❀ Glossary

ABCD	(American-born confused desi) refers to American-born children of Indian immigrants (see *desi*, below)
almirah	cupboard
alta cocker	Yiddish, mildly derogative, old fashioned, old folks
AFIS	automated fingerprint-identification system
apsara	heavenly nymph
baap, baap re	exclamation: oh, my father (oh, my god)
badmash	shady character, a bad man
bahu	daughter-in-law
bahut accha hai	that's very good
bai	respectful title for a woman; in Mumbai, refers to maid servants and domestics
banian	undershirt
bas	stop, enough
bastee	low-income area, slum
bed tea	early-morning tea or coffee served to hotel guests in their rooms or by servants in affluent families
bhabhi	respectful term for brother's (or cousin's brother's) wife
bhai	brother

bhai sahib	respectful term of address to an older brother or an adult man who is an acquaintance
bhajan	devotional song
bhangra	Punjabi folk music; global club music
bhel puri	spicy snack typical of Mumbai, sold from carts on streets and beaches
bhenji	respectful way of addressing older sister
bindi	traditionally, a red dot worn on the forehead of married Hindu women; more recently, a decorative accessory also worn by unmarried girls and non-Hindus
biryani	dish with meat (often lamb) and rice
bubbe	Yiddish, grandmother; also affectionate term for dear relatives, friends, or colleagues, especially in the theater.
burfi	a sweet dish made from thickened milk
burka	full body covering worn by Muslim women
CBI	Criminal Bureau of Investigation in India
chai	tea
channa	chickpeas
chapatti	round, flat Indian bread
chicken masala	refers to the many different dishes in which chicken is sautéed in a sauce with a mixture of spices
chicken tikka	a north Indian dish made of skewers of boneless chicken marinated in yogurt and baked in a clay oven
choli	blouse worn with sari or ghagra (skirt)
chowkidar	watchman
chutney	pickled fruit or vegetables that accompany food
dal	beans
desi	literally from the home or country
dharma	one's duty in life according to one's status
dholak	two-sided drum
dowry	a presentation of goods by the bride's family to the groom's family or to the married couple; tradition-

	ally dowry may have compensated for the fact that a woman could not inherit land or property. contemporary dowries mainly consist of jewelry and household goods
dupatta	scarf worn with shalwar-kameez
gobi-alu	cauliflower and potatoes
goonda	thug
guru	teacher
hai na?	literally, "isn't it?" meaning "isn't that so?" to confirm a statement of obvious truth
hijab	head covering for Muslim women
ji	respectful suffix
juldi, juldi	very quickly, in a rush
kaisi hai?	friendly greeting, "how are you?"
kirtan	a meeting for religious singing and recitations of religious books
kitty party	a rotating social gathering of a group of women
Kshatriya	warrior, second-highest caste in the Indian caste system
Kul Yug	the current age, one in which dharma becomes weak and sin and disorder reign
kurta	Indian garment worn by men or women, often embroidered
lakh	term for 100,000 of anything—could be people, dollars, rupees, stars, and the like; used like a million sometimes is in English
lungi	men's sarong
LUDs	Local Usage Details; records of all telephonic calls to and from specific phone lines indicating time of call and number of minutes the call lasted
masala	mixture
namaskar/namaste	respectful greeting using palms folded in front of chest
paan	palate cleanser made from various fillings folded within betel leaves

paanwallah	a person who makes and sells paan
pakoras	savory appetizer
palak panir	a baked dish of spinach and cheese
pallu	loose end of a woman's sari, worn over the shoulder
pappad	type of fried bread
paranda	decorative woven length of fabric intertwined with a woman's braided hair
puja	prayer
purdah	literally, the separation of women from men; in North India occurs as modified practices of respect, such as a woman covering her head in front of all elder males
saddhu	holy man
sas	mother-in-law
Sat Sang	group of women who gather to sing religious or folk songs
scheduled castes	very low or formerly untouchable castes
shalwar-kameez	typical North-Indian woman's dress consisting of long shirt and loose trousers
shehnai	Indian stringed instrument, used for classical music
sindoor	red powder traditionally worn in the hair parting of married Hindu women

 Sources

BOOKS AND ARTICLES

Abraham, Margaret. "Fighting Back: Abused South Asian Women's Strategies of Resistance." In *Domestic Violence at the Margins: Readings on Race, Class, Gender, and Culture,* edited by Natalie J. Sokoloff with Christina Pratt, 253–271. New Brunswick, NJ: Rutgers University Press, 2005.

———. *Speaking the Unspeakable: Marital Violence against South Asian Immigrants in the United States.* New Brunswick, NJ: Rutgers University Press, 2000.

Archer, William. *Songs for the Bride: Wedding Rites of Rural India.* Edited by Barbara Stoler Miller and Mildred Archer. New Yourk: Columbia University Press, 1985.

Buck, William, translator. *Ramayana.* New York: New American Library (Mentor), 1978.

Courtright, Paul B., and Lindsey Harlan. *From the Margins of Hindu Marriage: Essays on Gender, Religion, and Culture.* New York: Oxford University Press, 1995.

Dalrymple, William. "India: The Place of Sex." *New York Review of Books,* June 26, 2008: 33–36.

Dasgupta, S. Das, ed. *A Patchwork Shawl: Chronicles of South Asian Women in America*. New Brunswick, NJ: Rutgers University Press, 1998.

Divakaruni, Chitra Banerjee. *Arranged Marriage: Stories*. New York: Doubleday/Anchor, l995.

Dziech, Billie, and Linda Weiner. *The Lecherous Professor: Sexual Harassment on Campus*. Urbana: University of Illinois, l990.

Huyler, Stephen P. *Meeting God: Elements of Hindu Devotion*. New Haven: Yale University Press, 1999.

Kakar, Sudhir. *Intimate Relations: Exploring Indian Sexuality*. Chicago: University of Chicago Press, 1990.

Kalita, S. Mitra. *Suburban Sahibs: Three Immigrant Families and Their Passage to America*. New Brunswick, NJ: Rutgers University Press, 2003.

Khandelwal, Madhulika. *Becoming American, Being Indian: An Immigrant Community in New York City*. Ithaca, NY: Cornell University Press, 2002.

Marr, Sunaina. *Desis in the House: Indian American Youth Culture in New York City*. Philadelphia: Temple University Press, 2002.

Mukerji, Bharati. *Desirable Daughters*. Toronto: Harper Perennial, 2003.

Nankani, Sandhya, ed. *Breaking the Silence: Domestic Violence in the South Asian American Community*. Xlibris Corporation (http://www.xlibris.com), 2000.

Natarajan, Mangai. "Violence in Immigrant Communities from the Indian Subcontinent: What We Need to Know and What We Should Do." *International Journal of Comparative and Applied Criminal Justice* 26, no. 2 (2002): 301–322.

Rajagopalachari, C., translator. *Ramayana*. Bombay, India: Bharata Vidya Bhavan, 1979.

Stone, Linda, and Caroline James. "Dowry, Bride-Burning, and Female Power in India." In *Gender in Cross-Cultural Perspective*, eds. by Caroline B. Brettell and Carolyn F. Sargent, 4th ed., 310–320. Upper Saddle River, NJ: Pearson/Prentice Hall, 2005.

FILMS

Monsoon Wedding. Mira Nair, director. Distributed by Mirabai Films, Inc. USA, 2001.

My Wife's Murder. Ram Gopal, producer. Distributed by Eros International, 2005.

Provoked. Jag Mundhra, director. Distributed by Private Moments Ltd., UK, 2007.

Runaway Grooms. Ali Kazimi and Ish Amitoj Kaur, directors. Documentary, Canada, 2005.

WOMEN'S GROUPS

There are approximately fifteen to twenty women's groups that provide various kinds of services for South Asian women. These can be found on the Internet; among the most well-known are Sakhi (South Asian Women in New York City); Manavi, based in New Jersey, committed to ending violence and exploitation of South Asian women in the United States; Saheli, based in Austin, Texas, which provides assistance to Asian families; and Sawnet, a forum for and about women from India and other parts of South Asia who have experienced or otherwise have a link to domestic violence.

✿ Authors' Note

This story is an ethnographic fiction about violence against women. Consistent with the anthropological perspective, we set our central narrative in a particular cultural setting: that of an Indian community in New York City. We chose this context not because violence against women occurs more in the Indian diaspora than in other ethnic communities or indeed in the larger American community—it does not—but because by telling this one story we hope to illuminate how factors of culture, migration, and male dominance are woven together to impact women's lives and, too often, cause immense suffering.

Male dominance appears to be a universal context for violence against women. But like all cultural generalizations, this is expressed differently in different societies and different historical eras. As anthropologists we try to understand both the possible universal aspects of culture as well as the characteristics of particular cultures as we examine the diverse patterns of human behavior. Thus, while violence against women, particularly domestic violence, is a widespread, and indeed an increasing contemporary problem occurring on a global scale, its dimensions can perhaps be best understood through examination of a local, ethnographically specific setting.

Our story is set in the intersection of ethnography and fiction. While the story is fiction, the cultural background in which it is set is drawn from the standbys of the ethnographic method: participant-observation of informal and formal activities and gatherings, including rituals; individual and group interviews; ethnic media; genealogies; in-depth conversations with key interlocutors; historical and anthropological literature; and media accounts of actual cases of violence against Indian and other South Asian immigrant women.

No one book, whether ethnography or novel, can capture the great diversity of Indian culture or the adaptations of Indian immigrants. Thus, there is not just one but many families in our story, each giving a somewhat different perspective on gender roles, even as these are located within Hindu Indian culture.

Culture is never static: important cultural changes are occurring in India itself as well as within Indian immigrant communities, significantly because of processes associated with globalization and migration. With regard to gender roles, two important changes are an increase in more open sexuality, especially for women, and the increasing importance of love as a basis for marriages. But except for the extremely cosmopolitan, urban upper classes, these changes are coming very slowly. For many Indians, even those in large cities, these changes are constrained by traditional Indian cultural values and norms. There is still a huge Indian urban upper-middle class whose children are educated but whose lifestyles are still circumscribed by a more traditional Indian culture. They are less fast living and sexually active than the extreme cosmopolitans and still very committed to arranged marriages, though within this framework love does play a larger role than in the past. These are young adults who, during their college years, still do not date—in the American sense—but do spend much of their free time on group outings that include friends of both sexes. It is within this group that our story is set.

One of the distinguishing characteristics of Indian culture is the importance of the family, and family relationships shape much of an

Indian woman's life. This is true both in India and in the immigrant communities. While these family relationships form a matrix of security and satisfaction and successful adaptation for many, they also, unfortunately, may provide a context for abuse and violence. Thus, marriage and families are a central context of our narrative.

Interwoven with our primary narrative is a parallel depiction—again, fictional but ethnographically based—of the host society's cultural stereotypes and power structures that also bear on the subject of violence against women, both within and outside the family. This violence takes many forms, including psychological and physical abuse, sexual exploitation and rape, and even murder. We hope that our story will broaden the understanding of all our readers—students, social work and law enforcement personnel, and the professional and volunteer staffs of supportive agencies for women—about the issue of violence against women in all its forms and how it can more effectively be addressed.

Although our novel is an informed fiction, it *is* fiction. The specific situations and characters, with the exception of media reports in the public domain, are all products of the authors' imaginations. Any resemblance to actual persons or events is wholly coincidental. We happily acknowledge the many excellent printed sources on the topics addressed in our book. We especially applaud the many women's groups, some of which are listed on the sources pages, who are courageously and effectively addressing issues of violence against South Asian women. Many thanks to our families, friends, and colleagues, and to Simi Nallaseth for so generously providing the painting for the cover. We also want to thank Alan McClare, Krista Sprecher, Evan Wiig, and the staff at AltaMira Press for their interest in and support of this project.

We thank the staffs of the Faculty Resource Center and the Computer Center of New York City College of Technology (City University of New York) for their technical assistance.

We particularly acknowledge Ram and Santosh Mehta, Ravinder Nanda, and Arundhati Dheer for so generously sharing their knowledge about Indian culture and the Indian diaspora, but they in no way bear any responsibility for the ethnographic interpretations that appear in our story, which are completely our own.

Serena Nanda
Joan Gregg

❀ About the Authors

Serena Nanda, PhD anthropology, is professor emeritus at John Jay College of Criminal Justice, City University of New York. She has written widely on gender and is the author of *Neither Man nor Woman: the Hijras of India*, awarded the Ruth Benedict prize in 1990, and *Gender Diversity: Cross-Cultural Variations*. Professor Nanda has carried out fieldwork in rural and urban India and is the author of many articles on arranged marriage and family in Indian society. She is the coauthor of *Cultural Anthropology*, a text now in its ninth edition and *Culture Counts: A Concise Introduction to Cultural Anthropology*. She has also coauthored *American Cultural Pluralism and Law* and is the coauthor, with Joan Gregg, of a New York City guidebook.

Joan Young Gregg, PhD, comparative literature, is professor emeritus, English, at New York City College of Technology, City University of New York. She has taught English literature and English as a Second Language to faculty and students at colleges in China, Vietnam, and Indonesia. She is the author of *Devils, Women, and Jews*, a study of stereotypes of women and Jews in medieval European popular religious narratives, and coauthor of many ESL texts used both in the United States and Asia. She is coauthor, with Serena Nanda, of a New York City guidebook.

Breinigsville, PA USA
14 January 2010
230728BV00002B/2/P